CHILD NEUROPSYCHOLOGY

Volume 1

Theory and Research

This is a volume in

PERSPECTIVES IN
**NEUROLINGUISTICS, NEUROPSYCHOLOGY, AND
 PSYCHOLINGUISTICS: A Series of Monographs and Treatises**

A complete list of titles in this series is available from the publisher on request.

CHILD NEUROPSYCHOLOGY
Volume 1
Theory and Reseal Ch. 2 3
4 6
9 10 11

Edited by

JOHN E. OBRZUT

Department of Educational Psychology
College of Education
University of Arizona
Tucson, Arizona

GEORGE W. HYND

Departments of Educational Psychology and Psychology
University of Georgia
Athens, Georgia
and Department of Neurology
Medical College of Georgia
Augusta, Georgia

1986

ACADEMIC PRESS, INC.

Harcourt Brace Jovanovich, Publishers
Orlando   San Diego   New York   Austin
Boston   London   Sydney   Tokyo   Toronto

ACADEMIC PRESS, INC.
Orlando, Florida 32887

United Kingdom Edition published by
ACADEMIC PRESS INC. (LONDON) LTD.
24–28 Oval Road, London NW1 7DX

Library of Congress Cataloging in Publication Data

Child neuropsychology.

    (Perspectives in neurolinguistics, neuropsychology,
and psycholinguistics series)
    Includes indexes.
    Contents: v. 1. Theory and research — v. 2.
Clinical practice.
    1. Pediatric neurology.   2. Neuropsychology.
I. Obrzut, John E.   II. Hynd, George W.   III. Series:
Perspectives in neurolinguistics, neuropsychology, and
psycholinguistics.   [DNLM: 1. Child Development Disorders.
2. Nervous System Diseases—in infancy & childhood.
3. Neuropsychology—in infancy & childhood.   WS 340 C5357]
RJ486.C458   1986   618.92'89   86-3433
ISBN 0–12–524041–4 (hardcover) (v. 1: alk. paper)
ISBN 0–12–524043–0 (paperback) (v. 1: alk. paper)

PRINTED IN THE UNITED STATES OF AMERICA

86 87 88 89   9 8 7 6 5 4 3 2 1

To all the special colleagues and students who have both stimulated and encouraged this particular project from its inception. Also, special thanks to Krystopher, who provides the motivation to continue these professional endeavors.

J.E.O.

To W. Louis Bashaw, who provided the time, support, and friendship; and to Alphonse Buccino, who continues to facilitate our efforts to prepare psychologists to work with neurologically impaired children.

G.W.H.

Contents

Contributors   xi
Preface   xiii

Chapter 1   **Child Neuropsychology: An Introduction to Theory and Research**
John E. Obrzut and George W. Hynd

Introduction   1
Current Issues in Child Neuropsychology   3
Content of the Volume   8
References   10

Chapter 2   **Structure and Function in Prenatal and Postnatal Neuropsychological Development: A Dynamic Interaction**
W. Grant Willis and Anne H. Widerstrom

Introduction   13
Structural Development of the Central Nervous System   14
Luria's Conceptual Framework   29
Development of Motor and Sensory Functions   32
Concluding Remarks   47
References   48

Chapter 3 **Cortical Maturation and Developmental Neurolinguistics**
Sylvia Campbell and Harry Whitaker

Introduction   55
Anatomical Change and Asymmetry   57
Myelination   58
Neurodensity and Layer Width   60
Summary of Cortical Maturation Process   63
Neurolinguistic Research   63
Early Hemispheric Specialization   64
Summary and Conclusions   69
References   69

Chapter 4 **Developmental Aspects of Cerebral Lateralization**
M. P. Bryden and Lorie Saxby

Introduction   73
Handedness   75
Perceptual Asymmetries   79
Childhood Aphasia   84
Laterality and Reading   86
Conclusions   89
References   90

Chapter 5 **Psychophysiological Indices of Early Cognitive Processes and Their Relationship to Language**
Dennis L. Molfese and Victoria J. Molfese

Introduction   95
Voicing Contrasts   96
Place of Articulation   104
Auditory Evoked Responses as Predictors of Later Language Development   108
Predicting Language Performance at 3 Years of Age from AERs Obtained at Birth   109
Nonbrain Measures as Predictors of Language Performance: The Contribution of Perinatal and Infant Variables   111
Implications   112
References   113

Chapter 6   **Neuropsychological Functioning and
            Cognitive Processing**
            J. P. Das and Connie K. Varnhagen

Introduction   117
A Historical Perspective of the Search for Brain–Behavior
    Connections   118
The Information–Integration Model   121
Application of the Information–Integration Model to Studying
    Cognitive Processes   130
Summary   137
References   138

Chapter 7   **Plasticity and Recovery of Function in
            the Central Nervous System**
            *Francis J. Pirozzolo and Andrew C.
            Papanicolaou*

Introduction   141
Corticogenesis: Development of the Cytoarchitectonics of the Central
    Cortex   143
Nonlinguistic Recovery   149
References   150

Chapter 8   **Biological Interactions in Dyslexia**
            *Glenn D. Rosen, Gordon F. Sherman,
            and Albert M. Galaburda*

Introduction   155
Language and the Left Hemisphere   156
Neuropathological Anomalies in Developmental Dyslexia   160
Autoimmunity, Left-Handedness, and Developmental Disabilities   165
Discussion   168
References   170

Chapter 9   **Dementia in Infantile and Childhood
            Neurological Disease**
            *Paul Richard Dyken and Gerald E.
            McCleary*

Introduction   175
Special Considerations in Infants and Children   177
Cortical versus Subcortical Dementia   178

Infantile and Childhood Neurodegenerative Diseases Classification   179
Causes of Dementia   180
Evaluation of Dementia   181
Prototypical Diseases   184
Conclusion   187
References   188

Chapter 10   **Validity and Reliability of**
             Noninvasive Lateralization Measures
             Sidney J. Segalowitz

Introduction   191
Validity of Lateralization Measures   192
Reliability of Lateralization Measures   195
Problems with Noninvasive Lateralization Measures as Diagnostic
   Tools   203
Summary   204
References   205

Chapter 11   **Integrating Neuropsychological and**
             Cognitive Research: A Perspective
             for Bridging Brain–Behavior
             Relationship
             Marlin L. Languis and Merlin C.
             Wittrock

Introduction   209
Methods of Neurocognitive Assessment   211
A Research and Development Model: Integrating Neurocognitive
   Assessment, Diagnosis, and Metacognitive Intervention   225
Integrating Neurocognitive Assessment and Diagnosis with Meta-
   cognitive Intervention   226
Metacognitive and Cognitive-Control Intervention   231
Conclusion   234
References   235

Index   241

Contributors

Numbers in parentheses indicate the pages on which the authors' contributions begin.

M. P. Bryden (73), Department of Psychology, University of Waterloo, Waterloo, Ontario, Canada N2L 3G1

Sylvia Campbell (55), Department of Hearing and Speech Sciences, University of Maryland, College Park, Maryland 20742

J. P. Das (117), Centre for the Study of Mental Retardation, The University of Alberta, Edmonton, Alberta, Canada T6G 2G5

Paul Richard Dyken (175), Department of Neurology, University of South Alabama, College of Medicine, Mobile, Alabama 36617

Albert M. Galaburda (155), Charles A. Dana Research Institute and the Dyslexia Research Laboratory, and Department of Neurology, Beth Israel Hospital and Harvard Medical School, Boston, Massachusetts 02215

George W. Hynd (1), Departments of Educational Psychology and Psychology, University of Georgia, Athens, Georgia 30602, and Department of Neurology, Medical College of Georgia, Augusta, Georgia 30912

Marlin L. Languis (209), Department of Educational Theory and Practice, College of Education, Ohio State University, Columbus, Ohio 43210, and Brain Behavior Laboratory, Columbus, Ohio 43210

Gerald E. McCleary (175), Department of Neurology, University of South Alabama, College of Medicine, Mobile, Alabama 36617

Dennis L. Molfese (95), Department of Psychology and School of Medicine, Southern Illinois University at Carbondale, Carbondale, Illinois 62901

Victoria J. Molfese (95), Department of Psychology and School of Medicine, Southern Illinois University at Carbondale, Carbondale, Illinois 62901

John E. Obrzut (1), Department of Educational Psychology, College of Education, University of Arizona, Tucson, Arizona 85721

Andrew C. Papanicolaou (141), Department of Neurosurgery, University of Texas Medical Branch, Galveston, Texas 77550

Francis J. Pirozzolo (141), Department of Neurology, Baylor College of Medicine, Houston, Texas 77030

Glenn D. Rosen (155), Charles A. Dana Research Institute and the Dyslexia Research Laboratory, and Department of Neurology, Beth Israel Hospital and Harvard Medical School, Boston, Massachusetts 02215

Lorie Saxby* (73), Lutherwood Children's Mental Health Centre, Waterloo, Ontario, Canada N2J 3Z4

Sidney J. Segalowitz (191), Department of Psychology, Brock University, St. Catharines, Ontario, Canada L2S 3A1

Gordon F. Sherman (155), Charles A. Dana Research Institute and the Dyslexia Research Laboratory, and Department of Neurology, Beth Israel Hospital and Harvard Medical School, Boston, Massachusetts 02215

Connie K. Varnhagen (117), Centre for the Study of Mental Retardation, The University of Alberta, Edmonton, Alberta, Canada T6G 2G5

Harry Whitaker (55), The Neuropsychiatric Institute, Fargo, North Dakota 58107

Anne H. Widerstrom (13), School of Education, University of Colorado at Denver, Denver, Colorado 80202

W. Grant Willis (13), School of Education, University of Colorado at Denver, Denver, Colorado 80202

Merlin C. Wittrock (209), Department of Educational Psychology, College of Education, University of California at Los Angeles, Los Angeles, California 90024

* Present address: Lincoln Country Roman Catholic Separate School Board, St. Catharines, Ontario, Canada L2P 3H1.

Preface

This book is one of a two-volume set, both of which are among the first major efforts devoted to the neuropsychology of children. This volume is intended to present the most current theory and research on important neurodevelopmental issues. The second volume is primarily intended to address specific clinical neurodevelopmental disorders. Our interest in this endeavor grew from the concern that much has been written about presumed child–adult differences but little has been synthesized. Generally, there appear to be enough child–adult differences to suggest that cerebral impairment in children is a unique phenomenon and needs to be studied in depth. Thus, from our perspective, one of the major limitations in child neuropsychology is the absence of a data base on child populations.

Although interest in neurodevelopmental issues in behavior has been slow to develop, recent research has been widespread and is beginning to make a significant impact in shaping the field of child neuropsychology. In particular, recent research in the fields of developmental neuroanatomy, neurology, neuropsychology, speech and hearing, clinical child psychology, and school psychology has provided the necessary data base for one to hypothesize brain–behavior relationships in children on a more systematic basis. However, the field as it presently exists is in need of theoretical direction and data-based studies in order to accomplish its scientific and clinical goals.

A number of texts had appeared by the late 1970s and early 1980s addressing the neuropsychology of learning disorders, but most of these have not provided the wide-ranging yet comprehensive overview of theory and research necessary for the synthesis. Furthermore, most books currently on the market deal almost exclusively with disorders and research related to adult populations. This volume demonstrates that child neuropsychology includes theory and research similar in scope to that of adult neuropsychology, but different in emphasis and conceptualization.

A major goal of this volume is to provide the reader with recent theory and data pertaining to issues in neurodevelopment. We acknowledge that one volume cannot do justice to all of the theory and research and thus have chosen topics we feel are the most significant and provocative in the field at this time. Major topics include cortical and neurolinguistic maturation, functional cerebral lateralization, and neurophysiological and neurocognitive processing. Also, considerations of some of the major issues and trends in research in neuropsychological disorders in children, including plasticity and recovery of function, brain electrical mapping, and postmortem studies and measurement, are presented and discussed in a thorough and scholarly fashion. Each chapter provides the researcher and/or student with the most up-to-date literature review, analysis of past experimentation, and suggestions for future research design.

The contributors to each area are eminently qualified to address their particular chapter topics. All have made important contributions to the research literature, are recognized leaders in the field of developmental neuropsychology, and, most important, are exemplary in their ability to relate difficult scientific concepts and principles in an understandable manner.

This book is addressed primarily to neuropsychologists, experimental psychologists, neurologists, neuropediatricians, and educational researchers interested in children who are neurologically impaired. Specifically, this volume is designed to introduce beginning graduate students and researchers in the abovementioned allied fields to the latest theory and research in child neuropsychology.

This volume does not, however, provide an integrated theory of developmental neuropsychology. As is the case in other fields of psychology, there is little evidence to support any one general principle regarding the developmental course of brain functioning. At present, most of the research is of an inferential nature and has been conducted on adult populations. More experimentation needs to be conducted on child populations before a comprehensive theory of developmental neuropsychology can be put forth. In the meantime, this book should be helpful in providing some direction for future studies.

It is our hope that the volume will sufficiently guide the researcher to conduct methodologically improved experimentation in developmental neuropsychology. Only in this way are we assured that greater advancements will be made in our understanding of brain–behavior relationships in children.

John E. Obrzut

George W. Hynd

CHILD NEUROPSYCHOLOGY

Volume 1

Theory and Research

Chapter 1

Child Neuropsychology: An Introduction to Theory and Research

JOHN E. OBRZUT

Department of Educational Psychology
College of Education
University of Arizona
Tucson, Arizona 85721

GEORGE W. HYND

Departments of Educational Psychology and Psychology
University of Georgia
Athens, Georgia 30602
and
Department of Neurology
Medical College of Georgia
Augusta, Georgia 30912

INTRODUCTION

Since the late 1960s, remarkable advances have been made in the neuropsychology of childhood. Yet, much of this knowledge has been accessible only to a few psychologists who have specialized in research or clinical practice. Little has been done to provide a comprehensive synthesis of either the research or the data pertinent to clinical practice with children who experience neuropsychologically based disorders. Federal legislation (Federal Register, 1976), for example, Public Law 94-142 (The Education for All Handicapped Children's Act), has made it

1

imperative that children with special learning disorders be evaluated, identified, and placed in special educational programs for appropriate educational services. This law and associated shifts in federal funding to expand both research and clinical services to these children has made it necessary for a wider potential audience of researchers and clinicians to have the most recent information relevant to their professional needs. Specifically, the legislation and shifts in federal funding have led to more professionals recognizing the need for more information on brain–behavior relationships involved in the learning process, knowledge of specific neuropsychological disorders of childhood, more strategies, and more-varied strategies for clinical intervention, and more-valid neuropsychological information pertinent to prognosis.

Although a number of texts appeared by the end of the 1970s and early 1980s addressing the neuropsychology of learning disorders (see, e.g., Chall & Mirsky, 1978; Gaddes, 1980; Hynd & Obrzut, 1981; Knights & Bakker, 1976), most of these have not provided the wide-ranging yet comprehensive overview of neuropsychological research. Of those recently released (see, e.g., Rourke, Bakker, Fisk, & Strang, 1983; Hynd & Cohen, 1983), none were designed with the aforementioned comprehensiveness in mind. In addition, most volumes in neuropsychology deal almost exclusively with disorders and research related to adult populations.

One of the major limitations in child neuropsychology is the development of a database on child populations. Much has been written about presumed child–adult differences, but little has been synthesized. Thus, the attempt with this two-volume set is to highlight those neuropsychological issues deemed pertinent to researchers and clinicians working with child populations and to provide a synthesis of the available data. It is likely that we may find specific areas of neuropsychological functioning in children, which yield results comparable to those of adults. Other syndromes in children may yield vastly different clinical and research findings.

Recent research developments from the fields of neuroanatomy, neurology, neuropsychology, speech and hearing, clinical child psychology, and school psychology have provided the necessary database for one to hypothesize brain–behavior relationships in children on a more systematic basis. In fact, as Barkley (1983) so aptly points out, enough research and practice specific to children with neurologic syndromes has accumulated that a new subspecialty has developed which may be termed *clinical child neuropsychology*.

What does one consider to be the pertinent issues that comprise the field of child neuropsychology? Both of the present volumes attest to the fact that the field includes research and clinical issues similar in scope to that of adult neuropsychology, but different in emphasis and conceptualization. Most would agree that the field includes the study of developmental changes of the nervous system and its behavioral correlates. In addition, these developmental changes interact in a complex manner with biochemical and/or environmental alterations of the nervous system caused by trauma. Although interest in neurodevelopmental issues in behavior has been slow to develop, recent research has been widespread and is beginning to make a significant impact in shaping the field of child neuropsychology. However, the field, as it presently exists, is in need of theoretical direction and data-based studies in order to accomplish its scientific and clinical goals.

The nature and scope of child neuropsychology has broadened considerably in recent times, and therefore it was decided that the material should be organized into two volumes, one labeled theory and research, the other clinical practice. While both volumes contain an update of the most current research data on the particular topic discussed, each has its own focus, depending on the reader's interest in either theory or clinical practice.

This volume examines a number of important issues directly related to theory and research in child neuropsychology. Topics such as developmental neuroanatomy, cortical and neurolinguistic maturation, developmental cerebral lateralization, psychophysiological indices of early language, neuropsychological functioning and cognitive processing, plasticity and recovery of function, biological interactions in developmental dyslexia, measurement issues in child neuropsychology, and neuropsychological–cognitive research are presented and discussed in a thorough and scholarly fashion.

CURRENT ISSUES IN CHILD NEUROPSYCHOLOGY

At this point, several issues of prime importance to the study of child neuropsychology need to be considered as a prelude to the rest of the book. These issues include (1) the definition of child neuropsychology, (2) procedures used for conducting research in child neuropsychology, (3) developmental factors affecting child neuropsychology, and (4) generalization of neuropsychological findings from adult data to children.

Definitional Concerns
of Child Neuropsychology

It is fairly well established that child neuropsychology is concerned with the study of brain–behavior relationships as they apply to the developing human organism. More specifically, the discipline could be conceived as an attempt to discover and understand the exact neurological mechanisms involved in the learning process. If these were identified, it would allow one to determine indices of the particular way brain areas were functioning or malfunctioning. Kinsbourne (in press) suggests that such measures could then be used to assess the efficacy of remedial or other therapeutic efforts for the specific purpose of correcting the abnormality in the brain. It is projected that this approach would lend additional *depth* to the study of child neuropsychology. As Tramontana (1983) indicates, there is also a great need to distinguish whether impaired performance is the result of a neuropsychological deficit, psychiatric disturbance, or a developmental delay. It seems reasonable that this approach could have far-reaching effects in aiding the task of conducting accurate differential diagnoses.

Research Procedures Used in Child Neuropsychology

The usual approach to research in child neuropsychology is to compare results of matched experimental and control subjects on several neuropsychological measures or on various dimensions of processing abilities. Differences found are then attributed to some underlying basic dysfunctional process. However, little validity has been established for this approach. Kinsbourne (in press) suggested ways of establishing such validity. First, show that the degree of impairment of the assumed responsible underlying brain function is commensurate with the severity of the child's problem. Second, show that the types of difficulty encountered are face-valid expressions of deficiency in the hypothesized basic function. Third, use the child as his/her own control: for example, the child with acquired focal brain damage, who has lost an ability that he/she is known to have possessed previously. Although most research fails to satisfactorily meet these criteria, evidence is available as to the neurodevelopmental abnormalities that may disrupt the functional system of cortical zones important in learning among children (see Rosen, Sherman, & Galaburda, Chapter 8 in this volume). For example, the work of Duffy, Denckla, Bartels, and Sandini (1980) and Duffy, Denckla, Bartels, Sandini, and Kiessling (1980) provides evidence as to the disrupted cortical zones implicated in reading-disabled children's brains. Reports by Drake (1968), Galaburda and Kemper (1979), and Galaburda and Eidelberg (1982) further provide information about the correlated neurodevelopmental deficits. The research on cerebral asymmetries (e.g., dichotic listening, visual half-field, verbal–manual time sharing), as well as behavioral investigations, elaborate on the cognitive effects of these neurodevelopmental abnormalities (see Obrzut, Hynd, & Boliek, in press, for a review). Also, Volume II of this series is intended to provide the reader with available validation data for some of the major neurodevelopmental syndromes.

Scientific technologies have provided the means by which direct assessment of brain-behavior correlates could be found. Measurement using computerized axial tomography (CAT), positron emission tomography (PET), in addition to regional cerebral blood flow (rCBF), and electrophysiological techniques are among the most sophisticated methods being employed.

Developmental Factors in Child
Neuropsychology Research

Of all the developmental factors affecting child neuropsychology, the one eliciting greatest debate continues to be age of onset of the injury. Based on their review of the literature, Chelune and Edwards (1981) concluded that two consistent findings on the effect of early brain lesions are suggested. First, "long term deficits associated with static cerebral lesions are rarely as severe as the initial deficits." Second, "the earlier the brain damage is sustained in life, the less deleterious its essential impact on behavior than similar damage incurred by the mature brain" (p. 779).

While some theorists adhering to a structural position such as Isaacson (1976) and Reitan (1974) accept that brain damage negatively affects the developmental potential of the child, others such as Alajouanine and Lhermitte (1965), Basser (1962), and Hecaen (1976) concluded that young children show a greater restoration (i e., plasticity) of functions following brain damage than do adults. Still others, like Lenneberg (1967) and more recently Golden and Wilkening (1986), suggest that there are critical periods for successful transfer of, for example, language functions after brain damage occurs. Although these authors may disagree on the optimal times when damage can be minimized, they do agree that the earlier the damage, the better the chance for transfer of function. Further, Kolb and Whishaw (1980) have reported on studies with hemispherectomy patients and concluded that when hemidecortications were performed prior to the development of language (before age 2), transfer of function is possible. These studies support the notion that there is plasticity in the young brain but not equipotentiality. Perhaps the point of confusion may be that major structural changes observed are basically limited to animals who have sustained damage at early ages (Hicks & D'Amato, 1970; Isaacson, Nonneman, & Schmaltz, 1968).

Boll and Barth (1981) have outlined several important variables that have relevance for the study of the effects of neuropsychological dysfunction in childhood. These authors conclude that the age of the child at the time of injury, type and size of lesion, extent and location of damage, as well as the specific mental activity involved and its cognitive complexity, must all be considered. Wilkening and Golden (1982) also show that factors such as the socioeconomic status of the family, previous CAT-scan results, presence and length of unconsciousness, and treatment of injury, for example, surgery, irradiation, or chemotherapy, can influence the outcome of injury. Thus, it is becoming clearer that the relationship of brain injury to later development is based on many factors and must be viewed as a complex interaction.

There is less agreement over whether or not young children have an advantage over older children with regard to recovery of function (see Pirozzolo, Chapter 7 of this volume). Some authors, such as Black, Blumer, Wellner, Jeffries, and

Walker (1970), earlier suggested that young children do not have an advantage over older ones in the recovery process, and children experience a higher frequency of psychological disturbance following head injury while adults are more prone to complaints of a physical nature such as headaches. It has likewise been reported (Boll & Barth, 1981) that, in adults at least, by removing a damaged region of the brain, the abnormal influence of this system on mental activity may be less than the effects of a continued influence from dysfunctional brain tissue. This suggests that milder impairment can actually be more detrimental to the overall functioning of the brain than the complete absence of localized brain tissue. However, these same effects need to be examined in neuropsychological disorders of childhood. This topic is discussed at some length later in this chapter when comments regarding the validity of generalizing adult neuropsychological findings to child populations is presented. However, we must mention the difficulties of conducting neuropsychological research with children as opposed to adults.

Reed (1979) and Chelune and Edwards (1981) have identified obstacles confronting researchers who conduct neuropsychological research with children. Briefly, Reed (1979) suggests that because (1) adult brain injuries are often more subject to diagnostic and surgical procedures, they receive more intensive exploration than that of childhood cerebral dysfunctions, (2) assessments of children are made more difficult because of the complex nature of the interaction between brain-injury and the natural progressive changes due to development, (3) the limited range of dependent variables that are appropriate for use with children, and (4) difficulty of obtaining a representative sample of brain-damaged children to study. Chelune and Edwards (1981) related the difficulties inherent in neuropsychological research with children more succinctly by stating that the minds of children and adults are different, and the age of the individual at the time brain damage occurs is one of the main factors involved in determining patterns of behavioral deficits. Earlier, Boll (1974) had suggested that the factors to consider when evaluating a child should include chronological age, general developmental status, chronicity of the injury, and age of onset of the injury.

The return of speech is often cited to substantiate the belief that greater recovery occurs after early versus late brain damage. There is in fact a greater incidence of full recovery from aphasic dysfunction in children than in adults after brain damage. However, it should be recalled that no evidence exists suggesting that the causes of aphasia in childhood and adult life are similar.

On the other hand, Boll (1974) and Teuber and Rudel (1962) argued that the effect of the age at which brain damage occurs depends heavily on the type of human activity measured. For example, language understanding appears to lateralize more slowly than expression, such that lateralization of language understanding goes on probably until midadulthood. Rudel and Teuber (1971) also showed that brain-damaged children were worse than controls, beyond differences in their respective mental ages (M.A.s), in a spatial-orientation task. The deficits were not associated with either language or somatosensory impairment. Isaacson (1976) concluded, when considering all of the studies demonstrating "sparing" or "recovery" of behavioral abilities after early damage, it would seem that the reduced debilitation, if any, is always found in relation to some particular problem or task-specific event. However, very few studies have compared children who have sustained lesions early and those who experienced them late. Woods and associates (Woods & Carey, 1979; Woods & Teuber, 1973) have been investigating the subject in detail. From their studies, they have concluded that complementary specialization of the two hemispheres is already established in early childhood, even though effects of early left lesions on language tend to be more sutble than effects of corresponding lesions acquired later in life. Smith (1979) has suggested that generally his studies comparing children and adults have increasingly indicated an enduring hierarchy in the development and preservation of the various higher functions following brain insults in early life. However, he cautions that we need studies that carefully differentiate the evolving and resolving neuropathologic processes.

Reitan (1984) is very critical of generalization from animal research because of the inability to study higher-level brain functions in monkeys. In regard to children, he concluded that (1) early brain lesions, regardless of lateralization, cause devastating effects on the child's potential for developing normal abilities, especially if the lesion is severe, and (2) damage later in childhood is often more selective because the normal developmental process has already permitted production and organization of abilities as compared with the infant or young child.

Generalization of Adult Data to Children

Although the age of onset of brain injury has been of greatest concern in the child neuropsychology literature, generalization of neuropsychological findings from adults to children is also of considerable concern. Despite the vast amount of data that have been learned from the study of adults with brain lesions, as has been documented by Luria (1973, 1980), Reitan (1966), and Benton (1969), the adult models have provided little in the way of basic understanding of the neuropsychological functioning of the developing child. As Rourke et al. (1983) have pointed out, research in human neuropsychology has been largely dependent on the evaluation of behavior in individuals with documented lesions of the central nervous system (CNS). It is fairly well established that children experience much greater *generalized* rather than *localized* brain damage (Kinsbourne, 1974), the opposite being true for adults, and very different neuropsychological profiles emerge between the two types. For example, damage seen in adults is typically localized and results from cerebral vascular accidents, traumatic head injuries, and intracerebral tumors, while children more frequently experience epilepsy, anoxia, birth trauma, postnatal infections, and closed-head injuries. Therefore, as Barkley (1983) states, each field must possess a different fund of knowledge because the diseases children experience differ from those that adults experience. There is currently a trend for child neuropsychologists to study head trauma, tumors, Reye's syndrome, Tourette's syndrome, brain infections, and congential, biological disorders (Barkley, 1983).

More generally, the CNS of the child is quite different from that of the adult, not only in its anatomical characteristics, but also in its cognitive and behavioral capacities. Because the child's brain is in a constant process of evolving and resolving compared to the adult static brain, observed dysfunction should yield vastly different cognitive and behavioral sequalae.

Finally, there have been some data to indicate that even the type of injuries children experience at various developmental ages can have a significant effect in terms of eventual neuropsychological functioning. Klonoff and Paris (1974), as reported by Boll (1983), in their epidemiological study of head injuries of preschool and school-age children, noted some differences in the type and the location of occurrence of head injury. For example, these authors found that younger children appear to experience more serious intellectual deficits than do similarly injured adolescents. In addition, "children with mild injuries showed personality changes, headaches, irritability, school learning difficulties, memory and attention deficits which also tended to characterize the older and adolescent groups" (Boll, 1983, p. 76). Boll (1983) interpreted the Klonoff and Paris (1974) data to suggest that children may be more resilient to severe trauma on a physiological basis, but optimism regarding children's recovery from cerebral and psychological consequences is not supported by the available data.

In conclusion, we have attempted to outline some of the more interesting and provocative topics in child neuropsychology. Generally, there appear to be enough child–adult differences to suggest that the study of cerebral impairment in children is a unique area of inquiry and needs to be studied in depth. Now we say a few words on the content of the various chapters and authors who have contributed.

CONTENT OF THE VOLUME

This volume is designed to introduce beginning graduate students and to update advanced graduate students, clinicians, and researchers on the latest theory and research in child neuropsychology. We acknowledge that one volume cannot do justice to all of the theory and research, and thus we have chosen topics we feel are the most significant ones in the field at this time. We have also chosen authors who are on the forefront of this subspecialty area of psychology.

bidirectional relationships between structures and functions in prenatal and postnatal neuropsychological development. The research review focuses on selected motor and sensory aspects and attests to a dynamic interaction between changing neural structures and changing functions. Chapter 3, co-authored by S. Campbell and H. Whitaker, reviews the current state of knowledge regarding cortical maturation and developmental neurolinguistics. Neurophysiological and behavioral data are presented to demonstrate changes in linguistic development over the early years.

Chapter 4, written by M. P. Bryden and L. Saxby, summarizes the immense literature, primarily gathered since the late 1970s, on the lateralization of the child. The chapter addresses the definition of lateralization, how it is measured, and the relationship between deficient lateralization and cognitive abilities. Chapter 5, co-authored by D. Molfese and V. Molfese, reviews recent developmental research on the neuropsychological indices of early cognitive processes. The chapter also explores the possible relationship between hemispheric responses to speech cues early in development with later language performance.

Chapter 6, co-written by J. P. Das and C. Varnhagen, evaluates a neuropsychological model of information processing which has been validated by factor analytic and experimental research conducted primarily on children. The chapter further delineates the developmental changes in cognitive processes with a view toward understanding them in the theoretical context of the model. Chapter 7, co-authored by F. J. Pirozzolo and A. Papamicolaou, provides a discussion of the basic principles of plasticity and recovery of function, with particular emphasis on language and linguistic recovery. The chapter reviews studies that have utilized modern technical methods in establishing patterns of hemispheric activity during linguistic and nonlinguistic cognitive tasks.

Chapter 8, co-written by G. D. Rosen, G. Sherman, and A. M. Galaburda, provides data as to the neurobiological abnormalities associated with dyslexic brains. Cases are presented of five dyslexic individuals who have similar neuroanatomical anomalies. The chapter traces the development of these anomalies and provides evidence to show the particular biological interactions in dyslexia. Chapter 9, authored by P. Dyken and G. McCleary, discusses the neuropsychological aspects of dementia in infantile and childhood neurological disease. The chapter also provides a format for conducting a neuropsychological evaluation of this neurodegenerative disease in childhood.

Chapter 10, written by S. J. Segalowitz, discusses the validity and reliability of noninvasive lateralization measures. The chapter provides data to show that the most popular lateralization measures have considerable stability as group measures and can validly reflect cerebral specialization, but they are not as valid and stable when used with individual cases. Chapter 11, co-authored by M. L. Languis and M. C. Wittrock, demonstrates the use of electrophysiological approaches in conducting neurocognitive research. A model is proposed to integrate neuropsychological and cognitive research as a perspective for bridging brain–behavior relationships.

From reading the chapters contained in this volume, it is clear that research and theory specific to children with neurological disorders has increased since the late 1970s to the point where a new area of research could be identified as *developmental neuropsychology*. Although more neuropsychological data presently exist on adults, data on child populations are being gathered and synthesized at a fast rate. It appears that the benefits gained from taking a developmental neuropsychological perspective are potentially large. Because this volume consists of the most recent research and theory available in the area of developmental neuropsychology and has been contributed by some of the most experienced researchers in their respective fields, we think that the book has culminated into one that could shape the field into the next decade.

REFERENCES

Alajouanine, T., & Lhermitte, F. (1965). Acquired aphasia in children. *Brain, 88,* 653–662.
Barkley, R. A. (1983). Neuropsychology: Introduction. *Journal of Clinical Child Psychology, 12,* 3–5.
Basser, L. (1962). Hemiplegia of early onset and the faculty of speech with reference to the effects of hemispherectomy. *Brain, 85,* 427–460.
Benton, A. L. (1969). Constructional apraxia: Some unanswered questions. In A. L. Benton (Ed.), *Contributions to clinical neuropsychology.* Chicago: Aldine.
Black, P., Blumer, D., Wellner, A., Jeffries, J. J., & Walker, A. L. (1970). An interdisciplinary prospective study of head trauma in children. In C. R. Angle & E. A. Berring (Eds.), *Physical trauma as an etiological agent in mental retardation.* Bethesda, MD: U.S. Department of Health, Education, and Welfare.
Boll, T. J. (1974). Behavioral correlates of cerebral damage in children aged 9 through 14. In R. M. Reitan & L. A. Davison (Eds.), *Clinical neuropsychology: Current status and applications.* Washington, DC: Hemisphere.
Boll, T. J. (1983). Minor head injury in children—Out of sight but not out of mind. *Journal of Clinical Child Psychology, 12,* 74–80.
Boll, T. J., & Barth, J. T. (1981). Neuropsychology of brain damage in children. In S. B. Filskov & T. J. Boll (Eds.), *Handbook of clinical neuropsychology.* New York: Wiley.
Chall, J. S., & Mirsky, A. F. (1978). *Education and the brain.* (The Seventy-Seventh Yearbook of the National Society of Education, Part II). Chicago: University of Chicago Press.
Chelune, G. T., & Edwards, P. (1981). Early brain lesions: Ontogenetic-environmental considerations. *Journal of Consulting and Clinical Psychology, 49,* 777–790.
Drake, W. E. (1968). Clinical and pathological findings in a child with a developmental learning disability. *Journal of Learning Disabilities, 1,* 486–502.
Duffy, F. H., Denckla, M. B., Bartels, P. H., & Sandini, G. (1980). Dyslexia: Regional differences in brain electrical activity by topographical mapping. *Annals of Neurology, 7,* 412–420.
Duffy, F. H., Denckla, M. B., Bartels, P. H., Sandini, G., & Kiessling, L. S. (1980). Dyslexia: Automated diagnosis by computerized classification of brain electrical activity. *Annals of Neurology, 7,* 421–428.

Federal Register. (1976). *Education of handicapped children and incentive grants program.* U.S. Department of Health, Education, and Welfare, Vol. 41, p. 56977.

Gaddes, W. H. (1980). *Learning disabilities and brain function: A neuropsychological approach.* New York: Springer-Verlag.

Galaburda, A. M., & Eidelberg, D. (1982). Symmetry and asymmetry in the human posterior thalamus: II. Thalamic lesions in a case of developmental dyslexia. *Archives of Neurology, 39,* 333–336.

Galaburda, A. M., & Kemper, T. L. (1979). Cytoarchitectonic abnormalities in developmental dyslexia: A case study. *Annals of Neurology, 6,* 94–100.

Golden, C. J., & Wilkening, G. N. (1986). Neuropsychological bases of exceptionality. In R. Brown & C. Reynolds (Eds.), *Psychological perspectives on childhood exceptionality.* New York: Wiley (Interscience), pp. 61–90.

Hecaen, H. (1976). Acquired aphasia in children and the ontogenesis of hemispheric functional specialization. *Brain and Language, 3,* 114–134.

Hicks, S., & D'Amato, C. (1970). Motor-sensory behavior after hemispherectomy in newborn and mature rats. *Experimental Neurology, 29,* 416–438.

Hynd, G. W., & Cohen, M. (1983). *Dyslexia: Neuropsychological theory, research, and clinical differentiation.* New York: Grune & Stratton.

Hynd, G. W., & Obrzut, J. E. (Eds.). (1981). *Neuropsychological assessment and the school-age child: Issues and procedures.* New York: Grune & Stratton.

Isaacson, R. L. (1976). Recovery from early brain damage. In T. D. Tjossen (Ed.), *Intervention strategies for high risk infants and young children.* Baltimore, MD: University Park Press.

Isaacson, R. L., Nonneman, A., & Schmaltz, L. (1968). Behavioral and anatomical sequelae of damage to the infant limbic system. In R. L. Isaacson (Ed.), *The neuropsychology of development.* New York: Wiley.

Kinsbourne, M. (1974). Mechanisms of hemispheric interaction in man. In M. Kinsbourne & W. L. Smith (Eds.), *Hemispheric disconnection and cerebral function.* Springfield, IL: Charles C. Thomas.

Kinsbourne, M. (in press). Monitoring how disabled learners think with laterality tests. In S. J. Ceci (Ed.), *Handbook of cognitive, social, and neuropsychological aspects of learning disabilities.* Hillsdale, NJ: Laurence Erlbaum Associates.

Klonoff, H., & Paris, R. (1974). Immediate, short-term and residual effects of acute head injuries in children: Neuropsychological and neurological correlates. In R. M. Reitan & L. A. Davison (Eds.), *Clinical neuropsychology: Current status and applications.* Washington, DC: Hemisphere.

Knights, R. M., & Bakker, D. J. (Eds.). (1976). *The neuropsychology of learning disorders.* Baltimore, MD: University Park Press.

Kolb, B., & Whishaw, I. Q. (1980). *Fundamentals of human neuropsychology.* San Francisco: Freeman.

Lenneberg, E. H. (1967). *The effect of age on the outcome of central nervous system disease in children.* New York: Wiley.

Luria, A. R. (1973). *The working brain.* New York: Basic Books.

Luria, A. R. (1980). *Higher cortical functions in man.* New York: Basic Books.

Obrzut, J. E., Hynd, G. W., & Boliek, C. A. (in press). Lateral asymmetries in learning disabled children: A review. In S. J. Ceci (Ed.), *Handbook of cognitive, social, and neuropsychological aspects of learning disabilities.* Hillsdale, NJ: Lawrence Erlbaum Associates.

Reed, H. (1979). Biological defects and special education—An issue in personnel preparation. *Journal of Special Education, 13,* 9–33.

Reitan, R. M. (1966). A research program on the psychological effects of brain lesions in human beings. In N. R. Ellis (Ed.), *International review of research in mental retardation* (Vol. 1). New York: Academic Press.

Reitan, R. M. (1974). Psychological effects of cerebral lesions in children of early school-age. In R. M. Reitan & L. A. Davison (Eds.), *Clinical neuropsychology: Current status and applications*. Washington, DC: Hemisphere.

Reitan, R. M. (1984). *Aphasia and sensory-perceptual deficits in children*. Tucson, AZ: Neuropsychology Press.

Rourke, B. P., Bakker, D. J., Fisk, J. L., & Strang, J. D. (1983). *Child neuropsychology: An introduction to theory, research and clinical practice*. New York: Guilford Press.

Rudel, R., & Teuber, H. L. (1971). Spatial orientation in normal children and in children with early brain injury. *Neuropsychologia, 9,* 401–407.

Smith, A. (1979). Practices and principles of clinical neuropsychology. *International Journal of Neuroscience, 9,* 233–238.

Teuber, H., & Rudel, R. (1962). Behavior after cerebral lesions in children and adults. *Developmental Medicine and Child Neurology, 4,* 3.

Tramontana, M. G. (1983). Neuropsychological evaluation of children and adolescents with psychopathological disorders. In C. J. Golden & P. J. Vicente (Eds.), *Foundations of clinical neuropsychology*. New York: Plenum.

Wilkening, G. N., & Golden, C. J. (1982). Pediatric neuropsychology: Status, theory and research. In P. Karoly, J. Steffen, & D. Grady (Eds.), *Child Health psychology: Concepts and issues*. New York: Pergamon Press.

Woods, B. T., & Carey, S. (1979). Language deficits after apparent clinical recovery from childhood aphasia. *Annals of Neurology, 6,* 405–409.

Woods, B. T., & Teuber, H. L. (1973). Early onset of complementary specialization of cerebral hemispheres in man. *Transactions of the American Neurological Association, 98,* 113–115.

Chapter 2

Structure and Function in Prenatal and Postnatal Neuropsychological Development: A Dynamic Interaction

W. GRANT WILLIS
ANNE H. WIDERSTROM

School of Education
University of Colorado at Denver
Denver, Colorado 80202

INTRODUCTION

The theoretical orientation of this chapter is to consider the relationship between developing neural structures and functions as dynamic and bidirectional in nature. Neural structures often appear to determine associated functions at certain points in ontogenesis; however, it does not necessarily follow either that functions are an epiphenomenon of structures or that structures remain invariant in response to differential functioning. Neural structures are dynamic, functions are dynamic, and associations between structures and functions are dynamic; moreover, environments in which functions occur are dynamic, and the ontogeny of the organism is also dynamic.

There is experimental evidence from nonhuman animals supporting at least three possibilities for associations between structural maturation and organismic

13

CHILD NEUROPSYCHOLOGY, VOL. 1

functioning that are independent of the viewpoint that structure determines function (Gottlieb, 1983; Wolff, 1981). First, differential functioning may lead to differential maturation; in this sense, function may be considered as determinative or inductive in nature. Second, differential functioning may influence the time of onset or rate of maturation of particular neural structures; in this sense, function may be considered as facilitative in nature. Finally, the functioning associated with a particular system of neural structures may serve to maintain the integrity of that system; in this sense, function may be considered as maintenance in nature. These latter two possibilities, in particular, connote the susceptibility of the structure–function–behavior relationship to environmental influence.

Clearly, there are empirical relationships between the developing structures of the human nervous system and functions–behaviors of the organism both prenatally and postnatally. The precise nature of many of these relationships, however, has not been adequately delineated (Parmelee & Sigman, 1983). Consequently, the overspeculation concerning the nature of these relationships that is common to much of the research literature in this field is here avoided. Instead, the focus is to provide general overviews of selected aspects of both structures and functions in prenatal and postnatal human neuropsychological ontogenesis.

First, a selective overview of the structural development of the human nervous system is presented, beginning with the earliest differentiation of neural tissues in the embryo. The emphasis is directed primarily toward the gross morphology of the brain. Second, a theoretical framework for conceptualizing brain structures (Luria, 1980) is noted as a link toward the integration of structural and functional development. Third, an overview of selected developing prenatal and postnatal motor and sensory functions is presented, and associations between particular structures and functions are identified when data derived from human samples are available to support such conclusions. An appreciation of these issues is important for specialists in pediatric neuropsychology, both in research and in clinical settings. For example, hypotheses regarding etiology, syndrome analysis, course, and treatment may arise from the study of these issues.

STRUCTURAL DEVELOPMENT OF THE CENTRAL NERVOUS SYSTEM

Neurulation

The earliest differentiation of neural tissue in the human embryo is directed toward the formation of the neural tube. The process of neural-tube formation is termed *neurulation*. In a review of the mechanisms of this process, Karfunkel (1974) suggested that neurulation is both structurally and physiologically significant in human embryonic development. The process of neurulation is also significant in a functional sense because of the bidirectional associations between

TABLE 1

Sequential stages in neurulation

Carnegie stage	Gestational age (in weeks)	Structure
7	2	Neural plate appears.
8		Neural groove appears.
9	3	First pair of somites appear.
		Mesencephalic flexure.
		Neural groove deepens.
10		Neural crest migrates
		Neural tube closes.
11		Rostral neuropore closes (embryonic lamina terminalis).
12	4	Caudal neuropore closes.

structures and functions in the ontogeny of the human nervous system. Because of its structural, physiological, and functional significance, and because of the relationships between errors in neural-tube formation and various dysraphic congenital anomalies, the process of neurulation has received much attention, particularly in relation to the morphological, biochemical, and inductive forces that affect it (Gallera, 1971; Karfunkel, 1974; Saxen & Toivonen, 1962; Teidemann, 1967). As an initial period of embryonic development, neurulation consumes only approximately 2 weeks, yet the embryo's susceptibility to teratogenic influences may be highest during this critical period of development (Wilson, 1965).

The sequence of events in the process of neurulation is summarized in Table 1; Figure 1 shows schematic diagrams of horizontal sections of human embryos at sequential stages of neurulation. This process begins at approximately 2 weeks of gestation (defined as the length of time in utero) and is completed by approximately 4 weeks of gestation.

Formation of the Neural Tube

At approximately 2 weeks of gestation (Carnegie stage 7)[1], the ectoderm (i.e., the outermost germ layer) on the dorsal side of the embryo begins to thicken, forming the *neural plate*. In the middle of the neural plate, along what will later become the craniocaudal axis, a longitudinal fissure or trough, called the *neural groove*, appears. The neural groove first becomes evident between the second and third weeks of gestation during Carnegie stage 8. It is bounded on each side by thickened borders, or *neural folds*. During the third week of gestation, as the

[1]Carnegie stages refer to levels of prenatal development based on the collection of embryos at the Department of Embryology, Carnegie Institution of Washington.

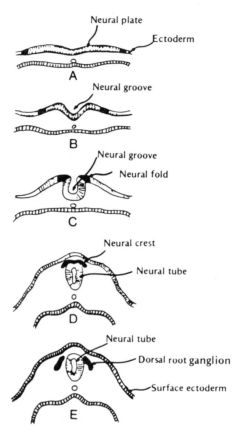

Figure 1. Diagrams of horizontal sections of human embryos at sequential stages of neurulation. (a) Carnegie stage 7: Neural plate develops; (b) Carnegie stage 8: Neural groove develops; (c) Carnegie stage 9: Neural groove deepens; neural folds thicken; (d) Carnegie stage 10: Neural folds begin to fuse; neural crest develops; (e) Carnegie stage 10: Neural tube fused; dorsal root ganglia develop.

first pair of somites begins to appear, the neural groove deepens and the neural folds thicken (Carnegie stage 9). Eventually, the neural folds meet and fuse together, forming the hollow, cylindrical shaped *neural tube*. The normal fusion of the neural folds in the formation of the neural tube begins in the cervical region and progresses in both rostral (i.e., cephalic) and caudal directions (Carnegie stage 10).

The Neural Crest

During that same stage (i.e., Carnegie stage 10), the *neural crest* begins to develop. As the neural folds fuse in their formation of the neural tube, the surface ectoderm (from which the neural structures are derived) is also drawn medially over the dorsal side of the craniocaudal axis of the human embryo. The ectoderm then separates from the neural tube. A layer of cells remains in the space between the dorsal craniocaudal axis of the neural tube and the overlying ectoderm. These cells comprise the neural crest. Eventually, the neural-crest substance divides longitudinally along the craniocaudal axis, and the cells migrate in lateral directions, forming right and left linear columns that are distinct from the neural tube.

The cells of the neural crest form segmented, bead-like aggregations of nerve-cell bodies known as *spinal ganglia*. In addition, neural fibers, originating from each spinal ganglionic mass, grow toward the neural tube, forming the *dorsal* or *sensory roots* of the spinal nerves. Similarly, in the lower cephalic region of the neural tube, neural-crest cells give rise to the sensory neurons that form ganglia for particular cranial nerves (Carpenter, 1976, p. 50). Thus, at approximately 3 weeks of gestation, structural precursors to gustatory, vestibular, and cutaneous sensations (i.e., functions associated with these cranial-nerve nuclei when mature) are evident.

Flexures

Also during Carnegie stages 9 and 10, due to differential rates of growth of particular regions of the neural tube, the craniocaudal axis bends such that at the completion of this process, the cephalic end is bent in an anterior direction (dorsal convexity), forming a right angle with the more caudal aspect of the neural tube. Three such *flexures* occur during embryonic development: (1) the (mesen)cephalic flexure, (2) the cervical flexure, and (3) the pontine flexure. In the course of ontogenesis, only the first of these flexures remains (Schade & Ford, 1973, pp. 8–9).

Motor and Sensory Precursors

The dorsal wall of the neural tube, the *roof plate,* is differentiated from the ventral wall, the *floor plate,* by a groove called the *sulcus limitans.* The sulcus limitans extends throughout the lumen (or cavity) of the future spinal cord and is also clearly identifiable in the floor of the fourth ventricle of the adult human brain. The sulcus limitans is an important structural division in a functional sense because it demarcates motor and sensory regions. The floor plate joins a pair of cell columns called the *basal plates* and, in a similar structural arrangement, the roof plate joins a pair of cell columns called the *alar plates.* The ventral gray columns (or horns) of the adult spinal cord are eventually formed from the basal plates; these columns are primarily motor in function. The dorsal gray columns (or horns) of the adult spinal cord are eventually formed from the alar plates; these columns are primarily sensory in function. The basal and alar plates further differentiate into columns of nuclei specialized for functions associated with various motor and sensory aspects of cranial nerves and other structures as well (Reinis & Goldman, 1980, pp. 72–73).

Closing of the Neural Tube

Between the third and fourth weeks of gestation (Carnegie stage 11) the more rostral opening of the neural tube, the *anterior neuropore*, closes. Subsequently (Carnegie stage 12), the more caudal opening of the neural tube, the *posterior neuropore*, closes. With the closing of the posterior neuropore, the process of neurulation is complete. Thus, by the fourth week of gestation, the basic structures of the neural tube have formed and the future functional significance of the associated neuroanatomical precursors is already apparent.

Differentiation of the Brain Vesicles

As the process of neurulation nears completion, the rostral lumen of the neural tube is characterized by three dilations, or *primary brain vesicles*. Figure 2 presents diagrams of the brain vesicles at two stages of embryonic development as well as divisions of the mature human brain derived from those vesicles. These three primary subdivisions of the human embryonic brain are called the *rhombencephalon* or hindbrain (most caudal aspect), *mesencephalon* or midbrain, and *prosencephalon* or forebrain (most rostral aspect). The narrowed region demarcating the junction of the mesencephalon and rhombencephalon is called the *isthmus*.

Although the mesencephalon remains undivided with further development, both the rhombencephalon and the prosencephalon are further subdivided, giving rise to the secondary brain vesicles. Initially, the prosencephalon subdivides into the more caudal *diencephalon* (future region of the thalamus, hypothalamus, epithalamus, and adjacent structures) and the more rostral *telencephalon* (future region of the cerebral hemispheres). Subsequently, the rhombencephalon subdivides into the more caudal *myelencephalon* (future region of the medulla oblongata) and the more rostral *metencephalon* (future region of the pons and cerebellum; see Figure 2, diagram b).

The Myelencephalon

The *medulla oblongata*, the most caudal aspect of the mature human brain (see Figure 2, diagram c), is derived from the myelencephalon. This brain structure is demarcated caudally by the first pair of spinal nerves in the cervical region of the spinal cord and rostrally by the beginning of the pontine flexure. Functions include life-supporting activities such as control of respiration, heart rate, and blood pressure. At lower (i.e., more caudal) regions, the medulla oblongata is structurally similar to the spinal cord. The features common to the spinal cord are thus continued into the medulla oblongata, where they are gradually displaced to

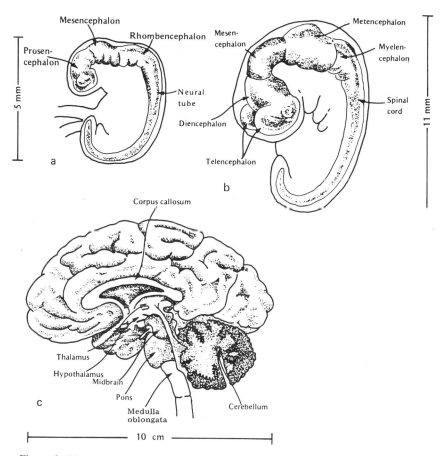

Figure 2. Diagrams of differentiation of the vesicles of the human brain at three levels of development. (a) primary brain vesicles at approximately 4 weeks of gestation. (b) secondary brain vesicles at approximately 6 weeks of gestation. (c) Midsagittal section of the mature human brain showing the right cerebral hemisphere.

different locations and undergo structural differentiation. For these reasons, the myelencephalon has been considered a transitional region between the spinal cord and the cerebral structures, linking the brain with the spinal cord in order to form an integrated functional system (Arey, 1966, p. 478).

In the most caudal aspect, the lumen of the medulla oblongata (i.e., the central canal) is present. The sulcus limitans, demarcating motor and sensory regions of specialization, is also clearly evident. Progressing in a rostral direction through the medulla oblongata, the central canal widens into the fourth ventricle and displaces the alar plates to a location lateral to the basal plates. Each of the alar and basal plates further differentiates into pairs of columns of nuclei, still retaining their sensory and motor functional specializations. The basal plates differentiate first, at about 6 weeks of gestation, followed by the alar plates (Arey, 1966, p. 481).

Cell Columns. Differentiated pairs of columns of motor (efferent) and sensory (afferent) nuclei extend throughout the rhombencephalon and mesencephalon. Medial to the sulcus limitans, specialized for motor functions, cell columns differentiate into general somatic efferent (GSE), special visceral efferent (SVE), and general visceral efferent (GVE), columns. Lateral to the sulcus limitans, specialized for sensory functions, cell columns differentiate into general somatic afferent (GSA), special and general visceral afferent (S/GVA), and special somatic afferent (SSA) columns.

In this and subsequent sections, the cranial-nerve nuclei arising from these motor and sensory cell columns are noted as they appear in the various regions of the brain. Table 2 presents levels of neuraxis and cell columns associated with particular cranial-nerve nuclei. Especially for the afferent nuclear columns, however, there is a consensus of opinion among various authors regarding neither the level of neuraxis at which all cranial-nerve nuclei are most prominent nor the way in which all nuclei are best classified (Arey, 1966; Brodal, 1981; Carpenter, 1976; Schade & Ford, 1973). Resolution of these issues is beyond the scope of this chapter, and designations presented in Table 2 are intended solely as organizational aides.

Within the medulla oblongata, the most lateral of the nuclear columns are the SSA columns. At this level of neuraxis, components of the vestibulocochlear (VIII) cranial-nerve nuclei are evident. Medial to these columns are the S/GVA

TABLE 2

Cranial nerve nuclei associated with differentiated cell columns

	Cell column					
Level of neuraxis	SSA	S/GVA	GSA	GVE	SVE	GSE
Myelencephalon (medulla oblongata)	VIII	VII	IX	IX	IX	XII
		IX	X	X	X	
		X	XII		XI	
Metencephalon (pons)			V	VII	V	VI
			VII		VII	
Mesencephalon			III	III		III
			IV			IV
			VI			
Prosencephalon	I					
	II					

columns comprising the *solitary nuclei* eventually functionally associated with taste sensations and involving the sensory nuclei of the facial (VII), glossopharyngeal (IX), and vagus (X) cranial nerves. The most medial of the alarplate derivatives are the GSA columns, which differentiate into the *gracile* and *cuneate nuclei,* cells that will become functionally specialized for ipsilateral somatic sensations from lumbar/sacral and cervical/thoracic regions, respectively. Sensory nuclei associated with the glossopharyngeal (IX), vagus (X), and hypoglossal (XII) cranial nerves are also included in the GSA columns at this level of neuraxis. Here, mature functions include general sensations from the anterior tongue, auditory meatus, and tympanic membrane.

The most lateral of the basal-plate derivatives (medial to the sulcus limitans) are the GVE columns comprising motor components of the glossopharyngeal (IX) and vagus (X) cranial-nerve nuclei. When mature, these nuclei are functionally associated with salivation and motor control of the heart, bronchi, and gastrointestinal tract. Medial to these cell columns lie the SVE cell columns that, at this level of neuraxis, comprise the *nucleus ambiguus.* The nucleus ambiguus comprises components of the glossopharyngeal (IX), vagus (X), and accessory (XI) cranial-nerve nuclei, eventually associated with motor control of the pharynx and larynx and innervation of the trapezius and sternocleidomastoid muscles. Finally, most medial, are the GSE cell columns giving rise to the motor components of the hypoglossal (XII) cranial-nerve nuclei eventually associated with motor control of the tongue.

Other Features. Along the ventral aspect of the medulla oblongata are the *corticospinal* (or pyramidal) *tracts,* where 75% to 90% of these descending fibers decussate, forming the contralateral structural and functional arrangements for motor control. Additionally, nuclei of the reticular formation are found in the medulla oblongata, although reticular nuclei extend rostrally to other structures beyond as well. Nuclei of the reticular formation are central to particular aspects of a conceptual framework for brain organization (Luria, 1980), noted in a subsequent section of this chapter.

The Metencephalon

The more rostral portion of the hindbrain, the metencephalon, gives rise to two major neuroanatomical structures, the *pons* and the *cerebellum.* The metencephalon is demarcated caudally by the pontine flexure and rostrally by the isthmus. The pons occupies the ventral aspect of the metencephalon, and the cerebellum occupies the dorsal aspect (see Figure 2, diagram c). Functionally, the mature pons serves as a pathway (or "bridge") between the cerebral cortex and the cerebellar cortex. The function of the mature cerebellum is associated with the coordination of movement and kinesthetic abilities through feedback systems and, perhaps, by inhibiting the firing of particular neurons (Blomfield & Marr, 1970).

The Pons. Within the developing pons, the alar and basal plates give rise to nuclei associated with motor and sensory aspects of particular cranial nerves and the pontine reticular formation. At the most caudal region of the pons, the columnar arrangement of cells present in the medulla oblongata persists; however, cells from the alar plates migrate dorsally to form the deep nuclei of the cerebellum.

At this level of neuraxis, the GSA columns give rise to the sensory nuclei of the trigeminal (V) and facial (VII) cranial nerves, which are eventually functionally associated with general sensations from the front of the head, including the nasal and oral cavities and meninges. The *pontine nuclei* in the ventral aspect of the pons are also derived from the alar plates. These nuclei are involved in a feedback system with the cerebellum regarding impending movement.

There are also several cranial-nerve nuclei derived from the basal plates at the level of the pons. The GVE columns comprise the *superior salivatory* nuclei associated with the facial (VII) cranial nerves. More medially positioned, the SVE columns comprise the motor nuclei of the trigeminal (V) and facial cranial nerves. When mature, the functional specializations of these nuclei include chewing, swallowing, and controlling the tympanic membrane, ossicles, stapes, hyoid bones, and facial muscles. Finally, the GSE columns at the level of the pons comprise the nuclei associated with the abducens (VI) cranial nerves, which, when mature, are functionally associated with the innervation of the lateral rectus muscles of the eyes.

The Cerebellum. The cerebellum is derived from the dorsolateral regions of the alar plates. Prior to the development of the pontine flexure, these regions migrate in posterior and medial directions, forming the *rhombic lips.* The rhombic lips eventually fuse in the midline, forming the *transverse cerebellar plate.* At 3 months of gestation, this structure shows the beginnings of the *cerebellar hemispheres,* represented as bulgings at its lateral aspects. The medial aspect is the *vermis.*

Between the third and fifth months of gestation, fissures begin to appear that section particular divisions of the cerebellum into lobes. The *posterolateral fissure* is the first to appear, and it differentiates the *flocculonodular lobe* from the rest of the vermis. This lobe, phylogenetically the oldest part of the cerebellum, is often termed the *archicerebellum.* As Brodal (1981, p. 296) noted, it is also sometimes simplistically referred to as the vestibulocerebellum because of its extensive connections with and influences on vestibular nuclei.

Rostral to the posterolateral fissure develops the *primary fissure* that separates the anterior and posterior lobes. These two lobes are called the *paleocerebellum* and *neocerebellum,* which exert influences on the spinal cord and cerebral cortex, respectively (Brodal, 1981, p. 296). The cerebellar hemispheres begin to undergo further specialization by the fifth month of gestation, and Arey (1966, p. 483) noted that, in fetuses of 7 months of gestation, the cerebellum has attained its mature configuration. Although not essential for life, given the extensive neural connections of the mature cerebellum, its activities may be associated with the coordination and control of almost any function in which the central nervous system is involved (Brodal, 1981, p. 294).

The Mesencephalon

The mesencephalon or *midbrain*, is demarcated caudally by the isthmus, dorsorostrally by the posterior commissure, and ventrorostrally by the mammillary bodies (Arey, 1966, pp. 484–485; see also Figure 2, diagram c). The midbrain undergoes little structural differentiation with development relative to the other brain vesicles. Mature functions are primarily associated with visual and auditory reflexes. Important motor as well as sensory pathways are also eventually represented in this intermediately situated structure.

Within the midbrain, the alar plates give rise to the *tectum* in which the laterally paired *colliculi* appear. A caudal pair of these colliculi, the *inferior colliculi*, are functionally associated with the auditory system. In a similar location, but more rostrally situated in the midbrain, are the *superior colliculi*. The superior colliculi are functionally associated with the visual system.

Although primarily motor in function, there are afferent components associated with the oculomotor (III), trochlear (IV), and abducens (VI) cranial-nerve nuclei at this level of neuraxis. The sensory aspects of these nuclei are derived from the GSA columns in the midbrain and, when mature, are functionally associated with sensations and proprioceptive feedback from the extrinsic muscles of the eyes. The nuclei of the *midbrain reticular formation* are also derived from the alar plates.

Motor aspects of the oculomotor (III) and trochlear (IV) cranial-nerve nuclei are derived from the GSE columns at the midbrain level of neuraxis. These nuclei, well defined by the third month of gestation (Schade & Ford, 1973, p. 15), are eventually functionally associated with control of the extrinsic eye muscles. The GVE columns are also represented at this level of neuraxis by the nucleus of *Edinger-Westphal* associated with the oculomotor (III) cranial nerve. The mature functions of this nucleus are associated with pupillary constriction and lens accommodation for near vision.

Derived from the basal and floor plates are a number of structures, including the *basal ganglia* (or corpus striatum), eventually functionally associated with the motor system.

The Diencephalon

The diencephalon is demarcated caudally by the rostral limits of the midbrain (see Figure 2, diagram c) and rostrally by the intraventricular foramen. Major neuroanatomical structures derived from the diencephalon include the *thalamus* and the *hypothalamus*. The *epithalamus* is also derived from the diencephalon.

As Brodal (1981, p. 99) noted, the thalamus comprises numerous nuclei, differing with respect to their connections. As such, when mature, these nuclei are functionally dissimilar, being related to motor control, maintenance of conscious states, hearing, vision, and other perceived sensations. The hypothalamus also comprises differing groups of nuclei that, when mature, are specialized for various functions. These functions include (1) the influence of the pituitary gland, which, in turn, influences the endocrine glands, (2) the influence of both the sympathetic and the parasympathetic divisions of the autonomic nervous system, and (3) significant involvement with motivation, emotional behavior, and physiological regulatory activity.

The hypothalamus and epithalamus appear phylogenetically, as well as ontogenetically, earlier than the thalamus. The epithalamus lies dorsocaudal, and the hypothalamus lies ventrorostral to the thalamus. The pituitary gland is attached to the most ventral aspect (i.e., infundibulum) of the hypothalamus and undergoes structural differentiation during the third through sixth weeks of gestation (Reinis & Goldman, 1980, p. 75). The two egg-shaped thalami, eventually connected by the *massa intermedia,* rapidly outgrow the epithalamus and hypothalamus, however, and, as previously noted, differentiate into a large number of nuclei that, when mature, are specialized for various functions.

The optic (II) cranial-nerve nuclei develop from the SSA columns in the caudal aspect of the diencephalon, eventually functionally specialized for vision. Fibers of the optic cranial nerves cross in the region of the *optic chiasm,* ventral to the hypothalamus. This crossing of nerve fibers is associated with the eventual contralateral cerebral representation of the visual hemifields.

The Telencephalon

The most rostral brain vesicle, the telencephalon, is demarcated caudally by the intraventricular foramen and gives rise to the two *cerebral hemispheres* (see Figure 2, diagram c). The prominence of the cerebral hemispheres begins to become evident during the sixth week of gestation (Arey, 1966, p. 489), and the cerebral hemispheres soon conceal the diencephalic structures, the midbrain, and some of the cerebellum when viewed laterally. In early prenatal development, the cerebral hemispheres are connected only by the *lamina terminalis* (i.e., the most rostral aspect of the neural tube). The telencephalon becomes the most functionally specialized region of the human nervous system. Three groups of structures arising from (or associated with) the telencephalon are (1) the *corpus striatum,* (2) the *paleopallium* and *archipallium,* and (3) the *neopallium.*

The corpus striatum. The corpus striatum, sometimes considered as synonymous with the term *basal ganglia,* includes the *caudate nucleus, putamen,* and *globus pallidus.* These structures, the eventual functional specializations of which include motor movement, are closely associated with particular diencephalic (especially thalamic) and midbrain nuclei. In prenatal development, the corpus striatum initially is distinct from the thalamus, being separated by a deep fissure. By the beginning of the fourth month of gestation, however, both of these groups of nuclei have enlarged, the fissure has disappeared, and the thalamus and corpus striatum appear as one continuous mass (Arey, 1966, p. 491). The anterior limb of the *internal capsule,* a tract of fibers, projects between the caudate nucleus and the putamen to and from the regions of the cerebral cortex eventually functionally specialized for motor movement. The posterior limb of the internal capsule separates the globus pallidus from the thalamus and eventually descends to the pyramids of the medulla oblongata, where the majority of these fibers decussate.

The Paleopallium and the Archipallium. The paleopallium includes the ventral surfaces of each of the cerebral hemispheres. These structures enlarge during the sixth week of gestation and become the *olfactory lobes.* The olfactory lobes, eventually functionally associated with the sense of smell, remain relatively small in the human central nervous system (Arey, 1966, p. 492), as compared with other species for which olfaction presumably assumes greater importance. Other structures are also associated with the paleopallium (e.g., parts of the amygdaloid complex), all of which receive fibers from the olfactory lobes (Carpenter, 1976, p. 52). The nuclei of the olfactory (I) cranial nerves are also located in this basal region of the telencephalon, arising from the SSA cell columns.

The archipallium gives rise to the *hippocampal region,* which develops along the medial aspect of each cerebral hemisphere. The neuroanatomy of the hippocampal region is complex, and associated functions are currently insufficiently defined (Brodal, 1981, pp. 683–689).

The Neopallium. The neopallium is the largest, most lateral aspect of the telencephalon and gives rise to the *cerebral cortex,* a highly specialized and differentiated structure forming the outer convoluted layer of the brain. Cortical regions are connected with subcortical structures via *projection fibers,* with other cortical regions in the same cerebral hemisphere via *association fibers,* and with cortical regions in the opposite hemisphere via *commissural fibers.*

Commissural fibers occur at several levels of neuraxis from the spinal cord through the telencephalon. The three telencephalic commissures are the *corpus callosum, anterior commissure,* and *hippocampal commissure.* The first commissure to develop is the anterior commissure. This bundle of fibers appears in the third month of gestation (Carpenter, 1976, p. 69) and connects particular aspects of the temporal lobes as well as olfactory regions in the two cerebral hemispheres. The second telencephalic commissure to develop is the hippocampal commissure, interconnecting hippocampal regions. Rostral and dorsal to the hippocampal commissure develops the corpus callosum, the largest mass of connecting fibers in the human nervous system (Walsh, 1978, p. 53). These fibers interconnect corresponding neocortical areas in the two cerebral hemispheres.

During the early stages of prenatal neuroanatomical development, the surfaces of the cerebral hemispheres are *lisencephalic* (i.e., smooth). During later prenatal development, however, the rapidly growing cerebral hemispheres develop convolutions called *gyri*, which are separated by fissures of varying depths called *sulci*. In an extensive study of over 200 serially sectioned human fetal brains, Dooling, Çhi, and Gilles (1983) investigated changing gyral patterns in telencephalic development. Dooling et al. concluded that

1. The lisencephalic surfaces of the cerebral hemispheres become deeply enfolded according to an orderly asymmetric pattern.
2. There is a marked increase in the number of gyri appearing at 26 to 28 weeks of gestation; moreover, this increase follows a fetal brain growth spurt in terms of brain weight at 24 to 25 weeks of gestation.
3. By parturition, full-term neonates show nearly all the gyri that are identifiable in the adult brain.

The major fissures and sulci demarcating the various *lobes* of the cerebral hemispheres are listed in Table 3 with the gestational age at which they appear according to the study conducted by Dooling et al. (1983). As noted in Table 3, the major sulci that demarcate the four lobes of each cerebral hemisphere are evident by 20 weeks of gestation. The *longitudinal fissure* separates the two cerebral hemispheres; the *lateral sulcus* (also called the Sylvian fissure) demarcates the dorsal boundary of the *temporal lobe;* the *parietooccipital sulcus* differentiates the caudal *pariental lobe* from the rostral *occipital lobe;* and the *central sulcus* (also called the Rolandic fissure) differentiates the rostral parietal lobe

TABLE 3

Development of major fissues/sulci in the central hemispheres[a]

Gestational age (in weeks)	Fissure/sulcus
10	Longitudinal fissure
14	Lateral sulcus
16	Parietooccipital sulcus
16	Calcarine sulcus
20	Central sulcus

[a] Adapted from Dooling, Chi, & Gilles (1983).

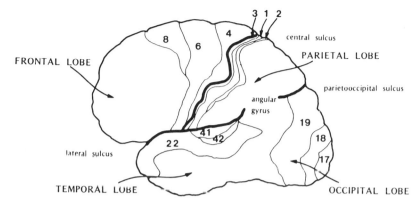

Figure 3. Diagram of left lateral view of the mature human brain.

from the caudal *frontal lobe*. Figure 3 presents a left lateral view of the mature human brain with the major sulci and lobes labeled, as well as several of Brodmann's cytoarchitectonic areas that are identified subsequently.

The cerebral cortex is of particular interest to neuropsychologists, although important subcortical structures should not be ignored. Research techniques for investigating functions associated with mature and developing cortical structures include resection of commissural fibers (Gazzaniga & LeDoux, 1978; Levy & Trevarthen, 1976; Sperry, 1968; Springer & Deutsch, 1981; Zaidel & Sperry, 1973), Wada procedures (Bogen & Gordon, 1971; Milner, Branch, & Rasmussen, 1964; Wada & Rasmussen, 1960), dichotic listening techniques (Kimura, 1961, 1973), visual half-field techniques (Heron, 1957; Kimura, 1966; Ley & Bryden, 1979; Mishkin & Forgays, 1952), and, more recently, time-sharing paradigms (Kinsbourne & Hiscock, 1983; Willis & Hynd, in press) and regional cerebral blood-flow techniques (Prohovnik, 1980). These research methods have varied considerably with respect to procedural aspects, yet many results have been robust to these differing methodologies. Most notable have been the relative left-cerebral-hemispheric superiority for language processing and the relative right-cerebral-hemispheric superiority for visuospatial processing (Hynd & Willis, 1985).

Although the functional asymmetries of the cerebral hemispheres have been documented for many years, neuroanatomical substrata supporting these asymmetries have been reported more recently. Geschwind and Levitsky (1968), for example, reported autopsy data derived from human adults revealing neuroanatomical asymmetries between the left and right cerebral hemispheres in the caudal region of the superior surface of the temporal lobe, that is, the *planum temporale*. This region, noted for its functional specialization for language, was found to be larger in the left than right cerebral hemisphere in 65 of 100 human,

adult brains examined. Geschwind and Levitsky suggested that the morphological asymmetry was of sufficient magnitude to be comparable with the
known functional asymmetry. There has ensued some controversy regarding
such functional and morphological asymmetries, with some contending that cerebral hemispheric functional asymmetries develop in the course of ontogenesis
and are influenced by environmental factors, and other contending that those
asymmetries result from a biological preprogramming (Kinsbourne, 1975;
Lenneberg, 1967).

Research conducted with human fetuses, neonates, and infants provides more
support for the latter view, assuming a positive relationship between structure
and function. Here, autopsy data have revealed a larger left than right planum
temporale as early as 29 weeks of gestation (Wada, Clarke, & Hamm, 1975;
Witelson & Pallie, 1973). More-recent evidence supports these findings and
documents other neuroanatomical asymmetries between the cerebral hemispheres during prenatal telencephalic development (Dooling et al., 1983).

Development of Brain Weight

Although the gross structural morphology of the human brain has nearly
attained its mature appearance by birth, brain weight continues to increase
postnatally. Brain weight increases in the human until adulthood, peaks at about
18 to 30 years, and subsequently gradually declines (Dekaban & Sadowsky,
1978). The ratio of brain to body weight decreases progressively throughout
postnatal development. Thus, at 3 months of gestation the brain comprises approximately 18% of body weight, at 4 months 16%, at 5 months 14%, at birth
12%, at 1 postnatal year 10%, and at age 20 2.5% (Jacobson, 1978, p. 108).

Rate of brain growth, however, is neither prenatally nor postnatally uniform.
In their study of telencephalic development, Dooling et al. (1983) noted a prenatal brain-growth spurt occurring at about 24 to 25 weeks of gestation, just prior
to the greatest proliferation of sulci and gyri. Another major growth spurt of the
human brain occurs during the first postnatal year. Here, brain weight increases
from about 350 grams at birth to 1000 grams. This later growth spurt is primarily
associated with the differentiation, growth, and maturation of existing neurons as
well as elaboration of dendrites and synapses (Jacobson, 1978). Additionally, the
accumulation of myelin accounts for a significant proportion of the increase in
brain weight during this period of development.

Dendrites (i.e., the branching processes of neurons through which neural
impulses propagate) increase substantially in terms of both length and complexity; *synapses* (i.e., the connections where neural impulses are transmitted from
one neuron to another) also increase at a rapid rate during this period of development. Consistent with the view of a bidirectional relationship between structure
and function in the human nervous system, some research has suggested an

association between sensory stimulation–deprivation and dendritic–synaptic development in nonhuman animals (Jacobson, 1978, pp. 202–206).

The process of the accumulation of myelin around the *axon* (i.e., the conducting process) of a neuron is called *myelination. Myelin* facilitates the propagation of neural impulses through the axons, greatly increasing their speed of conduction. Myelin is composed primarily of lipids and proteins; thus, nutritional deficiencies in the early postnatal period may be associated with degeneration of the myelin sheaths. Reinis and Goldman (1980, p. 187) suggested that myelination occurs first in the neural pathways of greatest importance for survival. Others (see, e.g., Arey, 1966, p. 463) have suggested that the oldest tracts phylogenetically and ontogenetically are the soonest to myelinate. The entire process of myelination is nearly completed by the second postnatal year, although some systems may still be myelinating many years later (Luria, 1980). There is apparently a great deal of biological variation, however, in the myelination process (Gilles, Shankle, & Dooling, 1983). Moreover, different neural tracts are associated with different rates of myelination. Thus, for example, although the pathway involved in the sucking reflex (with high survival value) is myelinated early in development (Reinis & Goldman, 1980, p. 187), inferences suggesting causal relationships between myelination and the emergence of neurological functioning should be avoided. As Gilles et al. noted, the different times of appearance, rates of development, and biological variation in the process of myelination may be associated with an interaction of several forces and processes, including structure, function, and environment.

LURIA'S CONCEPTUAL FRAMEWORK

The conceptual framework of brain organization proposed by Luria (1980) is useful for understanding relationships between structures and functions. Such a framework aids in the synthesis of these two literatures into an integrated whole, that is, the discipline of neuropsychology. A comprehensive review of Luria's conceptual framework is beyond the scope of this chapter; however, three units in this framework are briefly described.

The Arousal Unit

An important group of cells throughout the rhombencephalon, mesencephalon, and diencephalon comprise the arousal unit (including the reticular formation). The arousal unit, with its many neural connections with the frontal lobe, is functionally specialized for the maintenance of particular levels of cortical tone (or arousal) and, thus, the regulation of consciousness. Injuries at levels of neuraxis comprising reticular-formation cells may lead to a reduction in level of

consciousness, coma, or even death. Symptoms associated with various developmental learning disorders, such as developmentally inappropriate attention and
hyperactivity, may also be related to dysfunctions or delayed maturation associated with the arousal unit of the brain (Hynd & Willis, 1985; Obrzut & Obrzut,
1982). Moreover, Golden (1981) suggested that an explanation for the reduction
of hyperactive behaviors noted in some children at puberty may be associated
with the cerebral control exerted on the reticular formation by the maturing
cortical regions of the frontal lobes.

The Sensory-Input Unit

The sensory-input unit of the brain comprises those cortical regions caudal to
the central sulcus and includes the parietal, occipital, and temporal lobes (see
Figure 3). Each of these three lobes contains a nuclear zone of *analyzers,* functionally specialized for cerebral processing associated with a particular sensory
modality (Luria, 1980, pp. 37–77). Within each parietal lobe is the nuclear zone
of the cutaneous-kinesthetic analyzer; within each occipital lobe is the nuclear
zone of the optic analyzer; within each temporal lobe is the nuclear zone of the
auditory analyzer.

The nuclear zones of these analyzers are further differentiated as *primary* (or
central), *secondary* (or peripheral), and *tertiary* (or overlapping) fields. These
differentiated fields comprise the neuroanatomical substrata for different kinds of
functional processing. It is significant that their appearance follows a distinct
ontogenetic course.

Primary Fields

The primary fields in the caudal regions of the cerebral cortex are clearly
identifiable in terms of their cellular structures as well as their functional associations. These fields are Brodmann's areas 3 (cutaneous-kinesthetic zone), 17
(visual zone), and 41 (auditory zone; see Figure 3). In the course of ontogenesis,
the primary fields, with their connections to subcortical structures, are the first to
develop prenatally (Luria, 1980, pp. 58–59). These fields, which have the most
direct connections of the cortical regions with their corresponding sensory
organs, are dynamic, highly specialized zones. General, functional specializations of the primary fields are associated with the direct, unimodal perception
and differentiation of particular stimuli.

Secondary Fields

The secondary fields of the caudal regions of the cerebral cortex comprise
Brodmann's areas 1 and 2 (cutaneous-kinesthetic zone), 18 and 19 (visual zone),
and 22 and 42 (auditory zone; see Figure 3). Luria (1980, p. 59) noted that the

secondary fields develop relatively much later in the course of ontogenesis than the primary fields, coinciding with the first postnatal weeks and months. Moreover, the myelination of the neural pathways associated with these fields also occurs at correspondingly later periods. General functional specializations of the secondary fields are associated with the integration (or synthesis) of the components of groups of unimodally perceived stimuli.

Tertiary Fields

The parietooccipitotemporal areas of overlap of the nuclear zones of analyzers comprise the caudal tertiary fields of the cerebral cortex. The *angular gyrus* (see Figure 3), is functionally specialized for the integration of groups of multimodal stimuli. The tertiary zones are among the last cortical regions to mature, occupying the first few postnatal years (Luria, 1980, p. 59). Based on their review of the literature, Hynd and Cohen (1983) proposed that the angular gyrus may be an important component of the functional system of reading; case-study data have supported this hypothesis (Drake, 1968; Galaburda & Kemper, 1979; see also Rosen, Sherman, & Galburda, chap. 8, this volume).

The Organizational and Planning Unit

The organizational and planning unit comprises the cortical regions of the frontal lobes. Similar to the sensory-input unit, this unit of the brain may be subdivided into three groups of fields. In contrast to the sensory-input unit, however, this unit of the brain is functionally specialized for the performance of coordinated and goal-directed behavior in response to the perceived groups of stimuli processed in the sensory-input unit (Luria, 1980, p. 52).

The primary field of the third unit comprises Brodmann's area 4 (see Figure 3), and this precentral region is often referred to as the *motor strip*. The functional specialization of this area is associated with the initiation of contralateral movement. The secondary fields comprise Brodmann's area 6 and 8 (see Figure 3). Area 6 functions as a kind of association area (Filskov, Grimm, & Lewis, 1981) and is involved with the automatization of complex, coordinated movements (Luria, 1980, p. 53). The general functions of Area 8 may be associational as well, but this region is primarily involved with eye movement. The tertiary fields, the most rostral cortical regions of the frontal lobes, are functionally specialized for highly integrated forms of goal-directed activity (Luria, 1980, p. 56).

The structural formations and connections to the cortical regions of the frontal lobes (similar to the tertiary zones of the sensory-input unit) may be among the last cortical regions to mature, coinciding with the first few postnatal years (Luria, 1980, p. 59). Functionally, some recent data suggest that a number of behaviors often associated with frontal-lobe processing are mature at 6 postnatal years, although other behaviors so ascribed do not reach maturity until 10 to 12 postnatal years (Passler, Issac, & Hynd, 1985).

DEVELOPMENT OF MOTOR AND SENSORY FUNCTIONS

An examination of neurological function in the developing fetus and young infant may be divided into three parts: (1) motor function, (2) sensory function, and (3) autonomic responses. In each area of function, the focus is on normal development, where function connotes a dynamic aspect of the human neurological system and illustrates the complexity of the system at fetal and neonatal stages of development. Also noted are instances of abnormal development, however, for much that is presently known concerning normal neurological function has been learned through research conducted on infants with identified sensory or motor dysfunctions, or on preterm and low birthweight infants who are at risk for sensorimotor handicaps.

Motor Function

Early students of neural function based understanding of fetal and neonatal development on pathology of the human or animal adult nervous systems, resulting in at least two misconceptions (Prechtl, 1981). First, early neural function was considered to consist of a bundle of reflexes which with later development of the cortex became incorporated into more complex mechanisms, but which reappeared in the adult if brain damage occurred. Second, the development of neural function was seen to consist of the simple adding of more rostral structures to the earlier-developed spinal cord and brainstem, resulting in a hierarchy of reflexes associated with increasingly rostral structures.

Systems analyses of the brain have refuted the latter of these premises (Prechtl, 1981), and recent studies of the neural functions of healthy infants, providing evidence of the qualitatively different organization of the young nervous system from that of the adult, have refuted the former premise. Prechtl (1981, p. 198) pointed out that contrary to earlier views of the infant as dominated by involuntary, rigid motor patterns, the infant's behavior is complex, variable, and graceful. He stated, "At the onset of extrauterine life the neural mechanisms for vital functions such as breathing, rooting, sucking and swallowing, crying, spatial orientation, sleeping and waking are fully developed as very complex control systems and not as simple reflexes."

Prechtl (1981) and Touwen (1978) rejected the view of early or primitive reflexes coming under increasingly voluntary control as the infant nervous system develops as too imprecise a concept to explain motor development. They pointed out that certain later-developing reflexes often appear concurrently with the primitive reflexes, thus contradicting the idea that the former somehow inhibit the latter. Others (see, e.g., Capute, Pasquale, Vining, Rubenstein, & Harryman, 1978; Fiorentino, 1973; Zelazo, 1976) maintain that primitive reflexes become incorporated or integrated into more complex movement patterns associated with voluntary movements as the infant matures. In the following section, the development of primitive and automatic reflexes is traced in the prenatal and postnatal periods to illustrate the neuropsychological relationship between structures and functions in the developing infant.

Fetal and Neonatal Reflexes

In the normally developing fetus and neonate, early reflexes follow an orderly sequence of appearance and integration (Capute et al., 1978). Early work conducted with human embryos (first 8 weeks of gestation) and fetuses (8 weeks of gestation to parturition) from artificially terminated pregnancies (Hooker, 1938, 1939a, 1944, 1950, 1969; Humphrey, 1964, 1969; Minkowski, 1922) demonstrated that the human embryo is capable of movement as early as the 5th week of gestation. The fetus first responds to tactile stimulation during the 8th week, and generally the mother can feel fetal movements by the 12th week of gestation. At first these movements are undifferentiated, but between 9 and 12 weeks, they become more localized (Hooker, 1939a; Humphrey, 1964). Beginning at 12 weeks, combinations of two movements have been observed, such as swallowing and mouth closure or tongue movement and mouth closure (Humphrey, 1964).

The earliest reflexes appear to be evoked by oral stimulation (Hooker, 1944), beginning at the 8th week of gestation. Initially, the lips become sensitive, followed by the mouth (including tongue and mucous membranes, nose and chin areas). The reflex response to stimulation is avoidance, manifested in neck and trunk flexion or head and trunk rotation away from the stimulus. By 12 weeks, the *swallow reflex* is evident and, as previously noted, may be combined with tongue or lip movements.

Subsequent to 14 weeks of gestation, stimulation of the soles of the feet produces dorsiflexion of the foot, fanning of the toes, and flexion of the knee and hip (Hooker, 1939a). Photographic sequences of this reflexive movement are available from Hooker (1939b). All of these reflexes are mediated at spinal or myelencephalic levels of neuraxis.

At 23 weeks of gestation, the fetus has been observed to sneeze when the inside of the nostrils were tickled (Humphrey, 1964). By 24 weeks the *sucking reflex* can be elicited by stimulating the mouth region, and at 29 weeks, Hooker (1969) reported the onset of audible sucking when the lips were stimulated. Hooker 1969) also reported that the first spontaneous cry of the fetus occurs at 25 weeks; other authors (see, e.g., Carmichael, 1970) have corroborated this age.

According to Taft and Cohen (1967) the *positive support reflex,* seen in neonates at about 3 postnatal months, is present in the fetus at 8 months of gestation. In this reflex, stimulation of the hallucal area is associated with co-contraction of opposing muscle groups, fixing the joints of the legs so they can support weight. This may aid in the maintenance of erect posture in the infant (Capute et al., 1978).

All of these reflexes may generally be categorized as (1) avoiding/protecting or (2) later functioning in feeding, and are observed prenatally. Two other reflexes observed in neonates (i.e., during the first 4 postnatal weeks) seem more directly related to feeding: the Babkin reflex (Parmelee, 1963) and the rooting reflex (Prechtl, 1958). The *rooting reflex* consists of the turning of the head and mouth toward a stimulus applied to the lips. In the *Babkin reflex,* pressure on both palms of the hand simultaneously causes the infant to bring the head to midline, open the mouth, and elevate the tongue.

From this brief description of reflex development in the fetal and neonatal periods, it is apparent that, as early as 12 weeks of gestation, the fetus's movements are differentiated.

Primitive Reflexes in the Postnatal Period

During the first month following birth, the neonate's motor activity is primarily expressed through primitive reflexes. As previously described, some of these are present in the fetus; others appear at or soon after birth and may serve the purpose of preparing the infant for later, more complex, movement (Fiorentino, 1973).

The postnatal reflexes, like those observed prenatally, normally develop in a prescribed sequence dependent on the level of structural maturation within the central nervous system. The primitive reflexes are limited to the first 6 postnatal months in the normal infant; they are gradually inhibited, and patterns of righting and equilibrium reactions (also known as automatic or postural reflexes) become manifested (Zelazo, 1976). When inhibitory controls are disrupted or delayed, primitive patterns dominate motor responses to the exclusion of more adaptive automatic reflexes. The manifestation of primitive reflexes beyond normal age limits (usually from 4 to 6 postnatal months) may indicate neurological dysfunction. The automatic reflexes are not present at birth, but they develop during the first 2 years of life. They remain an important means by which upright posture is maintained in the growing child and adult (Thurman & Widerstrom, 1985).

The First Postnatal Month. To a great extent motor activity in the neonate is a continuation of fetal movement. *Rooting* and *sucking reflexes* persist approximately until age 3 to 4 months and are elicited through oral stimulation. The *grasp reflex,* elicited through pressure to the palm of the hand from the ulnar side, persists for approximately 3 to 4 months, and *withdrawal* and *extension reflexes* of the legs and feet generally persist for the first or second postnatal month. The *crossed extension reflex* is present prenatally and at birth but normally is suppressed at 3 to 4 months of age. When stimulated on the sole of the foot, the infant extends that leg; the opposite leg remains in flexion. This reflex interferes with crawling if it is not suppressed at the proper time, because the infant cannot make reciprocal movements, extending one leg after the other.

The *Moro* response, also present prenatally, is observable in the newborn but reaches its maximum expression at approximately 2 postnatal months. It is suppressed in the normal infant by 4 months of age. The Moro is elicited by sudden lowering of the head in the supine position, causing the infant to extend arms and legs away from the trunk, then flex arms into a clasping position with legs following in a milder flexion pattern. Clinically, absence of the Moro response may be diagnostic of central nervous system dysfunction in the neonate (Capute et al., 1978). Not only is the Moro reflex diagnostically important, but also it can interfere with normal motor functioning if it is not suppressed on schedule. The protective extensor reaction that normally replaces the Moro response at about 6 months of age is suppressed if the Moro is too strong. If this occurs, the infant's arms continue to extend to either side, rather than downward, when thrown off balance, a movement that is not useful in preventing a fall. In addition, a sudden change of position will elicit the response, upsetting balance and interfering with voluntary movement.

Another fetal reflex, present in the neonate until the second month following birth, is the *Galant reflex,* named for the man who first described it in 1917 (Capute et al., 1978). This reflex is elicited by stroking the back between the 12th rib and the iliac crest. This stroking is associated with lateral flexion of the trunk toward the stimulated side in order to avoid the stimulus. The reaction is observable in the fetus as early as 20 weeks of gestation (Capute et al., 1978) and is mediated at the spinal level of neuraxis. Absence of this response may indicate a spinal cord lesion; its persistence beyond 6 months is associated with athetoid cerebral palsy and interference with development of trunk stabilization, head control, and sitting balance.

The *positive supporting reflex* is present at birth, lasts until 6 to 8 weeks of age, and finally is suppressed at about 10 months in normal infants. This reflex is elicited by touching the soles of the feet on a hard surface, and associated with extensor tone in the hips and knees so that the legs straighten and support the body's weight. There is the tendency to stand on the toes, bringing the legs together. While this reflex encourages extension patterns in the young infant that are necessary for standing, it interferes with learning to walk if it persists after 10 months of age because reciprocal movement of the legs is blocked. Balance and coordinated bending of the knee and ankle joints are also inhibited by the increased tone in the leg muscles.

The Second Postnatal Month. The 6-week-old infant is strongly dominated by flexor tone in prone and supine positions. The primitive grasp reflex and the

Moro response are strong. At this time, an important and controversial reflex appears, the *asymmetrical tonic neck reflex* (ATNR). (See Capute et al., 1978, pp. 36–37, for a review of contradicting opinions concerning this reflex.) Turning the infant's head is associated with the extension of the arm and leg on the ipsilateral side of the body, while the contralateral arm and leg remain in a flexed position.

The ATNR is seen in nearly all premature neonates and in about half of all normal neonates during the first week of life (Capute et al., 1978). It normally disappears by the fifth month, although it may last until the ninth month during sleep. The ATNR is associated with basal ganglia structures. Maintenance of this reflex beyond normal age limits interferes with voluntary reaching and self-feeding. When it is not suppressed, the ATNR also prevents the learning of many important gross-motor movements such as turning from back to stomach, crossing the midline, and crawling on hands and knees. Conversely, in the young infant, the ATNR encourages extension of the arms to prepare for reaching and grasping.

The Third Postnatal Month. As the infant reaches about 3 months of age, there is still a predominance of flexor tone, but extensor tone is increasing, particularly in the upper half of the body. This is due partly to the effect of the extension reflexes: the Moro, the crossed extension, and the ATNR. This increase in extensor tone facilitates development of head control and raising of the upper trunk in prone position, which activates the deep postural muscles of the neck and back required for standing. At 3 months, the infant engages in bilaterally symmetrical hand and foot patterns because the ability to use only one side of the body has not yet developed. Consistent with the cephalocaudal principle of developmental sequence, unilateral patterns emerge first in the upper extremities, only later appearing in the lower extremities.

At this time, an important reflex emerges, the *Landau reflex.* It is not present at birth but usually appears by 3 months and lasts until the second year of life. In a prone position, the infant extends arms and legs when the head is raised and flexes these limbs when the head is lowered. It is, therefore, a useful reflex for encouraging extension of the hips and legs, which is necessary for crawling and standing.

The Sixth Postnatal Month. By the sixth month in the normally developing infant, many motor-controlling reflexes are mediated at the midbrain level of neuraxis. Reflexes mediated at this level are the protective and righting reactions. With the equilibrium reactions, the pathways of which include areas of the cerebral cortex, they influence the infant's motor development during the second 6 months of the first postnatal year and into the second year. Thus, by 6 months of age, the early patterns of total extension or flexion as seen in the Moro and Landau responses have been suppressed, and the normal infant is able to extend some muscles while flexing others. The infant is able, for example, to extend head and trunk muscles while flexing the hips, a necessary combination for sitting.

Early reflexes appear to facilitate the following early skills: (1) head control, (2) trunk control, (3) extension of limbs, (4) grasping, (5) eye-hand coordination, and (6) coordination of movements. It is apparent that these reflexes serve a useful purpose in the very young infant. Their persistence beyond the first year of life, however, may interfere with more differentiated or complex development. This is not true of the automatic reflexes that emerge as the infant begins to crawl, stand, and walk, because they complement rather than inhibit voluntary movement. In children with motor delays, these automatic responses do not develop at the normal rate and so are not available to the child for facilitating motor development.

Automatic Reflexes in the Postnatal Period

As neural structures develop in the second 6 months after birth, the righting, protective, and equilbrium responses emerge. The righting reactions, mediated at the midbrain level of neuraxis, appear first, initially manifested in the neonate and becoming fully established by 8 postnatal months. They are followed by the equilibrium reactions, beginning at about 6 months and, at the same time, the protective extensor reaction (Fiorentino, 1973).

Righting Reactions. The righting reactions inhibit the tonic reflexes. They originate in the labyrinths, proprioceptors of the neck muscles, trunk and limb receptors, and eyes. The *neck righting reaction,* present in the neonate, consists of the rotation of the entire body in the direction the head is turned. The reflex is integrated at approximately 6 months.

The *labyrinthine righting reaction* appears at approximately 2 months. In this reaction, the infant lifts the head to a vertical orientation when placed in a prone or supine position. It is the labyrinthine reaction that prevents the head lag in the 3-month-old infant when pulled to sit. This reflex continues to offer protection throughout life by maintaining the head in an upright position.

The *optical righting reaction* normally appears soon after the labyrinthine righting reaction and continues throughout life. Similar to the labyrinthine reaction, this reaction is elicited by tipping the child forward, backward, or to one side. The infant uses visual cues to aid in the righting of the head.

The *body righting reaction* does not emerge until 6 months of age. This reaction is elicited in a manner similar to the neck-righting reaction, by placing the infant in a supine position and turning the head to one side. Unlike the neck righting reaction, in which the body rotates as a whole, the body righting reaction (which replaces neck righting in the more mature infant) causes segmental rotation of the trunk in the direction of the head turn.

Protective Extensor Thrust. Also known as the *parachute reaction,* this reflex emerges at approximately 6 months and remains throughout life. It replaces the Moro and Landau responses. Whereas the latter cause the child to throw the arms out to the sides, a nonfunctional movement for protecting the head during a fall, the parachute reaction is associated with the extension of the arms above the head so that the hands bear the brunt of the fall. This is an example of an automatic reflex replacing a primitive one as the child's needs change. Although the Moro response is functional for the neonate in developing extensor muscles, the parachute reaction better meets the needs of the older, more active infant who requires protection from falls. This reflex continues throughout life.

Equilibrium Reactions. These reactions are the last to emerge, appearing when the righting reactions are fully extablished. They gradually modify the righting reflexes, emerging as the child's motor development begins to be characterized by voluntary, upright, reciprocal, and controlled movement.

The equilibrium reactions are associated with neural structures such as the basal ganglia, the cerebellum, and the cerebral cortex. Efficient interaction among these neural structures in the normal infant, beginning at about 6 months of age, provides body adaptation in response to change of center of gravity. These reactions continue throughout life.

Equilibrium reactions may be elicited in the infant or young child in any position from prone- or supine-lying to kneeling, sitting, or standing. Developmental ages for first appearance of the reactions in each of these positions begin at 6 months (prone or supine) and progress to 8 months (kneeling), 12 months (sitting), and 15 to 18 months (standing). In each position, the reaction is elicited by tilting the child to one side, forward, or backward, requiring adjustments in body positions to maintain equilibrium.

Although a comprehensive description of abnormal motor development is beyond the scope of this chapter, it is noted that children with cerebral palsy are dominated by the involuntary postures dictated by abnormal tonic reflexes and uninhibited primitive reflexes. Domination of movement by involuntary rather than voluntary patterns may be due to a lesion in some area associated with motor pathways of the central nervous system (Capute et al., 1978).

Sensory Function

In considering sensory functioning in the perinatal period, tactile, vestibular, olfactory, auditory, and visual sensory processing are examined. First considered is prenatal development, with an examination of cutaneous, proprioceptive, and labyrinthine receptors and the senses of taste, smell, hearing, and vision. These senses are then discussed as they develop in the neonate, citing research on both preterm (less than 37 weeks of gestation) and full-term (40 weeks gestation) infants. Finally, the development of sensory functioning is traced through the first year of postnatal life.

Prenatal Sensory Function

Gottlieb (1976, 1983) stated that, in contrast to motor development, the rate of sensory development in the human is so accelerated that all sensory systems are capable of function before birth. He described the ontogenetic sequence of development of cutaneous, vestibular, auditory, and visual sensory systems in the prenatal period. He cautioned, however, against defining function in the developing sensory systems too rigidly, because the function of developing senses may be different from that of the completely mature sensory system. Consistent with our bidirectional view of the structure–function relationship, Gottlieb (1983) noted that sensory structures may alter function throughout development while sensory function may contribute to further advancement of structural development.

Although early researchers concluded that sensory function was evident in the fetus (Bradley & Mistretta, 1975), methodological problems with much of that research makes it of questionable validity (Parmelee & Sigman, 1983). It probably can be concluded that the fetus is capable of sensing certain external stimuli, but how early in fetal development this is possible and at what level of neurological organization it occurs remains unclear.

Cutaneous Receptors. The most easily observed sense organ in the developing fetus is the skin. *Cutaneous receptors* include both deep-lying proprioceptors and tactile receptors, both of which are sensitive to *pressure.* As already noted, reflex responses are elicited tactually in the fetus as early as $7\frac{1}{2}$ to 8 weeks from conception. Humphrey (1969) reported that the growing nerve fibers are still some distance from the basement membrane at this time. Apparently, therefore, these nerve fibers must be sensitive to tactile stimulation mechanically transmitted through the fetal skin.

Cutaneous sensitivity begins in the oral–nasal region, spreading over the facial region and then to the entire body surface cephalocaudally (Carmichael, 1970). Research conducted in the 1930s (Windle & Griffin, 1931; Holt, 1931) suggested that motility precedes the ability to be stimulated cutaneously, and that fetal reflex movements may be a means of self-stimulation in the developing organism. (Related to this is Connolly's, 1981, suggestion that vestibular stimulation may lead to accelerated motor development in the neonate.)

Deep and light cutaneous pressures have been found to elicit different responses in the preterm infant, leading to speculation that two distinct functional systems may be at work, one elicited by weak stimulation of a receptor field, the other by strong stimulation (Carmichael, 1970). Many of the fetal reflexes described in the preceding section are elicited by stimulation of the cutaneous pressure receptors of the skin: specifically, the sucking, grasping, sweating, abdominal, and foot reflexes.

There is little information on the functional properties of *temperature recep-tors* in the fetus. Warm and cold stimuli have been used to elicit reflex responses in fetal guinea pigs, with greater sensitivity to cold observed. Sensitivity was seen to increase with fetal age, and the area from which a reflex could be initiated spread in a cephalocaudal direction (Bradley & Mistretta, 1975). In the human fetus, responses to hot and cold stimuli have been observed by midgestation (Carmichael, 1970).

There exists little information concerning fetal response to *pain*. It appears that pain receptors are poorly developed in the neonate and may not function pre-natally at all. Carmichael (1970), for example, reported that even though stim-ulation strong enough to destroy tissue was applied to the fetus, no response was recorded.

Proprioceptive Receptors. By the fourth month of fetal life, neuromuscular spindles are found in nearly all the muscles, including those of the tongue and eye, and perhaps also in the tendons and joints. These are sensory receptors located deep in the tissues, which respond to electrochemical changes within the muscle. Thus, they are activated by kinesthetic rather than tactile stimulation and are responsible for early fetal movements associated with breathing, sucking, and locomotion. By the time of birth, there are highly developed proprioceptors involved in all body movements.

Labyrinthine Receptors. Vestibular nuclei form a large complex in the brain-stem and are connected to the semicircular canals through the vestibulocochlear nerve. This complex integrates information from labyrinthine receptors centered in the inner ear and occular receptors in the eye to regulate posture, locomotion, vision, and space perception (Precht, 1979), thus resulting in a link between vestibular, occular, and cerebellar pathways (Schmid & Jeannerod, 1979).

Labyrinthine afferents form the largest input group to vestibular nuclei. The vestibular (or labyrinthine) sense is stimulated by the pull of gravity and by fetal-head movements, aiding in body righting, position in space, and balance during motion in the extrauterine environment. In the developing fetus, it is difficult to differentiate effects of the labyrinthine receptors from proprioceptors and certain tonic reflexes such as the tonic neck reflex. It has been suggested that during the fifth month of gestation, the labyrinths acquire adult size (although further mye-lination takes place), and the vestibular system facilitates birth positioning (Eliot & Eliot, 1964). Further research is necessary to test this hypothesis.

Taste. Mature taste receptors appear in the fetus after 12 weeks of gestation (Bradley & Mistretta, 1975; Carmichael, 1970). It is presumed that the human gustatory system is functional before birth because neonates have been found to prefer sweet solutions (Bradley & Mistretta, 1975; Carmichael, 1970), and it is unlikely that the taste receptors suddenly begin to function at birth. Additionally, because the fetus swallows amniotic fluid, which is of constantly changing composition, it is possible that taste receptors are stimulated by substances dissolved therein (e.g., fetal urine). There is some question about the degree of sensory discrimination within the fetal gustatory system, however, because neonates are not able to distinguish salty, sour, or bitter tastes.

Olfaction. Neural pathways associated with olfactory and tactile stimulation are among the first sensory areas to be myelinated in the fetus. Although no information exists regarding functional activity of the olfactory receptors before birth, there is evidence of function at birth (Bradley & Mistretta, 1975) and in preterm infants (Carmichael, 1970). It was once assumed that chemicals must be in a gaseous state to be detected by olfactory receptors. That assumption, however, is now known to be incorrect, and it is presumed that the fetus could detect odorants in the amniotic fluid (Bradley & Mistretta, 1975).

Audition. Although recordings of fetal responses to auditory stimuli have been reported in early literature (Bernard & Sontag, 1947; Forbes & Forbes, 1927; Johansson, Wedenberg, & Westin, 1964; Peiper, 1925), the design of the studies precluded any definite conclusions (Carmichael, 1970; Parmelee & Sigman, 1983). Consistent fetal responses to sound have been found only after 34 weeks of gestation. Responses in younger, preterm infants (28 to 32 weeks) are brief and inconsistent, disappearing with repeated stimulation (Parmelee & Sigman, 1983). Stimuli of 100 dB (decibels) or more were found to be necessary to evoke the response in the preterm infants. This is thought to be related to the fact that the fetus is exposed to a background intrauterine noise level ranging from 72 to 95 dB. Bench (1968) identified the source of the internal noise as the maternal cardiovascular system. Against this changing background of maternal sounds, it is probable that only very loud external sounds can reach the fetus (Aslin, Pisoni, & Jusczyk, 1983; Bradley & Mistretta, 1975). A contributing factor may be the closure of the external ear or of gelatinous liquid filling the middle ear in the fetus. Thus it is not clear whether the fetus responds to auditory stimuli before birth or whether the responses may be tactile rather than auditory.

Some evidence that fetal auditory receptors are functional at birth comes from records made during labor of evoked responses from electrodes attached to the scalps of term fetuses. Auditory evoked responses were recorded in only some fetuses, with wide individual variations (Bradley & Mistretta, 1975). Auditory evoked responses also have been obtained at both brainstem and cortical levels from preterm infants from 25 weeks of gestation (Parmelee, 1981). Latency at this age is long, and stimulation thresholds are high. These rapidly decrease until 36 weeks of gestation, then decrease more gradually until term and beyond. The long latency is presumed to be due to the limited functioning of the transducers of the vestibulocochlear (VIII) cranial nerve and to incomplete dendritic branching in the auditory cortex. However, as Aslin et al. (1983) have pointed out, methodological problems associated with this relatively improved method of measuring fetal or neonatal responses continue to make it difficult to determine exactly when the auditory system begins to function. The cortical evoked response (CER), the monitoring of heartrate (HR), and the high amplitude suck (HAS) have all been used in recent years to measure various responses of the fetus or neonate to sensory input; these response systems are themselves developing as the fetus develops and so may change independently of sensory input. These response measures are discussed in more detail in the following section.

In summary, research on fetal response to auditory stimuli is equivocal. It is likely that the auditory system of the human fetus is functional in a rudimentary sense several weeks before birth, given the presence of structural precursors, but we have as yet no conclusive evidence of the onset of auditory functions in utero.

Vision. The developing visual system of the human fetus has not been extensively studied. Carmichael (1970) suggested that because there is an absence in the uterus of radiation of the sort necessary to activate the retina, the fetus is probably incapable of true vision. Nevertheless, evidence of opening and closing of the eyes in premature infants from 29 weeks of gestation (Bradley & Mistretta, 1975) suggests that such movements occur in the fetus. Carmichael (1970) associated these eye movements with vestibular stimulation as the fetus reorients in the uterus, rather than ontogenetically later visual stimulation.

The developing fetus may be visually sensitive to changes in light intensity; experiments with premature infants have found the pupil to contract when exposed to strong light (Carmichael, 1970).

Because much of the knowledge concerning early visual processing comes from studies of preterm infants, a more extensive discussion follows. It is of interest to note that the visual system has been investigated more extensively in neonates and young infants than the auditory system, whereas the opposite is true of the fetus. Further, few differences exist in the auditory functioning between preterm and full-term infants, whereas significant developmental differences have been identified in the visual functioning between those two groups.

Postnatal Sensory Function

A perusal of the research literature indicates that many questions remain unanswered regarding sensory function in the prenatal period. This is primarily due to difficulties encountered in eliciting reliable information from the human fetus regarding the processing of sensory stimuli. Although the neonate is more available for study than the fetus, similar difficulties are encountered in interpreting responses to sensory stimuli after birth because verbal communication is impossible.

A variety of techniques for monitoring certain of the infant's responses to stimuli have been recently developed, based on technologically advanced apparatuses, resulting in more reliable information than was previously available. Such techniques have yielded accurate measures of habituation (Cohen, 1981; Fantz & Fagan, 1975; Friedman, Jacobs, & Werthmann, 1981; Rose, 1981), HR (Zeskind & Field, 1982), CER (Aslin et al., 1983; Banks & Salapatek, 1983; Parmelee & Sigman, 1983; Schulte, Stennert, Wulbrand, Eichorn, & Lenard, 1977), and HAS (Siqueland, 1981) in relation to a variety of auditory, visual, and tactile stimuli. Spectral analysis has been used to study infant crying (Zeskind, 1983) and HR patterns (Porges, 1983) as means of measuring the arousal capacity of the central nervous system. Although these methods represent an improvement on previous techniques, problems in interpreting data remain. For example, these kinds of responses may be a function of the peripheral sensory or visceromotor systems rather than the central nervous system; motor responses may be due to reflex movements rather than to sound or pattern perception (Parmelee & Sigman, 1983).

Sensory Processing in the Preterm Infant. The preterm infant's capabilities for sensory processing have been evaluated primarily by measurements of response latency, degree of initial responsiveness, amount of response decrement, and length of time to response decrement. *Response decrement* is a measure of habituation that may be confounded by sensory or motor fatigue; latency is considered to be a more reliable measure in the perinatal period (Friedman et al., 1981). Shorter response latencies, shorter initial responsiveness, and quicker response decrements are associated with more mature nervous systems and thus more efficient learning and memory (Friedman et al., 1981; Lipsitt, 1979). Habituation studies comparing preterm with full-term infants have identified a developmental sequence in tactile, auditory, and visual processing that appears to be related to fetal neurological development: Greater differences in response latency and decrement between preterm and full-term neonates matched for conceptional age (i.e., length of time since conception irrespective of length of time in utero) were found in visual than in auditory processing; differences in tactile processing were not found (Friedman et al., 1981; Rose, Gottfried, & Bridger, 1979; Katona & Berenyi, 1974; Sigman, Kopp, Littman, & Parmelee, 1977; Sigman & Parmelee, 1974; Siqueland, 1981). The fetal tactile system is the first of these to develop (Gottlieb, 1983) and is functional by 4 months of gestation (Hooker, 1969). The fetal auditory system is probably functional by the sixth to eighth month (Parmelee, 1981; Purpura, 1975) whereas the visual system is not structurally established until the ninth month (Purpura, 1975). These studies have reported an increase in the quality of visual attention from 32 weeks of gestation, with active attention commonly reported at 34 to 36 weeks. Visual recognition memory is in evidence by 35 weeks in studies of habituation measured by HAS (Siqueland, 1981).

Other studies have compared preterm and full-term infants on visual and

auditory CERs. Results of these studies support the described developmental
sequence. Schulte et al. (1977), for example, compared visual and auditory
CERs at 33, 37, and 40 weeks of conceptional age. The preterm neonates, born
at 28 to 31 weeks of gestation, were matched for conceptional age with full-term
neonates, resulting in the preterms having longer extrauterine life than the
matched full-terms who were tested at the end of their first postnatal week.
Results showed differences in visual but not auditory responses of the two groups
at 37 and 40 weeks; maturation of the visual CERs was delayed in the preterm
infants, whereas maturation of the auditory CERs was not. The authors concluded that the visual system is vulnerable to premature exposure to the extrauterine environment between 36 weeks and birth (a period of rapid dendritic
development in the human visual cortex), whereas the more mature auditory
cortex is not.

The results of Schulte et al. (1977) are consistent with those reported by
Parmalee and Sigman (1983) with reference to the auditory responses of preterm
infants in the neonatal intensive-care nursery. Auditory CERs elicited from preterm and full-term infants matched for conceptional age were the same, even
though the preterms were exposed to the continual noise pollution of the intensive-care unit and the full-terms remained in utero. Parmelee and Sigman (1983)
concluded, as did Schulte et al. (1977), that the auditory system is not vulnerable
to premature exposure to the extrauterine environment; the lack of vulnerability
was attributed to the limited capacity of the immature auditory cortex to process
auditory stimuli, thus protecting the preterm infant from destructive external
influences before birth. Schulte and Stennert (1978) have demonstrated that
exposure to incubator noise does not cause hearing loss in preterm infants.

Visual evoked responses show a sequence of development in the preterm
infant from 28 weeks of gestation (Banks & Salapatek, 1983). The sequence is
characterized by a gradual decrease in latency that is well documented. At 28 to
30 weeks, CERs suggest a predominance of apical dendritic synapses near the
cortical surface. By 32 to 34 weeks there is suggestion of development of some
axosomatic and axodendritic basilar synapses. At term (40 weeks), there is a
rapid decrease in latency and a dramatic increase in attention, leading Karmel
and Maisel (1975) to conclude that a different visual-processing mechanism
begins to function at approximately 6 postnatal weeks of age. By the third
postnatal month, the CERs are well formed and stable as in the adult. Latencies
are still decreasing, not reaching adult levels until between 2 and 4 years of age.
Nevertheless, the 3-month-old infant can visually discriminate and generalize on
the basis of form, an ability not reliably demonstrated in younger infants.

In summary, research on sensory function in preterm infants suggests that
neural maturation rather than environmental experience is associated with im-
provements in sensory processing in the perinatal and postnatal periods. Neonates demonstrate congenitally organized responsiveness to novel stimuli that

may be mediated by maturation of the autonomic nervous system in terms of increased myelination and dendritic branching.

Postterm Sensory Processing. Brainstem evoked potentials (auditory brainstem responses, ABR) have been used by Aslin et al. (1983) as a means for studying the infant's auditory processing abilities. They reported that the ABR waveform does not resemble the adult pattern until 12 postnatal months, reflecting development of the peripheral and central auditory systems during this period. The primary maturational changes observed in auditory processing during the second 6 postnatal months are increased sensitivity to low frequencies, lowered thresholds of intensity, and shorter latency periods. (These are positively correlated with conceptional rather than postnatal age.) Aslin et al. (1983) further reported that neonates can reliably orient their heads toward sound, an ability that decreases during the second and third postnatal months to reemerge stronger during the fourth month.

A thorough review of the literature on visual processing in neonates and infants is beyond the scope of this chapter (see Banks & Salapatek, 1983); in order to illustrate the developing infant's neurosensory capacities, pattern vision, visual acuity, and visual recognition memory during the first 12 postnatal months are examined here.

Beginning in the early 1960s, studies were conducted of infants' differential fixation responses to various pattern stimuli (Fantz, 1963; Karmel, 1969). Since that time, much information has been gained concerning *pattern preferences* in the neonate and young infant. The literature suggests that infant preferences before 3 months are governed by responses of neurons in the visual cerebral cortex (Haith, 1980). Certain patterns evoke greater firing of the neurons and thereby hold fixation. It has been hypothesized (Banks & Ginsburg, in press; Haith, 1980) that the infant's exposure to visual patterns facilitates the postnatal development of the visual cortex. The infant's fixation behavior may stimulate cortical development by exposing the central retina to salient patterns.

Numerous researchers have determined that whereas the neonate's *visual acuity* is quite poor in comparison to the adult's, it improves significantly during the first half postnatal year due to maturation of the lateral geniculate body and increased development of cortical neurons, retinal ganglion-cell receptive fields, and photoreceptors (Banks & Salapatek, 1983).

In addressing the related topic of infant *visual recognition memory*, the work of Rose and colleagues (Rose, Gottfried, & Bridger, 1978; Rose et al., 1979; Rose, 1980, 1981) is of interest. In studies of preterm and full-term infants at 6, 9, and 12 months of age, these authors found that younger full-term (6 and 9 months), preterm (6 and 12 months), and lower-socioeconomic-status infants both demonstrated less-developed visual recognition memory and lacked the ability to transfer information from one sensory modality (i.e., tactile) to another (i.e., visual). Only middle-class full-term infants were found able to perform this crossmodal transfer (Luria, 1980, p. 59). In the less-capable subjects, the added sensory input appeared to interfere with visual-memory processes, leading the authors to conclude that simultaneous sensory processing is not possible before 12 months after birth.

Autonomic Responses

The nervous system coordinates the interplay of numerous physiological systems via complex homeostatic feedback mechanisms. Coordination reflects dynamic interactions and interdependencies among the systems, and presents the possibility of analyzing central nervous system function by measuring such autonomic activity as HR, respiration, and cry threshold. Such a model has been used to study neonatal neurological function by measures of cry threshold (Zeskind, 1983), HR variability (Parmelee, 1981; Porges, 1983; Zeskind & Field, 1982), and arousal state (Aylward, 1982; Gardner & Karmel, 1983; Parmelee & Sigman, 1983).

Whereas sympathetic functions are present at birth, maturation of the parasympathetic nervous system continues throughout infancy, resulting in an increasingly great capacity for inhibition, mediated primarily by particular cranial nerves. By measuring this inhibitory capacity, an indirect measure of central nervous system maturation is obtained. For example, estimates of the tone of the vagus (X) cranial nerve (i.e., vagal tone) have been obtained by measures of HR variability and of neonatal cry threshold. Porges (1983) reported partitioning of HR variability by means of spectral analysis in order to differentiate normally functioning from neurologically impaired neonates. HR variability is controlled primarily through the vagus (X) cranial nerve, which mediates respiratory influence on the HR by means of inhibitory efferents. This vagal control of the heart has been shown in rats to increase with age (Larson & Porges, 1982; Porges, 1983).

Vagal nerve tone affects the infant's laryngeal and respiratory muscles, and thus the frequency of the cry sound. Zeskind and colleagues (Lester & Zeskind, 1982; Zeskind, 1983; Zeskind & Field, 1982) employed spectral analysis to analyze the frequency (pitch) of neonatal cries. Comparing groups of normal and at-risk neonates, they measured HR variability and threshold, duration, and frequencies of cry to pain. They found higher-pitched, shorter cries, higher cry thresholds, and greater HR variability to be associated with poor muscle tone and poor motoric activity. The results were interpreted as providing evidence of the degree of integrity of the infant's autonomic nervous system. Zeskind (1983) theorized that the at-risk infant may have less controlled parasympathetic functions; immature vagal functioning may be responsible for poor motoric activity associated with laryngeal and respiratory muscles used for crying. Greater HR variability may reflect autonomic instability.

The neonate's physiological states have been extensively studied (Als, Tronick, Lester, & Brazelton, 1979; Parmelee & Stern, 1972); it is thought that arousal-state modulating abilities provide indications of the infant's neurological functioning (Sameroff, 1978). Relations have been reported between infant state and response to visual, auditory, tactile, and vestibular stimulation, with best performance in a low state of arousal (Gardner & Karmel, 1983). Gardner and Karmel (1983) suggested that because the neonate lacks inhibitory cortical control over subcortical structures, resulting in the lack of ability to inhibit internal levels of arousal, regulation of external stimulation is substituted. Thus, in a state of low internal arousal, the infant is attracted to high-intensity stimuli and vice versa. This theory assumes that there is a maximum amount of stimulation, internal and external, that the infant can tolerate at any given time. Parmelee and Sigman (1983) interpreted the slower response decrement to visual stimulation of preterm infants as evidence of their inability to inhibit visual responsiveness. Consistent with this interpretation are Aylward's (1982) findings that preterm infants had higher levels of arousal and of irritability than full-term infants under similar environmental conditions, and demonstrated more-extreme responses to stimulation.

CONCLUDING REMARKS

The theoretical orientation of this chapter has emphasized the bidirectional relationships between structures and functions in prenatal and postnatal neuropsychological development. In this respect, we have presented selective aspects of development and have identified the specific nature of associations between structures and functions at particular points in ontogenesis only when data from human samples were available to empirically support such conclusions. In emphasizing the dynamic aspects of both structures and functions, we have also recognized the changing nature of their associations.

The changing nature of these associations, however, is compounded by the interdependence of the dynamic structures of the human nervous system. Thus, although our discussion was organized in terms of five structural divisions of the brain and three groups of functions, we stress that such organization is intended as meaningful primarily for pedagogical purposes.

In discussing prenatal and postnatal structural development of the human central nervous system, we began with the process of neurulation. This process of neural-tube formation is significant structurally and physiologically; we emphasized its functional significance as well. We next considered the differentiation of the rostral aspect of the neural tube into three primary and five secondary brain vesicles. In describing each of these subdivisions, we focused on selected aspects of their gross morphology and suggested structures as dynamic precursors for particular functions. We cannot overemphasize, however, that the emergence of structural precursors does not necessarily imply capability of function (Wolff, 1981). Our less-detailed coverage of finer levels of brain development (considered in terms of brain weight) should not be construed as suggesting that those dynamic processes are of lesser importance than gross morphology. Rather, our coverage is admittedly selective in nature.

We suggested that the conceptual framework proposed by Luria (1980) is useful for understanding functions in terms of structures as well as structures in terms of functions; it is not simply a bridge between two disciplines. Rather, this framework helps synthesize these two bodies of literature into an integrated whole.

Our summary of functional prenatal and postnatal development focused on selected motor and sensory aspects. The survey illustrated the equivocal nature of the research literature at these levels. Nevertheless, two primary generalizations can be stated. First, there is a distinct ontogenetic sequence of reflexive behaviors initiated as early as 8 weeks of gestation. Here, the innervation of these reflexes is associated with neural structures that are progressively more specialized for function (in both phylogenetic and ontogenetic development). Second, some sensory functions, such as tactile, vestibular, and proprioceptive sensations, have been assessed prenatally, whereas others, such as olfactory, auditory, and visual sensations, appear functional by birth.

Finally, the research literature on prenatal and postnatal neuropsychological development attests to a dynamic interaction between changing neural structures and changing functions. Given the dynamic nature of these components, it is not surprising that the nature of the associations between structures and functions is also dynamic. Moreover, changing structures, functions, and associations are further complicated by their susceptibility to the influences of a dynamic environment in which the organism behaves. It is this dynamic interaction that provides the foundation for research and practice in child neuropsychology.

REFERENCES

Als, H., Tronick, E., Lester, B., & Brazelton, T. B. (1979). Specific neonatal measures: The Brazelton Neonatal Behavioral Assessment Scale. In J. D. Osofsky (Ed.), *Handbook of infant development* (pp. 185–215). New York: Wiley.

Arey, L. B. (1966). *Developmental anatomy: A textbook and laboratory manual of embryology* (7th ed.). Philadelphia: Saunders.

Aslin, R. N., Pisoni, D. B., & Jusczyk, P. W. (1983). Auditory development and speech perception in infancy. In P. H. Mussen (Ed.), *Handbook of child psychology: Vol. 2. Infancy and developmental psychobiology* (4th ed., pp. 573–687). New York: Wiley.

Aylward, G. P. (1982). Forty-week full-term and preterm neurological differences. In L. Lipsitt & T. Field (Eds.), *Infant behavior and development: Perinatal risk and newborn behavior* (pp. 67–84). Norwood, NJ: Ablex.

Banks, M. S., & Ginsburg, A. P. (in press). Early visual preferences: A review and a new theoretical treatment. In H. W. Reese (Ed.), *Advances in child development and behavior*. New York: Academic Press.

Banks, M. S., & Salapatek, P. (1983). Infant visual perception. In P. H. Mussen (Ed.), *Handbook of child psychology: Vol. 2. Infancy and developmental psychobiology* (4th ed., pp. 435–572). New York: Wiley.

Bench, J. (1968). Sound transmission to the human fetus through the maternal abdominal wall. *Journal of Genetic Psychology, 1/3,* 85–87.

Bernard, J., & Sontag, L. W. (1947). Fetal reactivity to tonal stimulation: A preliminary report. *Journal of Genetic Psychology, 70,* 205–210.

Blomfield, S., & Marr, D. (1970). How the cerebellum may be used. *Nature, 227,* 1224–1228.

Bogen, J. E., & Gordon, H. W. (1971). Musical tests for functional lateralization with intracarotid amobarbital. *Nature, 230,* 524–525.

Bradley, R. M., & Mistretta, C. M. (1975). Fetal receptors. *Physiological Reviews, 55,* 352–382.

Brodal, A. (1981). *Neurological anatomy in relation to clinical medicine* (3rd ed.). New York: Oxford University Press.

Capute, A. J., Pasquale, J. A., Vining, E. P. G., Rubenstein, J. E., & Harryman, S. (1978). *Primitive reflex profile.* Baltimore: University Park Press

Carmichael, L. (1970). The onset and early development of behavior. In P. Mussen (Ed.), *Carmichael's manual of child psychology* (Vol. 1, pp. 447–563). New York: Wiley

Carpenter, M. B. (1976). *Human neuroanatomy* (7th ed.). Baltimore: Williams & Wilkins.

Cohen, L. B. (1981). Examination of habituation as a measurement of aberrant infant development. In S. Friedman & M. Sigman (Eds.), *Preterm birth and psychological development* (pp. 241–245). New York: Academic Press.

Connolly, K. J. (1981). Maturation and the ontogeny of motor skills. In K. J. Connolly & H. F. Prechtl (Eds.), *Maturation and development: Biological and psychological perspectives* (pp. 216–230). Philadelphia: Lippincott.

Dekaban, A. S., & Sadowsky, D. (1978). Changes in brain weights during the span of human life: Relation of brain weights to body heights and body weights. *Annals of Neurology, 4,* 345–356.

Dooling, E. C., Chi, J. G., & Gilles, F. H. (1983). Telencephalic development: Changing gyral patterns. In F. H. Gilles, A. Leviton, & E. C. Dooling (Eds.), *The developing human brain: Growth and epidemiologic neuropathology* (pp. 94–104). Boston: Wright.

Drake, W. E. (1968). Clinical and pathological findings in a child with a developmental learning disability. *Journal of Learning Disabilities, 1,* 486–502.

Eliot, G. B., & Eliot, K. A. (1964). Some pathologial, radiological, and clinical implications of the precocious development of the human ear. *Laryngoscope, 74,* 1160–1171.

Fantz, R. L. (1963). Pattern vision in newborn infants. *Science, 140,* 296–297.

Fantz, R. L., & Fagan, J. F. (1975). Visual attention to size and number of pattern details by term and preterm infants during the first six months. *Child Development, 46,* 3–18.

Filskov, S. B., Grimm, B. H., & Lewis, J. A. (1981). Brain–behavior relationships. In S. B. Filskov & T. J. Boll (Eds.), *Handbook of clinical neuropsychology* (pp. 39–73). New York: Wiley.

Fiorentino, M. R. (1973). *Reflex testing methods for evaluating C.N.S. development* (2nd ed.). Springfield, IL: Charles C. Thomas.

Forbes, H. S., & Forbes, H. B. (1927). Fetal sense reaction: Hearing, *Journal of Comparative Psychology, 7,* 353–355.

Friedman, S. L., Jacobs, B. S., & Werthmann, M. W. J. (1981). Sensory processing in pre- and full-term infants in the neonatal period. In S. Friedman & M. Sigman (Eds.), *Preterm birth and psychological development.* (pp. 159–178). New York: Academic Press.

Galaburda, A. M., & Kemper, T. L. (1979). Cytoarchitectonic abnormalities in developmental dyslexia: A case study. *Annals of Neurology, 6,* 94–100.

Gallera, J. (1971). Primary induction in birds. In M. Abercrombie & J. Brachet (Eds.), *Advances in morphogenesis* (Vol. 9, pp. 149–180). New York: Academic Press.

Gardner, J. M., & Karmel, B. Z. (1983). Attention and arousal in preterm and full-term neonates. In T. Field & A. Sostek (Eds.), *Infants born at risk: Physiological, perceptual and cognitive processes* (pp. 69–98). New York: Grune & Stratton.

Gazzaniga, M. S., & LeDoux, J. E. (1978). *The integrated mind.* New York: Plenum.

Geschwind, N., & Levitsky, W. (1968). Human brain: Left–right asymmetries in temporal speech region. *Science, 161,* 186–187.

Gilles, F. H., Shankle, W., & Dooling, E. C. (1983). Myelinated tracts: Growth patterns. In F. H. Gilles, A. Leviton, & E. C. Dooling (Eds.), *The developing human brain: Growth and epidemiologic neuropathology* (pp. 118–183). Boston: Wright.

Golden, C. J. (1981). The Luria–Nebraska Children's Battery: Theory and formulation. In G. W. Hynd & J. E. Obrzut (Eds.), *Neuropsychological assessment and the school-age child: Issues and procedures* (pp. 277–302). New York: Grune & Stratton.

Gottlieb, G. (1976). Conceptions of prenatal development: Behavioral embryology. *Psychological Review, 83,* 215–234.

Gottlieb, G. (1983). The psychobiological approach to developmental issues. In P. H. Mussen (Ed.), *Handbook of child psychology: Vol. 2. Infancy and developmental psychobiology* (4th ed., pp. 1–27). New York: Wiley.

Haith, M. M. (1980). *Rules that babies look by.* Hillsdale, NJ: Erlbaum.

Heron, W. (1957). Perception as a function of retinal locus and attention. *American Journal of Psychology, 70,* 38–48.

Holt, E. G. (1931). *Animal drive and the learning process* (Vol. 1). New York: Holt.

Hooker, D. (1938). The origin of the grasping movement in man. *Proceedings of the American Philosophical Society, 79,* 597–606.

Hooker, D. (1939a). Fetal behavior. *Research Publications of the Association for Nervous and Mental Disorders, 19,* 237–243.

Hooker, D. (1939b). *Preliminary atlas of early human fetal activity.* Author.

Hooker, D. (1944). *The origin of overt behavior.* Ann Arbor: University of Michigan Press.

Hooker, D. (1950). Neural growth and the development of behavior. In P. Weiss (Ed.), *Genetic neurology* (pp. 212–213). Chicago: University of Chicago Press.

Hooker, D. (1969). *The prenatal origin of behavior.* New York: Hafner.

Humphrey, T. (1964). Some correlations between the appearance of human fetal reflexes and the development of the nervous system. *Progress in Brain Research, 4,* 93–135.

Humphrey, T. (1969). Postnatal repetition of human prenatal activity sequences with some suggestions of their neuroanatomical basis. In R. J. Robinson (Ed.), *Brain and early behavior* (pp. 43–84). New York: Academic Press.

Hynd, G. W., & Cohen, M. (1983). *Dyslexia: Neuropsychological theory, research, and clinical differentiation.* New York: Grune & Stratton.

Hynd, G. W., & Willis, W. G. (1985). Neurological foundations of intelligence. In B. B. Wolman (Ed.), *Handbook of intelligence: Theories, measurements, and applications.* (pp. 119–157). New York: Wiley.

Jacobson, M. (1978). *Developmental neurobiology* (2nd ed.). New York: Plenum.

Johansson, B., Wedenberg, E., & Westin, B. (1964). Measurement of tone response by the human fetus. *Acta Otolaryngologica, 57,* 188–192.

Karfunkel, P. (1974). The mechanisms of neural tube formation. *International Review of Cytology, 38,* 245–271.

Karmel, B. Z. (1969). The effect of age, complexity, and amount of contour density on pattern preferences in human infants. *Journal of Experimental Child Psychology, 7,* 339–354.

Karmel, B. Z., & Maisal, E. B. (1975). A neuronal activity model for infant visual attention. In L. B. Cohen & P. Salapatek (Eds.), *Infant perception: From sensation to cognition* (Vol. 1, pp. 77–131). New York: Academic Press.

Katona, F., & Berenyi, M. (1974). Differential reactions and habituation to acoustical and visual stimuli in neonates. *Activitas Nervosa Superior, 16,* 305.

Kimura, D. (1961). Cerebral dominance and the perception of verbal stimuli. *Canadian Journal of Psychology, 15,* 166–171.

Kimura, D. (1966). Dual functional asymmetry of the brain in visual perception. *Neuropsychologia, 4,* 275–285.

Kimura, D. (1973). The asymmetry of the human brain. *Scientific American, 288,* 360–368.

Kinsbourne, M. (1975). The ontogeny of cerebral dominance. *Annals of the New York Academy of Sciences, 263,* 244–250.

Kinsbourne, M., & Hiscock, M. (1983). Asymmetries of dual-task performance. In J. B. Hellige (Ed.), *Cerebral hemisphere asymmetry.* (pp. 255–334). New York: Praeger.

Larson, S. K., & Porges, S. W. (1982). The ontogeny of heart period patterning in the rat. *Developmental Psychobiology, 15,* 519–528.

Lenneberg, E. H. (1967). *Biological foundations of language.* New York: Wiley.

Lester, B. M., & Zeskind, P. S. (1982). A biobehavioral perspective on crying in early infancy. In H. Fitzgerald, B. Lester, & M. Yogman (Eds.), *Theory and research in behavioral pediatrics* (Vol. 1). New York. Plenum.

Levy, J., & Trevarthen, C. (1976). Metacontrol of hemispheric function in human split-brain patients. *Journal of Experimental Psychology: Human Perception and Performance, 2,* 299–312.

Ley, R. G., & Bryden, M. P. (1979). Hemispheric differences in recognizing faces and emotions. *Brain and Language, 7,* 127–138.

Lipsitt, L. P. (1979). Critical conditions in infancy: A psychological perspective. *American Psychologist, 34,* 973–980.

Luria, A. R. (1980). *Higher cortical functions in man.* New York: Basic Books.

Milner, B., Branch, C., & Rasmussen, T. (1964). Observations on cerebral dominance. In A. V. S. deKeuck & M. O'Connor (Eds.), *Ciba foundation symposium on disorders of language* (pp. 200–214). London: Churchill.

Minkowski, M. (1922). Ueber frühzeitige Bewegungen. Reflexe und muskulare Reaktionen beim menschlichen Fötus und ihre Beziehungen zum fötalen Nerven- und Muskelsystem. *Schweizerische medizinische Wochenschrift: Journal Suisse de Medecine (Basel), 52,* 721–724, 751–755.

Mishkin, M., & Forgays, D. G. (1952). Word recognition as a function of retinal locus. *Journal of Experimental Psychology, 43,* 43–48.

Obrzut, J. E., & Obrzut, A. (1982). Neuropsychological perspectives in pupil services: Practical application of Luria's model. *Journal of Research and Development in Education, 15,* 38–47.

Parmelee, A. H. (1963). The hand–mouth reflex of Babkin in premature infants. *Pediatrics, 31,* 734–740.

Parmelee, A. H. (1981). Auditory function and neurological maturation in preterm infants. In S. Friedman & M. Sigman (Eds), *Preterm birth and psychological development* (pp. 227–250). New York: Academic Press.

Parmelee, A. H., & Sigman, M. D. (1983). Perinatal brain development and behavior. In P. H. Mussen (Ed.), *Handbook of child psychology: Vol. 2. Infancy and developmental psychobiology* (4th ed., pp. 95–155). New York: Wiley.

Parmelee, A. H., & Stern, E. (1972). Development of states in infants. In C. Clemente, D. Purpura, & F. Meyer (Eds.), *Sleep and the maturing nervous system* (pp. 117–149). New York: Academic Press.

Passler, M. A., Isaac, W., & Hynd, G. W. (1985). Neuropsychological development of behavior attributed to frontal lobe functions in children. *Developmental Neuropsychology, 1,* 349–370.

Peiper, A. (1925). Sinnesempfindungen des Kindes vor seiner Geburt. *Monatsschrift für Kinderheilkunde, 29,* 239–241.

Porges, S. W. (1983). Heart rate patterns in neonates. In T. Field & A. Sostek (Eds.), *Infants born at risk: Physiological, perceptual, and cognitive processes* (pp. 3–22). New York: Grune & Stratton.

Precht, W. (1979). Labyrinthine influences on the vestibular nuclei. In R. Granit & O. Pompeiano (Eds.), *Progress in brain research: Vol 50. Reflex control of posture and movement* (pp. 369–381). New York: Elsevier/North-Holland.

Prechtl, H. F. (1958). The directed headturning response and allied movements of the human baby. *Behavior, 13,* 212–242.

Prechtl, H. F. (1981). The study of neural development as perspective of clinical problems. In K. J. Connolly & H. F. Prechtl (Eds.), *Maturation and development: Biological and psychological perspectives* (pp. 198–216). Philadelphia: Lippincott.

Prohovnik, I. (1980). *Mapping brainwork.* Gotab, Sweden: Gleerup.

Purpura, D. P. (1975). Dendritic differentiation in human cerebral cortex: Normal and aberrant developmental patterns. In G. W. Kreuzberg (Ed.), *Advances in neurology* (Vol. 12, pp. 115–141). New York: Raven Press.

Reinis, S., & Goldman, J. M. (1980). *The development of the brain: Biological and functional perspectives.* Springfield, IL: Charles C. Thomas.

Rose, S. A. (1980). Enhancing visual recognition memory in preterm infants. *Developmental Psychology, 16,* 85–92.

Rose, S. A. (1981). Lags in the cognitive competence of prematurely born infants. In S. Friedman & M. Sigman (Eds.), *Preterm birth and psychological development* (pp. 255–270). New York: Academic Press.

Rose, S. A., Gottfried, A. W., & Bridger, W. H. (1978). Cross-modal transfer in infants: Relationship to prematurity and socio-economic background. *Developmental Psychology, 14,* 643–652.

Rose, S. A., Gottfried, A. W., & Bridger, W. H. (1979). Effects of haptic cues on visual recognition memory in full term and preterm infants. *Infant Behavior and Development, 2,* 55–67.

Sameroff, A. J. (Ed.). (1978). Organization and stability of newborn behavior: A commentary on the Brazelton Neonatal Behavior Assessment Scale. *Monographs of the Society for Research in Child Development,43,* 5–6.

Saxen, L., & Toivonen, S. (1962). *Primary embryonic induction.* Englewood Cliffs, NJ: Prentice-Hall.

Schade, J. P., & Ford, D. H. (1973). *Basic neurology* (2nd ed). New York: Elsevier.

Schmid, R., & Jeannerod, M. (1979). Organization and control of the vestibulo-ocular reflex. In R. Granit & O. Pompeiano (Eds.), *Progress in brain research: Vol. 50. Reflex control of posture and movement* (pp. 477–489). New York: Elsevier/North-Holland.

Schulte, F. J., & Stennert, E. (1978). Hearing defects in preterm infants. *Archives of Disease in Childhood, 53,* 269–290.

Schulte, F. J., Stennert, E., Wulbrand, A., Eichorn, W., & Lenard, H. G. (1977). The ontogeny of sensory perception in preterm infants. *European Journal of Pediatrics, 126,* 211–224.

Sigman, M., Kopp, C. B., Littman, B., & Parmelee, A. H. (1977). Infant visual attentiveness as a function of birth condition. *Developmental Psychology, 13,* 431–437.

Sigman, M., & Parmelee, A. H. (1974). Visual preference of 4-month-old premature and full-term infant. *Child Development, 45,* 959–965.

Siqueland, E. R. (1981). Studies of visual recognition memory in preterm infants: Differences in development as a function of perinatal morbidity factors. In S. Friedman & M. Sigman (Eds.), *Preterm birth psychological development* (pp. 271–288). New York: Academic Press.

Sperry, R. W. (1968). Hemispheric deconnection and unity in conscious awareness. *American Psychologist, 23*, 723–733.

Springer, S. P., & Deutsch, G. C. (1981). *Left brain, right brain.* San Francisco: Freeman.

Taft, L. T., & Cohen, H. J. (1967). Neonatal and infant reflexology. In J. Hellmuth (Ed.), *Exceptional infant: Vol. 1. The normal infant* (pp. 79–120). New York: Brunner/Mazel.

Teidemann, H. (1967). Biochemical aspects of primary induction and determination. In R. Weber (Ed.), *The biochemistry of animal development* (Vol. 2, pp. 3–55). New York: Academic Press.

Thurman, S. K., & Widerstrom, A. H. (1985). *Young children with special needs: A developmental and ecological approach.* Boston: Allyn & Bacon.

Touwen, B. C. L. (1978). Variability and stereotype in normal and deviant development. *Clinics in developmental medicine* (No. 67). Philadelphia: Lippincott.

Wada, J., Clarke, R., & Hamm, A. (1975). Cerebral hemispheric asymmetry in humans. *Archives of Neurology, 32*, 239–246.

Wada, J., & Rasmussen, T. (1960). Intracarotid injection of sodium amytal for the lateralization of cerebral speech dominance: Experimental and clinical observations. *Journal of Neurosurgery, 17*, 266–282.

Walsh, K. W. (1978). *Neuropsychology: A clinical approach.* New York: Churchill Livingstone.

Willis, W. G., & Hynd, G. W. (in press). Lateralized interference effects: Evidence for a processing style by modality interaction. *Cortex.*

Wilson, J. G. (1965). Embryological considerations in teratology. In J. G. Wilson & J. Warkany (Eds.), *Teratology: Principles and techniques* (pp. 251–261). Chicago: University of Chicago Press.

Windle, W. F., & Griffin, A. M. (1931). Observations on embryonic and fetal movements of the cat. *Journal of Comparative Neurology, 52*, 149–188.

Witelson, S. F., & Pallie, W. (1973). Left hemisphere specialization for language in the newborn: Neuroanatomical evidence of asymmetry. *Brain, 96*, 641–646.

Wolff, P. H. (1981). Normal variations in human maturation. In K. J. Connolly & H. F. Prechtl (Eds.), *Maturation and development: Biological and psychological perspectives* (pp. 1–18). Philadelphia: Lippincott.

Zaidel, D., & Sperry, R. W. (1973). Performance on the Raven's Coloured Progressive Matrices Test by subjects with cerebral commissuriotomy. *Cortex, 9*, 34–39.

Zelazo, P. R. (1976). From reflexive to instrumental behavior. In L. P. Lipsitt (Ed.), *Developmental psychobiology* (pp. 87–108). Hillsdale, NJ: Erlbaum.

Zeskind, P. S. (1983). Production and spectral analysis of neonatal crying and its relation to other behavioral systems in the infant at risk. In T. Field & A. Sostek (Eds.), *Infants born at risk: Physiological, perceptual and cognitive processes* (pp. 23–44). New York: Grune & Stratton.

Zeskind, P. S., & Field, T. M. (1982). Neonatal cry threshold and heart rate variability. In L. Lipsitt & T. M. Field (Eds.), *Infant behavior and development: Perinatal risk and newborn behavior* (pp. 51–60). Norwood, NJ: Ablex.

Chapter 3

Cortical Maturation and Developmental Neurolinguistics

SYLVIA CAMPBELL

Department of Hearing and Speech Sciences
University of Maryland
College Park, Maryland 20742

HARRY WHITAKER

The Neuropsychiatric Institute
Fargo, North Dakota 58107

INTRODUCTION

In 1967, the concept of the biological basis for language capabilities was reinstated by Eric Lenneberg (Lennenberg, 1967). Setting forth cognition as the "behavioral manifestation of physiological processes" (p. 373), Lennenberg then defined language "as one of the species-specific cognitive propensities, differentiated spontaneously and developing ontogenetically in the course of physical maturation" (pp. 372, 344). His neurological, maturational model of language development was further expanded in his treatise and included the following now-well-known tenets:

1. Hemispheric equipotentiability exists for language mediation. Lenneberg claimed that at birth the hemispheres are equipotential in the ability to develop language.
2. Lateralization of language processes (generally to the left hemisphere) is realized gradually. Influenced by both maturational and environmental

55

factors (exposure to and use of language), the development of lateralization (subsequent decrease in equipotentiality) proceeds most rapidly between 2 and 3 years of age and more slowly after that until puberty, at which time the process is felt to be complete (loss of equipotentiality).

3. Interhemispheric plasticity exists for language development. This plasticity (actually denoting the combined effects of tenets 1 and 2) is necessary for learning language naturally and completely (critical age for language learning) and also enabled the right hemisphere to assume language mediation in cases of damage to the left, language-lateralized hemisphere.

In the years since Lenneberg's assertion regarding the biological basis for language processes, equipotentiality and plasticity/critical-age concepts have dominated developmental research and theory, and they have affected programming and planning for both normal and disordered populations. Models of the language acquisition process based on Lenneberg's tenets have ranged from simple restatements of the equipotentiality claim to attempts to associate specific language acquisition stages to maturation of central nervous system mechanisms (Milner, 1976). Perhaps the boldest interpretation and application of the Lenneberg model of language development was presented in 1974 by H. T. Epstein. With a biological basis for language as the foundation, Epstein claimed causal relationships between brain growth spurts (weight and skull size) and learning (cognitive) abilities. He then hypothesized four stages during which fairly abrupt changes in behavior reflected associated changes in biophysical properties of brains. The brain growth spurts occurring at 6–8 years, 10–12 years, 14–17 years and 2–4 years were determined to directly coincide with Piagetian stages of cognitive development (e.g., the 14–17-year spurt correlated with the Piagetian stage of formal operations.) From this basic framework, Epstein further suggested that these so-called brain-growth–cognitive-stages should govern what, when and how children are taught (Epstein, 1974b).

It is possible to establish relationships between neural mechanisms and language systems during the cortical maturation process. However, attempts like those of Milner (1976) and Epstein (1974a, 1974b), which conclude causal relationships between neural mechanisms and linguistic functions outside an early developmental model and without support of experimental data seem entirely inappropriate. Clearly, it is difficult, if not impossible, to signify a relationship between complex behaviors and neural functioning (Jacobson, 1975).

For example, what is the strength of the inverse of both Milner and Epstein's hypotheses? It seems just as reasonable to assume that the increase in complexity of linguistic and cognitive behavior brings about neurological change and reorganization. The point to be made is that hypotheses regarding complex behavior and biological interactions can not be based on correlational and anecdotal observations alone. Recently, however, experimental data have become available.

In the late 1970s, a new discipline attempting to clarify issues concerned with the form of representation of language in the human brain arose (Marshall, 1980). This discipline—neurolinguistics—serves as the interface between linguists and neuroscientists (concerned with neural systems and mechanisms involved in information sorting and control of behavior). As such, it offers an integrative approach to developmental issues involving language acquisition and its relationship with the human brain (Dingwall & Whitaker, 1977).

In light of the resulting studies in the field of neurolinguistics and the current level of knowledge regarding cortical maturation, the appropriateness and accuracy of the Lenneberg tenets and subsequent developmental models of acquisition must be seriously questioned. All currently available evidence indicates that a hemispheric specialization for language exists at birth, thus negating any claims of equipotentiality and limiting plasticity. Additionally, not only do the correlations that exist between cortical maturation and language development become less convincing as the complexity of the organism and function increases, the cortical maturation process appears to be 90% complete by age 5. The obvious implication is that after age 5, cortical maturation plays a minimal, if not completely insignificant, role in the development of higher-level syntactic, semantic, pragmatic, and cognitive functions.

The remainder of the chapter provides support for the preceding assertions. Cortical maturation is concisely reviewed relative to those processes most commonly felt to reflect the course to establishment of a mature system. Particular attention is paid to changes occurring across specific language areas of the brain. This is followed by a review of the neurolinguistic research involving hemispheric specialization and plasticity with respect of language function. Conclusions and suggestions for future research are provided.

The neuroanatomical apparatus governing the comprehension and projection of meaningful language is not known. Correlations do exist between changes in the human nervous system and behavior, which suggest a dynamic relationship between maturation and function. These relationships are most clear and most accurately interpreted at earlier, less-complex stages of cortical and linguistic development.

ANATOMICAL CHANGE AND ASYMMETRY

At birth, the human brain weights approximately 300–400 grams, or about one quarter of its adult weight. The neurons, sufficiently dense, but lacking the complexity of dendritic arborization, have completed the migration to the final location with the cortex, and the neocortical areas show their characteristic six-layer structure. Apparent is the common occurrence of the Yakovlevian anti-clockwise torque: the left occipital pole is longer and extends across the midline toward the right; the right hemisphere is wider in its frontal portion and the right frontal pole frequently protrudes forward (Lemay, 1976). The lobes are well defined, although fissurization is not complete.

Two commonly cited anatomic differences assumed to be related to language functioning are left–right asymmetries in the temporal and frontal lobes. The planum temporale, the superior surface of the temporal lobe posterior to Herchel's transverse gyrus and fissure, is markedly larger in the left than in the right hemisphere (an asymmetry visible at the 29th week of gestational age) (Teszner, Tzavaras, Gruner, & Hecaen, 1972; Clarke & Hamm, 1975; A. Witelson & Pallie, 1973). With respect to the frontal lobes, Adrianov (1980) reported results of Russian studies, which indicated functional interhemispheric asymmetry in the frontal lobes characterized by size of area, degree of vertical order of cells, intrasulcal components, and layer width and abundance. According to Adrianov (1980), the data indicated asymmetric growth-increases in area 45—a 22% increase in the right hemisphere versus a 54% increase in the left hemisphere during the first $2\frac{1}{2}$ months postnatally. In addition, late in postnatal development, area 44 is large in absolute area in the right hemisphere. Although these anatomical asymmetries seem to suggest a potential for functional asymmetry, they do not in and of themselves indicate that an actual functional asymmetry exists (S. Witelson, 1977).

Anatomically, the brain of the newborn clearly reflects an immaturity relative to gross measures in the adult brain. The cortex of the newborn, exhibiting a lack of dendritic arborization, limited and differential myelination, decreased width of cell layers and various other histological limitations (amount of chromophil in cell bodies, etc), also reflects an immaturity relative to the adult brain. The process of cortical maturation actually begins in utero and will proceed in a multidimensional manner varying temporally and spatially through the adult years (Whitaker, Bub, & Leventer, 1981). How is this multidimensional process of cortical maturation best defined? In attempting to relate those factors of cortical maturation most likely to reflect functional change in the organism, two criteria have been commonly used: myelination and histological changes within the neurons, specifically changes in neurodensity and cell width of cortical layers. Although somewhat speculative to use these criteria to narrowly define conclusions regarding cortical functioning, these maturational changes in the cortex do correlate with increased functional sophistication of the organism and, therefore, are assumed to at least grossly index functional change.

MYELINATION

The growth pattern of myelination follows an orderly sequence during fetal and postnatal life. Although the presence of a myelin sheath is not essential for conduction of action potentials, prior to myelination, neurons exhibit slower transmission times (conduction velocities) and repetitive firing rates, and they are more prone to fatigue effects (Bronson, 1982). These changes resulting from the completion of the myelogenetic cycle reflect a functional maturity, which can be related to the emergence of gradual behavioral changes (Yakolev & Lecours, 1967).

Myelination in the developing central nervous system has been extensively examined. Patterns of myelination across the cerebral cortex were identified by Flechsig in 1901. He found variations in the onset of the development of myelin across three cortical fields. The myelination process began first in the primordial fields—pre- and postcentral gyri, calcarine cortex, and retrosplenial, subcallosal, and septal areas, and the transverse temporal gyrus. This was followed by the onset of the process in the intermediate fields at approximately 3 months postnatally and the classical association areas (terminal fields) at approximately 4 months postnatally. Yakolev and Lecours expanded Flechsig's work (Lecours, 1975; Yakolev, 1962; Yakolev & Lecours, 1967) and concluded that the myelination process was best defined in terms of cycles of myelogenesis, with highly variable times from onset to adult status of myelination. This pattern of development offered support for the functional–structural relationship of myelination (Bronson, 1982; O'Brien, 1970) and provided for the role of stimulation in the myelination process: (O'Brien, 1970)

1. In man, the major part of myelination begins at birth or shortly thereafter.
2. Pathways in the central nervous system (CNS) become myelinated in the order in which they develop phylogenetically (efferent tracts from the cerebellar hemispheres myelinate before the afferent tracts).
3. Tracts in the CNS become myelinated at the time they become functional—
   a. The fetus receives tactile, auditory, proprioceptive stimuli; hence, these tracts begin the myelination process early during fetal life and are myelinated up to the thalamus at birth.
   b. The fetus does not receive pain, visual, or olfactory stimuli; these tracts begin the myelination process at birth.
   c. Myelination in a premature infant exceeds that of a full-term infant of the same gestational age, reflecting the influence of external stimuli and development of myelin relative to function.
4. The conduction velocities of neurons varies with age. In the child, they are slower than in adults (reflecting incomplete myelination). In general, the rate of velocity change follows the myelination pattern (O'Brien, 1970).

Specific data regarding the onset rate and completion of the myelination process can be expanded by summarizing data presented by Yakolev (1962) and Yakolev and Lecours (1967).

The myelination process begins in the peripheral system in the sensory and motor pathways of the spinal column at approximately 3 months of fetal life.

Myelination of the motor roots is essentially complete in the neonate. Myelination of the sensory system is less rapid and continues into the first 6 months after birth.

Marked differences are apparent among the various modalities of the sensory afferents extending into the subcortical areas. The vestibular system is most advanced with myelination complete at the time of birth. Myelination of the subcortical visual afferents begins somewhat earlier, at approximately 2 months of fetal life, but does not complete until approximately 3 months after birth. Following a similar pattern with a later onset, the inferior colliculus of the auditory system begins myelination at approximately 3 months prenatally and completes the process at approximately 3 months after birth.

Myelination of the sensory afferents to the neocortex does not begin until at birth, or as in the case of the somatosensory system, shortly before birth. The process is most rapid in the neocortical branch of the visual afferent system— completed by approximately 4 months postnatally. Myelination in the somato-sensory tracts is complete by the first year after birth. The auditory afferent system does not complete the process until well into the preschool years (5 years of age—Lecours, 1975).

At approximately 5 months of fetal age, the pyramidal tract descends. The myelination process begins in the major efferent pathway from the cortex approximately 2 months later and is completed by the first year of life.

The oculomotor, the motor divisions of the eighth nerve, are among the first of the cranial nerves to begin the process. The abducens, trochlear, facial, glossopharyngeal, vagus, spinal accessory and the hypoglossal myelinate in the order listed (Whitaker et al., 1981).

The pathways to and from the cerebellum follow two separate courses of development in the myelination process. The inner division, presumed to control the various motion-induced reflexes of the infant (Bronson, 1982), completes myelination at approximately 2 months before birth. The remainder of the cerebellum continues myelinating until 2 years of age.

Myelination of the cortical–subcortical pathways and short interneuron connections does not begin until as late as 4 months after birth (e.g., nonspecific thalamic nuclei and association areas), and this continues into midchildhood and beyond. Myelination of the *corpus callosum,* the major fiber bundle connecting the two cerebral hemispheres, nears completion by age 6 years then continues slowly until age 10 years.

NEURODENSITY AND LAYER WIDTH

The characteristics of the neurons are developmentally defined by Conel (1939–1967). Maturational change was measured by several criteria: myelination, development of cortical axons and exogenous fibers, development of bulbs, and growth of neurofibrils and chromophil in the cell bodies. For the purpose of this section of the chapter, only those histological changes in density and width within various cortical layers are considered.

Measured of neurodensity, reflecting the development of dendrites, sizes of cell bodies, and development of axons show important differences across cortical regions. Neurodensity is high in the visual cortex due to a predominance of axosomatic synapses. In the precentral cortex with the extensive surfaces of a large pyramidal cells and well developed dendrites, neurodensity is low (Whitaker et al., 1981). The changes in neurodensity reflected by the maturing brain are likewise not constant across regions. For example, in the primary motor cortex the average decrease in the number of cells is approximately 12 years. In Broca's and other frontal areas, the decrease is smaller—50%—and complete by $2\frac{1}{2}$ years.

Measures of the width of layers of the cortex, somewhat dependent on dendritic arborization, also provide some indication of the structural complexity of the cortex. Yakolev (1962) defines the maturational changes in width of cortical layers (percentages of increase) from birth to 20 years as follows:

Layer I   136% increase
Layer II   150% increase
Layer III 170% increase
Layer IV   66% increase
Layer V   133% increase
Layer VI   194% increase.

These percentages reflect width changes across both hemispheres for all areas within the cortex. When the percentages of width increase are analyzed relative to a specific hemisphere and/or specific areas of functioning, a differential pattern emerges. This is especially apparent across various language areas. Whitaker et al. (1981) defined the width changes in terms of peaks and drops in width ratios across language areas, and the following pattern emerged:

Layer I   —   All four language areas: Broca's, Wernicke's and the supramarginal and angular gyri peak at 4 years of age.
Layer II   —   Wernicke's area and the supramarginal and angular gyri have a peak at 15 months, a drop at 2 years of age, and peak again at 4 years.
Layer III —   Broca's and Wernicke's areas and the supramarginal gyrus peak at 4 years and show a drop at 6 years of age.
Layer IV   —   Wernicke's and Broca's areas and the supramarginal gyrus show a peak at 6 months of age and drop at 2 years of age.
Layer V   —   Broca's area and the angular and a supramarginal gyri peak at 6 months and show a drop at 2 years.
Layer VI   —   All areas peak at 15 months and show a drop at 2 years.

Some of the specific changes that result in the differential rates of increase in cell width are as follows.

In the 1-month-old cortex, the changes in width are due to increases in the size of the neurons as well as increases in the number of glial cells. Layers I and II show less consistent width increases than layers IV, V, VI. By 3 months of age, all layers have increased in width, although cells in the upper section III and those in layers I and II are poorly developed (Whitaker et al., 1981). Layer VI has increased in exogenous fibers and subcortical association fibers. The supramarginal and angular gyri are now essentially developed to the same degree in terms of cell width and cell differentiation. In the primary sensorimotor cortex, the areas serving the head and lower extremities are the least mature. By 6 months of age, subcortical association fibers have increased in the primary motor, visual, auditory, and somatosensory areas. By 15 months, increases in size of cells in layers IV and II have occurred in all areas.

In the frontal lobe, the greatest development has occurred in the pyramidal cells (layer III). An increase in the number of apical dendrites and ascending vertical exogenous fibers are evident as vertical striations in the supramarginal and angular gyri. There is an increase in size in the large pyramidal cells in Broca's area. The axonal networks of Golgi type II cells are present throughout all layers and areas. Horizontal exogenous fibers are not developed in layer II. Layer VI contains numerous subcortical association fibers. At 2 years of age, the horizontal exogenous fibers remain undeveloped in layers II and III. Myelinated exogenous fiber has increased in Broca's area, as well as other areas of the frontal lobe. By 4 years of age, layer III in the frontal lobe and layer VI in the temporal lobe have increased in width. Layers II, III, and IV are well developed in the head area in the frontal lobe, and horizontal exogenous fibers are increasing in this lobe in layers III and IV. Layer III of the supramarginal gyrus has increased its width. By 5 years of age, the width of all layers is less than that of

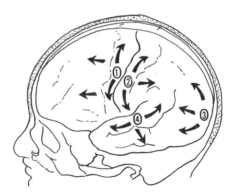

Figure 1. Cerebral-cortical maturation. Maturation processes begin first in area (1), last in area (4), and proceed in the direction of the areas.

the adult. A gradient in degree of development from layer VI (innermost) to layer I (outermost) is apparent. Vertical exogenous fibers end in layer IV in the most advanced areas.

Based on the specific criteria of myelination and neurodensity and layer width discussed in this chapter, and all other available criteria of neural maturation, the brain has reached 90% of adult values by 5 years of age (Whitaker et al., 1981). This maturational change to adult levels of cortical maturity reflects a growth pattern across the cortical mantle, as shown in Figure 1. The numbers 1–4 indicate the point at which maturation begins and the arrows indicate the direction in which it proceeds.

SUMMARY OF CORTICAL MATURATION PROCESS

The cortical maturation process defined by gross anatomical changes and asymmetries, the myelination process, and changes in neurodensity and layer width correlate well with functional changes occurring in the organism and seem to parallel the gradual emergence and refinement of cognitive and motor capabilities (Bronson, 1982).

The differential degrees of cortical maturation at birth, and the differential and rapid rates of change postnatally (the so-called growth spurts of development) lend themselves well to speculations regarding co-occurring behavioral changes in the maturing child and stages of developmental growth. Even grossly considered, the shift from the reflexive behaviors of the newborn to goal-directed behaviors and finally to behaviors guided by integrative processes involving several sensory modes and attribution of symbolic significance, accompanied by increasing levels of sophistication of neural processing and cortical maturation, tempts one to expand the correlations into direct and specific relationships between maturation and function. However, it must be remembered that this maturational process is 90% complete by age 5, thus limiting the time frame in which functional maturational relationships may occur.

With specific respect to language development, the data minimally suggest a preprogrammed hemisphere specialization for linguistic capabilities in humans. Clear causal relationships between cortical maturation and linguistic capabilities cannot be defined. In order to more precisely evaluate the "status of the relationship of man's language and her nervous system" (Dingwall & Whitaker, 1977), one must supplement this understanding of the central maturation process with data from research addressing the neurolinguistic performance of children.

NEUROLINGUISTIC RESEARCH

Traditionally, in the study of child language, the majority of the research has addressed the language acquisition process either in terms of cognitive, linguistic, or, more recently, pragmatic (functional) models. Investigators and theorists have attempted to define the process in terms of the various aspects and characteristics of each of the models and to provide normative data relative to age, manner, and course (stages) of the acquisition process. Performance of disordered populations has likewise been considered diagnostically, therapeutically, and prognostically in terms of the various models and specific normative populations. Evaluating child language capabilities with respect to neurolinguistic relationships is a relatively recent development within the area of child language research. Largely as a result of the basic tenets of Lenneberg presented in 1967 (discussed in the introduction), developmental neurolinguistic research has primarily addressed the mutually inclusive issues of hemisphereic specialization and interhemispheric plasticity within the maturing child. Based on data obtained from both normal and disordered populations, current neurolinguistic research does not support a strong *equipotentiality hypothesis,* which, as proposed by Lenneberg, holds that the lateralization of language abilities and loss if interhemispheric plasticity is a developmental phenomenon occurring gradually over time and completing at puberty. The evidence clearly suggests a left-hemispheric specialization for language, present from birth, which may limit the degree of interhemispheric plasticity available to the brain-damaged child (Dennis & Whitaker, 1977).

The remainder of the chapter provides an overview of current neurolinguistic research with infants and children followed by conclusions and implications for future research.

EARLY HEMISPHERIC SPECIALIZATION

Normal Populations

Behavioral studies designed to provide neurolinguistic data for normally developing infants and children can be categorized into two major types of tasks: those assessing speech preception (infants) and those assessing differential responses to verbal and nonverbal stimuli.

Results of speech perception studies have indicated that infants 4 months of age and younger can discriminate differences in essential parameters of acoustic signals for the processing of linguistic information—intensity, frequency and duration (Eisenberg, 1976). Using a habituation paradigm, Kaplan (1969, p. 55) demonstrated that infants could discriminate between falling intonation contours, thus exhibiting the ability to apply discriminatory skills for frequency, intensity, and duration to analyze linguistic information. Infants' perceptual sensitivity was related directly to the discrimination of speech sounds in several studies (Eimas, Siqueland, Juscyk, & Vigorito, 1971; Morse, 1974; Trehub & Rabinovitch, 1972).

In separate studies, Morse (1974), Moffitt (1971), and Trehub and Rabinovitch (1972) demonstrated infants' ability to discriminate the consonants /b/, /p/, /d/, /t/, and /g/. Eimas et al. (1971) found that the phonemic boundary for /b/ and /p/ relative to the voice-onset time continuum was the same for infants (6 weeks for age) as for adults. The investigators interpreted the results as suggesting that the categories for input for perception of stop-consonants are not dependent on experience with language. This interpretation was later expanded, and the presence of a feature-detector system, present at birth and specially tuned to certain features of sensory (linguistic) input, was postulated (Eimas & Corbit, 1973; Eimas, Cooper, & Corbit, 1973).

These consistent findings obtained regarding infants' early abilities both to respond differentially to acoustic features related to input and to perceive and discriminate speech phonemes suggests a possible biologically determined predisposition for linguistic capabilities.

A considerable number of studies evaluating early differential responses to verbal–nonverbal stimuli involve dichotic listening and tachistoscopic tasks. Problems of interpretation plague both groups of data. Springer and Deutsch (1981) list several inconsistencies and questions regarding interpretation of dichotic and tachistoscopic measures in adults. According to these authors and others, the measures typically underestimate the incidence of left-hemisphere language representation found in right-handed individuals through sodium amytal (Wada) testing. This inconsistency then leads one to question whether the behavioral measures actually reflect right–left hemispheric asymmetry for linguistic stimuli or other, less-lateralized abilities. Differences in response strategies and attention biases (selectively shifting attention to either left or right stimuli) have been shown to alter results. Finally, test results between the two measures are not highly correlated with one another, and both procedures exhibit low test reliabilities. While all of these issues may not be directly relevant to infant and child performance (e.g., attention bias), the factors affecting adult performance should be considered, and the data, if not skeptically, at least cautiously, considered.

Entus (1977) and Best, Hoffman, and Glanville (1982) investigated infant dichotic listening, using a high-amplitude sucking (HAS) and heart rate (HR) paradigm. All investigators obtained patterns of lateral asymmetry for speech and for nonspeech stimuli. For infants as young as 22 days, a right-ear superiority was found for speech stimuli. In another study by Vargha-Khadem and Corballis (1979), infants were able to discriminate consonant–vowel contrasts equally efficiently in either ear, thus suggesting no lateral asymmetry for processing. In an extensive review of dichotic listening studies with children aged 7 years and younger, S. Witelson (1977) reported "a marked consistency for greater right than left ear scores for children of all ages, even those as young as $2\frac{1}{2}$ years" (p. 230). S. Witelson interpreted these results as providing strong support for a greater participation of left than right hemisphere in tasks involving linguistic processing, although she did report difficulties in comparing results across studies and with broad interpretations of the data (e.g., increase in degree of specialization with increasing age). Also referenced by Witelson were investigations indicating left-hemisphere specialization for linguistic stimuli presented dichotically to school-age children (populations serving as normal controls for various clinical samples). (See S. Witelson, 1977, for specific references.)

Results of tachistoscopic studies offer little information regarding left-hemispheric specialization (S. Witelson, 1977). The difficulties in assessing exactly what is being measured by the studies as well as ascertaining what, if any, direct relationship exists between the responses to visually presented linguistic stimuli and biologically based linguistic capabilities preclude significant, relevant interpretations of tachistoscopic data. In addition, an abundance of methodological problems exist for all studies (e.g., subject selection, reading ability). For these reasons, tachistoscopic studies are not considered in this chapter; for a thorough, critical review, see S. Witelson (1977).

Finally, with reference to the development of early differential response to verbal–nonverbal stimuli, several studies have used electrophysiological measures to determine interhemispheric differences. Davis and Wada (1977) measured auditory evoked potentials (AEP's) to simple visual (flashes) and auditory (clicks) stimuli. A comparison of the tracings indicated hemispheric asymmetries in coherence and power spectra for infants 5 weeks of age. A number of other investigations with infants have reported similar findings with larger AEP's over the left hemisphere for verbal input and larger AEP's over the right hemispheres for noises (Molfese, Freeman, & Palermo, 1975; Molfese, D., & Molfese, V. J., 1979). Barnett, Vincentini, and Campos (1974) also reported greater amplitudes of AEP's in the left hemisphere for speech stimuli in infants. Asymmetries of electroencephalographic (EEG) power distributions in response to speech and music have also been reported in infants 6 months of age (Gardiner & Walter, 1977).

Brain-Damaged Populations

In 1962, Basser reported incidences of language dysfunction in children who had sustained unilateral (right or left) brain damage prior to 2 years of age. His data indicated that approximately 50% of the children presented speech delays, and that the distribution of disorder was the same for both hemispheres. Lenneberg (1967) subsequently based his equipotentiality theory primarily on this data, which by Lenneberg's interpretation indicated a period in infancy in which the two hemispheres are equipotential for language or function.

Just as there is behavioral evidence from normal populations for a hemispheric specialization for language present during infancy, so is there substantial evidence available from brain-damaged populations. The data generally reflect incidence of language disorder relative to site (hemisphere) of damage. Two patterns emerge regarding incidence: first, there is a greater occurrence of language disturbance following right-hemisphere damage in children than in adults, and second, in comparisons of right- versus left-hemisphere damage in children, the percentages indicate a greater occurrence of language disturbance following lesions to the left. Although the latter more clearly supports early hemispheric specialization for language functioning, the former appears to contradict such a claim. This greater incidence of language disturbance following right hemispheric lesions in children would seem to suggest a greater role in the right hemisphere in language functioning in children than in adults, and this would argue for equipotentiality of the two hemispheres with respect to language. Before attempting to clarify this apparent contradiction, let us first turn to incidences of language disturbance in which the two hemispheres are compared.

Evidence for the presence of early (left) hemispheric specialization for language has evolved from studies in which evidence of unilateral brain damage has been defined by the presence of hemiplegia. As early as 1868, Cotard found impaired language associated significantly more frequently with left-hemisphere damage than right-hemisphere damage in children (Cotard, 1868, p. 95). Numerous other nineteenth-century studies corroborated these findings with reported differences of language damage relative to hemisphere of damage as high as 78% by Bernhardt (1884, p. 95; see also Freud & Rie, 1891, p. 95; Gaudard, 1884, p. 95; Lovett, 1888, p. 95; Osler, 1888, p. 95; Sachs & Peterson, 1890, p. 95; Wallenberg, 1886, p. 95). For a thorough review of nineteenth-century studies, see Dennis and Whitaker (1977). Studies from the 1950s through the 1960s have also indicated similar incidence ratios and support an early hemispheric specialization of the left hemisphere for language (Bishop, 1967; Dundson, 1952, p. 95; Ingram, 1964, p. 96). The one exception within this period is Basser's (1962) report of equal distribution of language disorder for both right- and left-hemisphere damage. However, Basser's linguistic assessment included measures of age of acquisition of first words, a criterion which may not clearly reflect the presence of a specific language impairment (see remainder of chapter). In 1973, Annett provided further support for early specialization by evaluating the effects of damage incurred prior to 13 months of age. As in past studies, left-sided cerebral insult more frquently resulted in language impairments than did right-sided damage (32% versus 10%, respectively). Russell and Espir (1961) and Zangwill (1967) report a higher incidence of language impairment in children than in adults following damage to the right hemisphere [approximately 30% for children, as compared to 5–10% for adults (S. Witelson, 1977)].

If one considers incidence factors alone, the support the preceding data provides for an early (left) hemispheric specialization for language may seem obscured by the well-documented greater frequency of language disturbances fol-

lowing right-hemisphere damage in children than adults. To clearly understand
the data relative to early (left) hemispheric specialization issues, they cannot be
evaluated in terms of incidence alone. Detailed evaluation of the linguistic deficits consequent to right hemisphere damage must be made. Unfortunately, the
data in the early studies have been frequently difficult to interpret and compare
across studies due to a lack of specificity in detailing the severity, duration, and
type of aphasic symptomatology presented (S. Witelson, 1977). Bishop's study
(1967) is one of the earlier studies that provides detailed information regarding
linguistic abilities relative to damage site. According to his data, dysarthric
conditions were found in approximately equal proportions across left- and right-
damaged populations. However, when the damage was to the left hemisphere,
the dysarthria was accompanied by developmental delays in language acquisition
(Bishop, 1967). Further analysis indicates a delay in the acquisition of word-
combinations (syntax), but not for single words, in the left-hemisphere-damaged
population (Bishop, 1967). From these detailed results, one can infer that the
hemispheres are equally susceptible to articulatory deficits following damage;
however, only the left hemisphere is "additionally at risk for language disorders" (Dennis & Whitaker, 1977).

Several recent studies have documented the effect of early and extensive left-
hemisphere damage in children. Results indicate differential functioning of the
two hemispheres relative to syntactic abilities (Dennis & Kohn, 1975; Dennis &
Whitaker, 1976; Kohn, 1980). In his study of 12 children with epilepsy who
were found to have right-hemisphere mediation of language (as measured by
Wada testing), Kohn (1980) found 9 of the 12 children to exhibit deficits in
comprehension of syntax as measured by the Token Test and the Active–Passive
Test. Dennis and Kohn (1975) presented evidence from infants who sustained
early brain damage followed by therapeutic hemispherectomy. The authors
found that the understanding of syntactic forms in the left hemidecordicates was
deficient in both rate of acquisition and adult proficiency levels. Dennis and
Whitaker (1976) extensively evaluated the language abilities of three 9- and 10-
year-old children who had undergone hemidecordectomies before the onset of
speech. Language skills were clearly differentiated by the absence of a right or
left hemisphere. For all subjects, phonemic and semantic abilities were similarly
developed. As in the Dennis and Kohn (1975) study, syntactic abilities showed
differences relative to damage site. The left hemidecordicates were deficient in
(1) understanding syntactic meaning; (2) detecting and correcting errors of surface syntactic structure; (3) repeating stylistically permuted sentences; (4) producing tag questions that reflected the grammatical features of a presented statement; (5) determining implicature; (6) supplying missing pronouns by integrating
both semantic and syntactic information and by integrating lexical interre-
lationships in sentences (Dennis & Whitaker, 1976).

For aforementioned studies detailing incidence of occurrence of language impairment relative to the damaged hemisphere and across adult and child populations (as in the case of right-hemisphere damage) provide substantial evidence for the presence of hemispheric specialization for language abilities. In addition, a few studies provide specifically defined behavioral evidence that not only strengthens support for the presence of hemispheric specialization at birth, but also provides an excellent model for future research.

SUMMARY AND CONCLUSIONS

What can be concluded from the current state of knowledge regarding cortical maturation and developmental neurolinguistics? The evidence in this chapter identifies two clear aspects of a developmental neurolinguistic model: (1) there exists an early (left) hemispheric specialization for language development, and (2) cortical maturation is 90% complete by 5 years of age.

With respect to the first point—it is clear that the Lenneberg notion of equipotentiality is incorrect. Both the neurophysiological and the behavioral data presented in this chapter provide consistent evidence of an early left-hemispheric specialization for language development. In light of this, it seems appropriate to eliminate the equipotentiality notion from developmental models of language acquisition and descriptions of the recovery process in acquired childhood aphasia.

The obvious consequence of the second claim is to limit the relationship between cortical maturation and language to early developmental stages when the behaviors are less complex. With the process nearing completion by age 5 years, cortical maturation cannot account for the changes that occur in the complexity of the syntactic, semantic, and pragmatic aspects of the language system after age 5. Thus, cortical maturation appears basically irrelevant to language acquisition process after age 5. To what then can these changes in linguistic development be attributed? Clearly, an integrative approach must be used, which includes neurophysiological data and detailed behavioral evidence from both normal and disordered populations and considers the reciprocal relations between cognition and language. Only through such an approach, supported by carefully controlled and clearly defined studies, will we come closer to understanding the neurolinguistic mechanisms involved in the transition from child to adult representation of language in the brain.

REFERENCES

Adrianov, O. S. (1980). Structural basis for functional interhemispheric brain asymmetry. *Human Psychology, 5,* 359–363.

Annett, M. (1973). Laterality of childhood hemiplegia and the growth of speech and intelligence. *Cortex, 9,* 4–33.

Barnett, A. B., Vincentini, M., & Campos, M. (1974). Cited in Witelson, S. (1977). Early hemispheric specialization and interhemisphere plasticity. In S. Segalowitz & F. Gruber (Eds.), *Language development and neurological theory* (pp. 213–276). New York: Academic Press.

Basser, L. S. (1962). Hemiplegia of early onset and the faculty of speech with special reference to the effects of hemispherectomy. *Brain, 85,* 427–460.

Bernhardt, M. (1984). Cited in Dennis, M., & Whitaker, H. (1977). Hemispheric equipotentiality and language acquisition. In S. Segalowitz & F. Gruber (Eds.), *Language development and neurological theory* (pp. 93–107). New York: Academic Press.

Best, C., Hoffman, H., & Glanville, B. (1982). Development of infant ear asymmetries for speech and music. *Perception & Psychophysics, 31,* 75–85.

Bishop, N. (1967). Speech in the hemiplegic child. *Proceedings of the Eighth Medical Conference of Australian Cerebral Palsy Association.* pp. 141–153.

Bronson, G. W. (1982). Structure, status and characteristics of the central nervous system at birth. In P. Stratton (Ed.), *Psychobiology of the human newborn* (pp. 99–118). New York: Wiley.

Conel, J. L. (1939–1967). *The postnatal development of the human cerebral cortex* (Vols. 1–8). Cambridge, MA: Harvard University Press.

Cotard, J. (1868). Cited in Dennis, M., & Whitaker, H. (1977). Hemispheric equipotentiality and language acquisition. In S. Segalowitz & F. Gruber (Eds.), *Language development and neurological theory* (pp. 93–107). New York: Academic Press.

Davis, A. E., & Wada, J. A. (1977). Hemispheric asymmetries in human infants: Spectral analysis of flash and click evoked potentials. *Brain and Language, 4,* 23–31.

Dennis, M., & Kohn, B. (1975). Comprehension of syntax in infantile hemiplegics after cerebral hemidecortication: Left hemisphere superiority. *Brain and Language, 2,* 472–482.

Dennis, M., & Whitaker, H. (1976). Language acquisition following hemidecortication: Linguistic superiority of the left over the right hemisphere. *Brain and Language, 3,* 404–433.

Dennis, M., & Whitaker, H. (1977). Hemispheric equipotentiality and language acquisition. In S. Segalowitz & L. F. Gruber (Eds.), *Language development and neurological theory* (pp. 93–107). New York: Academic Press.

Dingwall, W., & Whitaker, H. (1977). Neurolinguistics. In W. Dingwall (Ed.), *A survey of linguistic science* (pp. 207–247). Stamford, CT: Greylock.

Dundson, M. (1952). Cited in Dennis, M., & Whitaker, H. (1977). Hemispheric equipotentiality and language acquisition. In S. Segalowitz & F. Gruber (Eds.), *Language development and neurological theory* (pp. 93–107). New York: Academic Press.

Eimas, P. D., Cooper, W. E., & Corbit, J. D. (1973). Some properties of linguistic feature detectors. *Perception & Psychophysics, 13,* 247–252.

Eimas, P. D., & Corbit, J. D. (1973). Selective adaptation of linguistic feature detectors. *Cognitive Psychology, 4,* 99–109.

Eimas, P. D., Siqueland, E. R., Juscyk, P., & Vigorito, I. (1971). Speech perception in infants. *Science, 171,* 303–306.

Eisenberg, R. B. (1976). *Auditory comprehension in early life.* Baltimore: University Park Press.

Entus, A. (1977). Hemispheric asymmetry in the processing of dichotically presented speech stimuli and non-speech stimuli by infants. In S. Segalowitz & F. Gruber (Eds.), *Language development and neurological theory* (pp. 64–75). New York: Academic Press.

Epstein, H. T. (1974a). Phrenoldysis: Special brain and mind growth periods in human brain and skull development. *Developmental Psychology, 7,* 207–216.

Epstein, H. T. (1974b). Phrenoblysis: Special brain and mind growth periods in human mental development. *Developmental Psychology, 7,* 217–224.

Flechsig, P. (1901). Developmental (myelogenetic) localization of the cerebral cortex in the human subject. *Lancet ii,* 1027–1029.

Freud, S., & Rie (1891). Cited in Dennis, M., & Whitaker, H. (1977). Hemispheric equipotentiality and language acquisition. In S. Segalowitz & F. Gruber (Eds.), *Language development and neurological theory* (pp. 93–107). New York: Academic Press.

Gardiner, M. F., & Walter, D. O. (1977). Evidence of hemispheric specialization from infant EEG. In S. Harnad, R. Doty, L. Goldstein, J. Janes, & G. Krauthamer (Eds.), *Lateralization in the nervous system.* New York: Academic Press.

Gaudard (1884). Cited in Dennis, M. & Whitaker, H. (1977). Hemispheric equipotentiality and language acquisition. In S. Segalowitz & F. Gruber (Eds.), *Language development and neurological theory* (pp. 93–107). New York: Academic Press.

Ingram, T. T. S. (1964). Cited in Dennis, M. & Whitaker, H. (1977). Hemispheric equipotentiality and language acquisition. In S. Segalowitz & F. Gruber (Eds.), *Language development and neurological theory* (pp. 93–107). New York: Academic Press.

Jacobson, M. (1975). Brain and development in relation to language. In E. H. Lenneberg & F. Lenneberg (Eds.), *Foundations of language development: A multidisciplinary approach.* (Vol. 1). New York: Academic Press.

Kaplan, E. L. (1969). The role of intonation in the acquisition of language. Cited in Snow, C., & Ferguson, C. A. (1977). *Talking to children* (chap. 2). London: Cambridge University Press.

Kohn, B., (1980). Right-hemisphere speech representation and comprehension of syntax after left cerebral injury. *Brain and Language, 9,* 350–361.

Lecours, A. R. (1975). Myelinogenetic correlates of the development of speech and language. In E. H. Lenneberg & E. Lenneberg (Eds.), *Foundations of language development: A multidisciplinary approach* (Vol. 1). New York: Academic Press.

LeMay, M. (1976). Morphological cerebral asymmetries of modern man, fossil man, and nonhuman primate. In S. R. Harnac, H. D. Steklis, & J. Lancaster (Eds.), *Origins and evolution of language and speech* (pp. 349–365). New York: New York Academy of Sciences.

Lenneberg, E. H. (1967). *Biological foundations of language.* New York: Wiley.

Lovett, R. (1888). Cited in Dennis, M., & Whitaker, H. (1977). Hemispheric equipotentiality and language acquisition. In S. Segalowitz & F. Gruber (Eds.), *Language development and neurological theory* (pp. 93–107). New York: Academic Press.

Marshall, J. (1980). On the biology of language acquisition. In D. Caplan (Ed.), *Biological studies of mental processes.* Cambridge, MA: MIT Press.

Milner, E. (1976). CNS maturation and language acquisition. In H. Whitaker & H. A. Whitaker (Eds.), *Studies in neurolinguistics* (Vol. 1). New York: Academic Press.

Moffitt, A. R. (1971). Consonant cue perception by twenty to twenty-four week old infants. *Child Development, 42,* 717–731.

Molfese, D., Freeman, R., Jr., & Palermo, D. (1975). The ontogeny of brain lateralization for speech and nonspeech stimuli, *Brain and Language, 2,* 356–368.

Molfese, D., & Molfese, V. J. (1979). VOT distinctions in infants: Learned or innate? In H. Whitaker & H. A. Whitaker (Eds.), *Studies in neurolinguistics* (Vol. 4, pp. 225–240). New York: Academic Press.

Morse, P. A. (1974). Infant speech perception: A preliminary model and review of the literature. In R. Schiefelbusch & L. Lloyd (Eds.), *Language perspectives: Acquisition, retardation and intervention.* Baltimore: University Park Press.

O'Brien, J. S. (1970). Lipids and myelination. In W. Himwich (Ed.), *Developmental neurobiology.* Springfield, IL: C. Charles Thomas.

Osler, W. (1888). Cited in Dennis, M., & Whitaker, H. (1977). Hemispheric equipotentiality and language acquisition. In S. Segalowitz & F. Gruber (Eds.), *Language development and neurological theory* (pp. 93–107). New York: Academic Press.

Russell, R., & Espir, M. (1961). *Traumatic aphasia*. London: Oxford University Press.

Sachs, B., & Peterson, F. (1890). Cited in Dennis, M., & Whitaker, H. (1977). Hemispheric equipotentiality and language acquisition. In S. Segalowitz & F. Gruber (Eds.), *Language development and neurological theory* (pp. 93–107). New York: Academic Press.

Springer, S. P., & Deutsch, G. (1981). *Left brain, right brain* (chaps. 3, 6, 7, 10). San Francisco: Freeman.

Teszner, D., Tzavaras, A., Gruner, J., & Hecaen, H. (1972). Cited in Witelson, S. (1977). Early hemispheric specialization and interhemisphere plasticity. In S. Segalowitz & F. Gruber (Eds.), *Language development and neurological theory* (pp. 213–276). New York: Academic Press.

Trehub, S., & Rabinovitch, M. S. (1972). Auditory linguistic sensitivity in early infancy. *Developmental Psychology, 6*, 74–77.

Vargha-Khadem, F., & Corballis, M. C. (1979). Cerebral asymmetry in infants. *Brain and Language, 8*, 1–9.

Wada, J., Clarke, R., & Hamm, A. (1975). Cerebral hemispheric asymmetry in humans. *Archives of Neurology, 32*, 239–246.

Wallenberg, A. (1886). Cited in Dennis, M., & Whitaker, H. (1977). Hemispheric equipotentiality and language acquisition. In S. Segalowitz & F. Gruber (Eds.), *Language development and neurological theory* (pp. 93–107). New York: Academic Press.

Whitaker, H., Bub, D., & Leventer, S. (1981). Neurolinguistic aspects of language acqusition and bilingualism. *Annals of the New York Academy of Sciences*, 59–74.

Witelson, A., & Pallie, W. (1973). Left hemisphere specialization for language in the newborn: Neuroanatomical evidence of asymmetry. *Brain, 96*, 641–647.

Witelson, S. (1977). Early hemispheric specialization and interhemispheric plasticity: An empirical and theoretical review. In S. Segalowitz & F. Gruber (Eds.), *Language development and neurological theory* (pp. 213–276). New York: Academic Press.

Yakolev, P. (1962). Morphological criteria of growth and maturation of the nervous system in man. Research publication of the A.R.N.M.D. *Mental Retardation, 39*, 3–46.

Yakolev, P., & Lecours, A. (1967). The myelogenetic cycles of regional maturation of the brain. In A. Minkowski (Ed.), *Regional development of the brain in early life* (pp. 3–70). Philadelphia: Davis.

Zangwill, O. C. (1967). Speech and the minor hemisphere. Cited in Witelson, S. (1977). Early hemispheric specialization and interhemisphere plasticity. In S. Segalowitz & F. Gruber (Eds.), *Language development and neurological theory* (pp. 213–276). New York: Academic Press.

Chapter 4

Developmental Aspects of Cerebral Lateralization

M. P. BRYDEN

Department of Psychology
University of Waterloo
Waterloo, Ontario, Canada N2L 3G1

LORIE SAXBY*

Lutherwood Children's Mental Health Centre
Waterloo, Ontario, Canada N2J 3Z4

INTRODUCTION

It has become very popular since the mid-1970s to be concerned about the lateralization of the child, and an immense number of books and articles have been written in which deficiencies in reading ability, language skills, or cognitive abilities have been attributed to abnormal lateralization (see, e.g., Corballis, 1983). The very fact that such concerns exist raises some very important questions. Just what is it that is meant by lateralization? How can it be measured? What does it mean to attribute cognitive deficiency to abnormal lateralization? In this chapter, we attempt to address these issues.

Although there are many instances in which the concern has focused on such overtly lateralized phenomena as hand preference (Porac & Coren, 1981) or eye dominance (Porac & Coren, 1976), it is implicit in most of the work on later-

*Present Address: Lincoln County Roman Catholic Separate School Board, Saint Catharines, Ontario, Canada L2P 3H1

CHILD NEUROPSYCHOLOGY, VOL. 1

alization that we are ultimately concerned with the lateralization of brain function. It has long been known that the left cerebral hemisphere is more important for language functions in the majority of individuals than is the right hemisphere (Bryden, 1982; Corballis, 1983; Segalowitz & Bryden, 1983; Springer & Deutsch, 1981). Thus, for example, disturbances of language (*aphasias*) follow unilateral left-hemisphere brain damage far more often than they follow right-hemisphere damage. We have come to appreciate that other functions are critically dependent on the integrity of the right hemisphere. Thus, unilateral right-hemisphere brain damage produces deficits in visuospatial processes, in face recognition, in some aspects of music perception, and in the perception of emotional expression (Perecman, 1983; A. W. Young, 1983). There are, however, considerable individual differences in brain organization, with the result that aphasia does not always follow left-hemisphere damage, nor visuospatial deficits right-hemisphere damage. If there are major differences in the pattern of cerebral organization, it is possible that they are related to individual differences in cognitive ability (see Levy, 1972, for one such argument).

The observation that aphasic disturbances appear more often with right-hemisphere damage in left-handers than in right-handers (Hécaen & Sauguet, 1971; Rasumussen & Milner, 1977; Segalowitz & Bryden, 1983) has led many researchers to focus on handedness differences rather than on some more direct measure of cerebral lateralization. It should be noted, however, that even in left-handers, the majority of individuals show left-hemisphere representation of language. Furthermore, there is little difference between left- and right-handers in the lateralization of visuospatial processes (DeRenzi, 1982). Thus, assessing handedness is not a particularly direct way of assessing cerebral lateralization.

If we attribute cognitive deficits to abnormal cerebral lateralization, then we are implicitly accepting one of two alternative views about the development of brain function. Lenneberg (1967) argued that cerebral lateralization for language develops gradually, becoming fully fixed only at puberty. By this view, one should be able to find evidence of the development of lateralization in normal individuals, and abnormal lateralization is the result of factors that delay or retard the normal processes of lateralization. A rather more pessimistic view is that language lateralization is determined by the time of birth, by genetic and/or ontogenetic factors, and does not change thereafter. By this view, a child with abnormal lateralization is stuck with it and must learn compensatory strategies to cope with the abnormal pattern of brain organization. A third alternative is that both views are partially correct: an initial lateralization is biologically determined, but it is modified by experience.

In the ensuing pages, we review the evidence for lateralization of both motor and perceptual functions in children, and we see how this lateralization relates to cognitive ability.

HANDEDNESS

Because handedness is so easily observed, many studies have focused on it rather than on some more direct measure of cerebral lateralization. Such an approach is implicitly based on the assumption that the patterns of cerebral organization will differ, on average, in large samples of left- and right-handers. Segalowitz and Bryden (1983), however, have estimated that one would need at least 50 subjects in each handedness group for a cerebral lateralization effect to be detectable. Investigating cerebral lateralization indirectly through handedness may well overestimate the small correlation between handedness and language lateralization (Segalowitz & Bryden, 1983), or what appears to be an even smaller association between handedness and visuospatial lateralization (De-Renzi, 1982). Further, some effects may be the result of handedness per se rather than of cerebral asymmetries.

Handedness is normally assessed by a measure of hand preference in different unimanual activities (Porac & Coren, 1981) or by comparing the two hands on some unimanual performance measure (Annett, 1970). While such procedures are easily implemented with kindergarten or school-age children, they are not appropriate for use with infants, and a variety of imaginative procedures for assessing motor laterality have been developed.

While handedness has been traditionally viewed as the preferred use of one hand over the other, researchers have recently identified difficulties with such a general, imprecise definition. For example, distinctions have been made between hand preference and proficiency (Porac & Coren, 1981) and between manual specialization and handedness (G. Young, Corter, Segalowitz, & Trehub, 1983). Further, some methods for determining hand dominance are questionable; for certain measures, hand dominance has been found to vary from day to day (O'Connor, 1970) and as a function of task complexity (Steingruber, 1975). Other assessment techniques may be suitable for determining hand use asymmetries in older children, but not in preschoolers or infants (e.g., handwriting). The development and adoption of more precise and nontraditional testing methods has further delineated the development of hand dominance for other activities and has made research on infants possible.

Indeed, studies indicate right-hand dominance in infancy for various activities requiring manual control. G. Young, Bowman, et al. (1983) reported that, in 1-month-olds, the right hand was generally used more than the left for reaching and touching, especially when the stimulus object was at midline or to the right side, whereas the opposite pattern was observed for nondirected activity. In a study by Hawn and Harris (1983), a reliable right-hand preference on a unimanual test of grasp duration was found for 2- and 5-month-old infants with no familial history of left handedness, although only older infants were found to prefer the right hand on a bimanual test. A small sample of familial left-handed infants showed a reverse, though less pronounced, effect favoring the left hand. A similar pattern favoring the right hand on a grasp duration task has been reported by Caplan and Kinsbourne (1976) for familial right-handed 2- to 4-month olds, though no consistent manual asymmetry was found for familial left-handed infants. In a replication of the Caplan and Kinsbourne study that involved neonates (1- to 5-day-olds) and infants (1 to 4 months of age), Strauss (1982) failed to find evidence for hand asymmetries in grasp duration, but did find a significant increase in right-hand grasp control over a number of weeks after birth. Ramsay (1980) reported a trend toward right-hand preference that appeared between 5 and 9 months of age for unimanual manipulation of toys. For baton tapping rate and transfer, a right-hand preference was found in infants as young as 15.3 months of age (Ramsay, 1979). Bresson, Maury, Pierault-LeBonniec, and de Schonen (1977) observed that successful right-handed reaching predominates by 22 weeks of age and is preceded by a stage of bimanual collaboration. In another study, a right-hand preference for bimanual manipulation of toys as assessed at 13 months has been found to correspond to unimanual hand preference observed at 7 and 9 months (Ramsay, 1979, 1983).

Other motor behaviors appear to be lateralized in infancy, and show a relationship to hand preference: Michel (1982) found infant supine head-orientation preference to be a significant predictor of hand-use preference during infancy, and Viviani, Turkewitz, and Karp (1978) reported a significant relationship between neonatal head turning and hand preference at age 7 years. Ramsay (1983) reported data suggesting that unimanual hand preference might be associated with the onset of duplicated babbling in 6-month-olds, though longitudinal investigation did not show clearly that the emergence of these two behaviors coincided in time. Other infant behaviors, though not as yet established as correlates of hand preference, are known to be lateralized, including a rightward bias in the stepping reflex in neonates (Melekian, 1981) and a rightward head-turning bias in response to stimulation in infants with two, but not one, right-handed parents (Liederman & Kinsbourne, 1980).

While the general consensus of these studies is that a clear right bias appears in the population by the age of 1 year and that this bias is related to subsequent hand preference, the proportion showing a right bias is not so extreme as that found in older children or adults. About 90% of adults are right-handed, yet the proportion of infants showing a right reaching, grasping, or head-turning bias is rather less. Somehow, more children who show left biases in infancy become right-handed than the reverse. Whether this is simply the result of a large measurement error in the infant studies or a manifestation of a significant developmental process is not presently clear. Corballis (1983), for example, sees a consistent handedness developing with speech and argues that right-handedness and left-hemispheric speech lateralization mutually facilitate one another.

Investigations into lateral asymmetries in noninfant samples also point to right-hand dominance in most children, although age trends vary with samples and testing methods used. In a study of manual responses in 8-week-olds to 10-year-olds, Gesell and Ames (1947) reported inconsistent handedness prior to age 2 years. A right-hand preference predominated between ages 4 to 6 years followed by a shift to left or bilateral preference, with consistent right-handedness being observed only from about 8 years of age on. Belmont and Birch (1963) reported a similar developmental pattern for four pantomimed handedness measures, with the majority of their subjects (87%) showing a right-hand preference at age 5 that did not reappear consistently until about age 9. A developmental increase in moderate to strong right-handedness (from 67.2% to 82.5%) and a decline in left-handedness (from 14.8% to 9.3%) from ages 7 to 9 years was obtained by Harris (1957) for five behavioral measures of handedness. In contrast, Van Camp and Bixby (1977) used two direct measures of handedness and found a small decline in the incidence of right-handedness (from 91% to 85%), along with an increase in left-handedness (from 9% to 15%), in 4- to 7-year-olds. Hardyck, Goldman, and Petrinovich (1975), also using direct handedness measures on almost 8,000 school-aged children, failed to find important age-related deviations from the incidence of 90.4% right-handedness and 9.6% left-handedness in their sample. Their choice of a large sample in a school district prohibiting enforcement of right-handedness in students may account for the developmental consistency in handedness pattern.

In their survey of hand preference studies, Porac and Coren (1981) indicated that right-hand preference appeared in about 80% of preschoolers, but in 90% of older children. In contrast, Annett (1970), using a peg-moving task, found no age-related increase in the incidence of right-handedness from ages 3 years on. Clearly, there is variability in performance in young children, but most of us seem to show a right-hand bias by the end of the first year of life.

Lateralization in other domains has also been investigated, but to a lesser degree than manual dominance. Several studies report the establishment of strong right-footedness by ages 4 or 5 years, with little evidence of subsequent change in degree or direction of lateralization (Belmont & Birch, 1963; Harris, 1957; Sinclair, 1971), although on the basis of their review of the literature, Porac and Coren (1981) report an increase in right-footedness with age. Further, Annett and Turner (1974) reported footedness for kicking to be related to handedness in their 5- to 10-year-old sample. Eyedness, while substantially less well-lateralized than handedness and footedness, appears to increase somewhat in right-sidedness with age (Belmont & Birch, 1963; Harris, 1957; Porac & Coren, 1981). There is evidence for a moderate relation between eye and hand preference (Annett & Turner, 1974) which increases somewhat with age (Belmont & Birch, 1963; Harris, 1957). However, for a large sample of kindergarteners and first graders, Van Camp and Bixby (1977) found essentially no relation between measures of ocular dominance and hand dominance. Available data on lateral dominance in audition indicate some inconsistency and shifting in ear preference between ages 4 and 7 years (Sinclair, 1971), with an apparent increase in left-earedness with age (Porac & Coren, 1981).

Regarding the issue of whether handedness and lateral dominance patterns relate to other factors, such as directional and spatial confusion (see Palmer, 1964, for a review), reading and language problems (see, e.g., Harris, 1957; Orton, 1937), and personal adjustment (Hanvik & Kaste, 1973), there is, at best, little evidence for a correspondence between dominance patterns and deficits in these areas. While Kaufman, Zelma, and Kaufman (1978) reported mastery of left–right discrimination to be associated with the establishment of consistent hand preference in 5- to 8-year-olds, such a correspondence between lateral awareness and hand, eye, or foot preference was not found in school-aged children by Belmont and Birch (1963). Harris (1957) reported more left–right confusion in 7-year-old reading disabled children than in agemates without reading difficulties, but Balow (1963) found no such relation between left–right knowledge and reading achievement. Absence of an association between lateral dominance and reading achievement at the 5- to 6-year level has also been reported (Balow, 1963; Sinclair, 1971), although Harris concluded mixed dominance to be more common among 9-year-old reading disabled subjects than among nondisabled agemates. However, as 87% of Harris's reading disabled sample was male as compared with 50% male in his nondisabled sample, his findings may simply reflect the commonly observed pattern of lower rates of right dominance in boys than in girls (see, e.g., Annett, 1970; Annett & Turner, 1974; Heim & Watts, 1976).

In a study of 5- to 14-year-olds, McCormick (1978) found no overall differences in hand preference in normals as compared to children with learning, emotional, and behavioral problems. For preschoolers with established hand dominance, but not older children, performance on cognitive and motor coordination tasks was found to be significantly, though not meaningfully, higher than that of children without established dominance (Kaufman et al., 1978). Similarly, Sabatino and Becker (1971) found no variations in scores for school-aged children on 17 behavioral and 3 cognitive measures as a function of hand, foot, and eye preference patterns. Children who are not consistent right-handers have been reported to have somewhat, though not significantly, lower vocabulary scores than right-handers (Annett, 1970; Annett & Turner, 1974). However, another investigation failed to find that left-handers do more poorly than right-handers on cognitive measures relating to verbal, visuospatial and numerical reasoning; in fact, left-handers, especially males, performed significantly better than right-handers on the numerical ability measure (Heim & Watts, 1976).

Studies of hand preference therefore, have indicated that a right preference exists in the majority of children after the age of 2 years, with little evidence for any developmental change other than increased consistency. There is somewhat more evidence that the percentage of right-handers is lower in infancy, but this shift may be as much the result of measurement technique as of any real shift in handedness. Finally, the data relating handedness and other motor asymmetries to cognitive abilities remains equivocal.

PERCEPTUAL ASYMMETRIES

An alternative way of assessing the functions of the two cerebral hemispheres is to take advantage of the fact that, in general, sensory inputs from the left side of the body are first transmitted to the right cerebral hemisphere, while sensory inputs to the right side of the body are first transmitted to the left hemisphere. Therefore, if the left hemisphere carries out the final analysis of the stimulus, right-side presentations are faster or more accurately identified because left-side input must pass through the corpus callosum before it can reach the left hemisphere. Thus, for example, verbal material, whether presented auditorily (Kimura, 1961) or visually (Bryden, 1965), shows a right-side advantage in normal adult subjects. Conversely, if the task depends on the right hemisphere, a left-side advantage is found, as is the case with musical passages (Kimura, 1964), lines of varying orientation (Kimura & Durnford, 1974), or faces (Geffen, Bradshaw, & Wallace, 1971). A number of thorough reviews of the procedures for demonstrating such perceptual asymmetries in adults have appeared (Beaumont, 1982; Bradshaw & Nettleton, 1983; Bryden, 1982; Corballis, 1983; Hellige, 1983).

Dichotic Listening Studies

The first report of a link between perceptual asymmetry and brain lateralization was that of Kimura (1961), and it made use of a procedure known as *dichotic listening*. Kimura presented two lists of numbers simultaneously, one to each ear, arranged in such a way that one number arrived at the left ear at the same time that a different number arrived at the right ear. Subjects were asked to listen to the numbers and then to report as many as they could, in any order. Kimura found that normal subjects were more accurate on the right ear than on the left, and that clinical patients with known language lateralization were better on the ear contralateral to their language-dominant hemisphere. This latter finding suggested that the dichotic listening task could be used to assess the language-dominant hemisphere in normal individuals. Kimura (1963) was also the first to apply the dichotic listening procedure to children. She tested both boys and girls between the ages of 4 and 9 years, and found significant right-ear effects for all groups but the 7- and 9-year-old girls. Overall, however, her data suggest a right-ear effect, and therefore a left-hemisphere language dominance, for all ages in the range tested.

One of the difficulties with the dichotic list task Kimura used is the fact that there are both perceptual and short-term memory components to the task. If a subject is expected to report 6 numbers, he/she must somehow organize them and report them in sequence. In so doing, numbers that are reported toward the end of the sequence are less likely to be remembered correctly than those re-corded at the beginning of the sequence, both because of decay and because of output interference. Thus, even if a subject hears the left-ear items poorly, he/she may obtain higher scores on the left ear by reporting the left-ear items first. The fact that such strategy effects can confound the observed laterality effect has led many researchers to use single pairs of words or nonsense syllables (Goodglass, 1973) or a detection task in which one signals the presence of a specific target (Geffen, 1976).

The developmental aspects of dichotic listening performance have been thor-oughly reviewed by Witelson (1977a), and we do not attempt to provide an exhaustive review of the literature here. However, we should treat a number of points critical to a general understanding of dichotic performance in children. These concern the development of dichotic laterality effects and the dependence of the results on the specific procedure used or on the type of material employed.

Lenneberg (1967) proposed that language functions gradually became later-alized to the left hemisphere, not reaching the adult state until about the age of puberty. By this view, one should expect to find that the dichotic right-ear effect for verbal material increases with age during the primary school years. Although there have been a few reports of a gradually increasing right-ear effect (Larsen, 1984; Satz, Bakker, Teunissen, Goebel, & Van der Vlugt, 1975), it is now generally agreed that there are no systematic changes in either the magnitude or the incidence of a right-ear effect in children in the age range 5 to 14 (Berlin, Hughes, Lowe-Bell, & Berlin, 1973; Bryden & Allard, 1981; Geffen, 1976, 1978; Goodglass, 1973; Hynd & Obrzut, 1977; Saxby & Bryden, 1984).

The Larsen (1984) paper is a particularly curious example, in that the author reports both a *decrease* in the absolute magnitude of the ear effect between 9 and 15 years, and a simultaneous *increase* in the percentage of the subjects manifest-ing a right-ear advantage (REA). These effects, however, may be more apparent than real. The specific index of laterality used by Larsen is one that has a greater range at low levels of accuracy than at high levels (Bryden & Sprott, 1981). Because the older subjects were more accurate than the younger ones, there may have been a restriction-of-range effect that led to the decrease in the absolute value of the laterality measure. At the same time, the task involved the free recall of three pairs of words, a task that is vulnerable to subject-initiated strategy effects (Bryden, 1978). Young children are behaviorally more variable than older ones, and the increasing porportion of subjects showing the right-ear effect may simply reflect this variability.

Taken together, these studies have employed a large number of subjects of both sexes, and have used pairs of meaningful words, pairs of nonsense syllables with initial stop consonants (e.g., "ba-ga"), and meaningful sentences. Such data have led Krashen (1973) to argue that language lateralization is fixed by the age of 5.

The data on preschool children are rather more equivocal, although it is not clear whether this is because language has not yet become fixed or because young children are variable in their performance. Typically, significant REAs are found, but specific age–sex groups fail to show the effect. Thus, for example, Nagafuchi (1970), using word lists, found a general REA in children from 3 to 6, but not in 4- or 6-year-old girls. Likewise, Ingram (1975) studied 3- to 5-year-olds with single pairs of words and found REAs in all groups but the 4-year-old girls. Although it is curious that it should be the 4-year-old girls who are so often the exception, it is difficult to know whether or not to attach any meaning to this. Ingram's (1975) paper, for example, implies that there is no significant age by sex by ear interaction, suggesting that the lack of REA in the one subgroup is a statistical happenstance. Furthermore, such anomalies do not appear in other studies (Hiscock & Kinsbourne, 1977).

The dichotic listening studies provide little evidence for any developmental change in the REA after the age of 3 years, when the procedure can be used in approximately the same form as is employed with adults.

Tactual Asymmetries

An alternative way of assessing cerebral lateralization involves the use of *dichhaptic* stimulation procedures (Witelson, 1974). In this procedure, subjects are given two different shapes to palpate simultaneously, one with each hand. Essentially, then, the procedure is a tactual analog to the dichotic listening task. Because the ascending somatosensory pathways are crossed, information from the right hand is transmitted first to the left hemisphere, while the reverse is true for left-hand information. This gives the dichhaptic procedure a superficial advantage over the dichotic procedure, in that there are no ascending ipsilateral pathways from the hands. In general, the dichhaptic procedure yields a left-hand superiority for random shapes and other nonverbal stimuli, and either a right-hand advantage or no hand difference for letters of the alphabet (Witelson, 1974).

As soon as one tries to use the dichhaptic procedure, however, a variety of problems become evident. Because active touch is far more accurate than passive touch (J. J. Gibson, 1962), it is necessary to permit the subjects to feel the stimuli actively if one is going to use any but the most elementary stimuli. As a result, researchers have used presentation times of up to 10 seconds. With a presentation of this length, it becomes difficult to ensure that the subject is exploring both shapes equally, and that he/she is not alternating attention from one hand to the other. When more than one pair of stimuli are presented before recall is required, the long time duration permits a reorganization in short-term memory that may well obscure any underlying laterality effect. Finally, the procedure tends to be time consuming, with the result that relatively few trials are administered to any one subject and the statistical precision tends to be low.

In Witelson's (1974) original study, she had children palpate two nonsense forms simultaneously for 10 seconds, and then had her subjects point to the two figures they had just felt in a 6-alternative visual display. Subjects in this study were 47 boys, ranging in age from 6 to 14 years; in general, they were better at identifying the shapes presented to the left hand. In later studies, Witelson (1976, 1977b) reported similar findings on much larger samples, although it is not clear whether the original 47 subjects are included in the later groups or not. Witelson also investigated dichhaptic letter perception in her 1974 study. She presented two pairs of letters for 2 seconds each, then asked subjects to report all four letters. There were no significant hand effects on this task.

Subsequent research has concentrated largely on dichhaptic shape recognition, perhaps because children do not normally identify letters by feel. The majority of other investigators have reported left-hand superiority for dichhaptic shape recognition, with little or no sign of any age-related changes (Dawson, 1981; Denes & Spinaci, 1981; C. Gibson & Bryden, 1983), although Flanery and Balling (1979) found left-hand superiority only in older children when tactual, rather than visual, response alternatives were used. Some investigators have failed to find even the left-hand effect (Cranney & Ashton, 1980; LaBreche, Manning, Goble, & Markham, 1977).

Little in the way of hand differences has been found with single letters (C. Gibson & Bryden, 1983; Witelson, 1974), although Cioffi and Kandel (1979) did observe a right-hand advantage for the identification of simple 2-letter words.

Basically, this research points to the same conclusion as does the dichotic research: There is little evidence for any consistent developmental change in lateralization effects in children beyond the age of 5 years.

Visual Asymmetries

In the visual system, the ascending sensory pathways are not fully crossed, but decussate at the optic chiasm. The result is that sensory input to the left of the line of sight is projected first to the right hemisphere, while input to the right of the line of sight is projected to the left hemisphere, no matter which eye is stimulated. In order to take advantage of this, it is necessary to restrict the subject's eye movements to ensure that the stimulus remains in a specified visual field. Most visual asymmetry studies, therefore, have employed *tachistoscopic* procedures, in which the stimuli are presented for very brief periods of time, usually less than 180 milliseconds.

Probably the most common procedure for assessing visual laterality involves presentation of one stimulus on each trial, presented randomly to either the left or the right of a central fixation point (*unilateral* presentation). The fact that the subject does not know on any one trial whether the material will appear on the left or the right helps ensure that he/she will maintain fixation at the center. Other researchers prefer to use *bilateral* presentation, somewhat more analogous to dichotic listening, in which different stimuli are presented simultaneously to the left and right of fixation. This procedure requires careful control over order both of report and of fixation.

While much of the adult literature on asymmetry involves visual presentation (Beaumont, 1982), visual studies on children are less common for a variety of reasons. First, children tend to perform very poorly at brief exposure durations, and it is often necessary to increase the exposure duration into the range in which eye movements are possible in order to raise accuracy to acceptable levels. Second, in order to identify verbal material, the child must be able to read it; consequently, there is an inevitable confound between reading ability and accuracy that may well influence observed laterality measures. It is well, therefore, to view the developmental literature on visual asymmetries with caution.

The earliest visual-field study of lateral asymmetry was perhaps that of Forgays (1953), who presented words to the left or right of fixation and reported that the right-visual-field superiority did not emerge until about age 12 years. Similar findings have been reported more recently by Miller and Turner (1973) and Reitsma (1975). In these studies, however, it is impossible to separate those effects resulting from the acquisition of reading skills from those due to altered cerebral lateralization, and it would be premature to conclude that the data require the assumption that visual laterality shows age-related changes.

Carmon, Nachshon, and Starinsky (1976) presented Israeli school children with single Hebrew letters, 2- and 4-digit numbers (conventionally read from left to right), and 2- and 4-letter Hebrew words (read from right to left), in an attempt to control directional scanning factors. They found a significant right visual field (RVF) superiority for all types of material except the single letters, leading them to conclude that scanning effects are relatively minimal. They also found age-related effects: 12-year-old children showed RVF effects under all conditions, while 6-year-olds showed an RVF effect only with two-letter words presented bilaterally. Carmon et al. argue that the left hemisphere becomes increasingly involved in the sequential processing necessary for the identification of words and numbers.

On the other hand, Saxby and Bryden (1985) found no age-related changes on a lateralized letter-matching task. They presented pairs of letters, one in upper case and one in lower case, to one visual field or the other. Subjects were asked to indicate whether the letters had the same name (e.g., "A, a") or not ("A, b"). A very strong RVF effect was found on this task at all ages from 6 to 14 years.

Unlike word-recognition tasks, this task does not require that the subject read, but only that he/she be familiar with the alphabet. It is, therefore, one that can be used with 6-year-olds, and it is notable that the data parallel those obtained with dichotic listening, in that no change in laterality with age was observed.

In many ways, the visual studies of lateralization are disappointing. It is unclear just how factors such as word orientation or the fact that the beginning of a horizontally presented word is further in the periphery when it appears in the LVF then when it appears in the RVF may affect the results (Kirsner & Schwartz, in press). The Saxby and Bryden (1985) procedure may be the best, and, like the dichotic and dichhaptic procedures, shows no evidence for a developing lateralization.

Other Asymmetries

Another approach to cerebral asymmetry involves dual-task performance. Basically, the idea is to occupy one hemisphere with a particular task, and to see how this affects performance of some other task. Thus, for example, reciting animal names or a familiar nursery rhyme should involve left-hemisphere activity and disrupt right-hand tapping more than left-hand tapping. White and Kinsbourne (1980) found such an effect, but reported no age-related changes between 3 and 12 years.

The general pattern emerging from all of the studies of perceptual asymmetry is that lateralization effects do not change significantly after the age of 3 years. There may be meaningful changes occurring in the first few years of life, but better techniques and careful longitudinal studies are needed to establish their significance.

CHILDHOOD APHASIA

Lenneberg's contention that speech lateralization gradually developed through childhood until puberty was based in part on the childhood aphasia literature. Lenneberg interpreted this as indicating that aphasia in right-handers was far more common following right-hemisphere lesions in children than it was in adults and that recovery from aphasic disturbance was better in children than in adults. By his argument, because language was not yet fully lateralized to the left hemisphere, the right hemisphere was more able to take over the lost functions. In fact, incidence and recovery data address two quite separate questions. If one becomes aphasic following cerebral damage, it tells us something about the localization of language at the time of damage, while the relative ease of recovery tells us something about the plasticity of the system. If childhood aphasics are more likely to recover, it may indicate that the system is more plastic, but does not necessarily mean that language was not well-established in the damaged hemisphere.

Satz and Bullard-Bates (1981) have recently provided an excellent review of the literature on childhood aphasia, in which they have concentrated on the well-documented cases of unilateral damage. According to their data, aphasia was evident in 28 of 35 (80.0%) right-handers following left-hemisphere damage, and in 4 of 22 (18.2%) right-handers following right-hemisphere damage. If we assume unilateral speech lateralization in right-handers and random sampling, then (80.0/80.0 + 18.2) or 81.5% of right-handed children have speech in the left hemisphere, 18.5% have speech in the right hemisphere, and there is a 98.2% likelihood that unilateral brain damage in the language-dominant hemisphere will produce aphasia. There were only 11 left-handers in the Satz and Bullard-Bates survey, so any statements about left handers must necessarily be preliminary, but the incidence of aphasia following right-hemisphere damage (3 of 5 cases) was much higher than it was in right-handers.

While these data indicate that the majority of children, like the majority of adults, have left-hemispheric language representation, the data differ from the adult data in several important respects. Most importantly, the incidence of aphasia following unilateral damage to either hemisphere is higher in children than in adults. This may indicate that children are more vulnerable to brain damage, but it may simply result from differing criteria for classifying children and adults as aphasic. The other point is that the estimates of the incidence of right-hemisphere language are much higher in right-handed children (18.5%) than in right-handed adults (5%) (Segalowitz & Bryden, 1983). While this may simply indicate a tendency to report cases of crossed aphasia, as Satz and Bullard-Bates (1981) imply, it may also indicate a real difference between children and adults. If so, one must account for why control of language should migrate from the right hemisphere to the left in approximately 13% of right-handers. Unfortunately, Satz and Bullard-Bates included cases with lesion onset prior to the age of 16, and provide no breakdown according to age of onset. Thus, their data do little more than to tell us that left-hemisphere language is prevalent in children.

It should be noted that the left temporal planum, a region of the brain important for receptive language, is larger than the right planum in about 88% of infants (Wada, Clarke, & Hamm, 1975). This would provide a neurological head start for the left hemisphere in the control of language, at least in those for whom the left temporal planum is larger.

Childhood hemiplegia presumably indicates rather massive damage to the cerebral cortex on the side opposite the hemiplegia. Annett (1973) reports that virtually all children showing language disturbance following hemiplegia of postnatal origin have a right hemiplegia, indicative of left-hemisphere damage. In those with hemiplegias of perinatal origin, however, language disturbance is also prevalent in the left hemiplegics (6 of 40, or 15%, as opposed to 13 of 42, or 32%, right hemiplegics). Using the statistical procedure applied earlier to the aphasia data, this would imply left-hemisphere language in about 68%. This figure is generally consistent with the data reviewed by Dennis and Whitaker (1977) and by Satz and Bullard-Bates (1981).

Taken together, these data present something of a problem. As we saw in earlier sections, there is little evidence for any developmental change in behavioral measures of cerebral asymmetry from the age of 3 on. However, virtually all right-handers are left hemispheric for speech, while estimates from infancy and childhood range from 68% to 88%. Thus, while there may be no general tendency for language to become more lateralized with age, it does seem that more adults than children are left-hemispheric for language. Interestingly, the same trend does not appear in left-handers. Satz and Bullard-Bates give about the same incidence of right-hemispheric speech in left-handed children as is seen in adults (Segalowitz & Bryden, 1983). Thus, being strongly right-handed may be enough to alter some individuals so that they become left-hemispheric for language.

LATERALITY AND READING

Cerebral lateralization becomes of considerable interest if it can be related to everyday behavior. One area in which it is often suggested that an abnormal pattern of lateralization is found is that of developmental dyslexia or reading disability. Here, it is often claimed that poor readers are less likely to show the normal pattern of lateralization than are normal readers (Corballis, 1983, chap. 8). Two different hypotheses have been advanced to account for the supposed weak lateralization in poor readers: a developmental lag hypothesis and an abnormal cerebral organization hypothesis.

According to the *developmental lag hypothesis,* poor readers lag behind normal readers in the development of linguistic skills, and therefore language has not not fully lateralized to the left hemisphere, leading to weak asymmetries on tests of perceptual laterality. Because we have been able to find virtually no support for Lenneberg's (1967) position of a gradual lateralization of language functions throughout childhood, the developmental lag hypothesis seems quite untenable. If there is nothing developing, there is nothing to lag. The alternative is that something has gone wrong, either in the genetics of cerebral organization or during prenatal or early development that has led to an abnormal cerebral organization. Evidence for a genetic factor in some types of reading disability (Smith, Pennington, Kimberling, & Lubs, 1983), and for cerebral abnormalities associated with dyslexia (Galaburda, 1983; Heir, LeMay, Rosenberger, & Perlo, 1978) are consistent with such a view. While the notion of an impairment being associated with a fixed but abnormal cerebral organization may seem to be a pessimistic one, such need not be the case. The identification of an abnormality makes it possible to develop compensatory strategies that will circumvent the potential problem.

While most recent reviews have been rather critical of the data supporting a relationship between cerebral lateralization and reading disability (Naylor, 1980; A. W. Young & Ellis, 1981), Corballis (1983) has argued rather strongly for such an effect. In his review of the literature, he indicates 19 studies that have indicated greater lateralization in normal readers than in dyslexics, and only 3 that have shown the reverse (Corballis, 1983, p. 167). There are also 21 studies that have shown no difference between the groups, but some of them do not have enough power to detect a difference. In any event, the large number of studies showing weaker lateralization in poor readers must be considered to be at least suggestive.

While metanalyses such as that offered by Corballis are often very useful, they fail to consider the quality of the studies, the magnitude of the effects reported, the sample sizes employed, or the procedural details of the studies. A. W. Young and Ellis (1981), for example, are highly critical of those studies that have attempted to show a relation between visual-field asymmetries and reading ability, on the grounds that good and poor readers may approach the task with quite different information-processing strategies and quite different knowledge bases. If a poor reader can't read the words being shown in a tachistoscope, he/she is not likely to show much of a laterality effect.

Because of such problems, we concentrate here on studies seeking to establish the relation between dichotic laterality and reading ability. In this area, Corballis's (1983) review indicates that poor readers are more likely to show weaker lateralization effects than normal children in the younger samples (below age 10), but that good–poor reader differences are less evident in older children.

It is not easy to do a good study of reading ability and dichotic listening laterality. Two major problems that one must face immediately are the selection of an appropriate dichotic listening task and the definition of what is meant by a poor reader. Much of the early dichotic work with poor readers involved the presentation of lists of numbers or words, and, as we have seen earlier, such tasks leave much to idiosyncratic subject strategies and also involve a large short-term memory component (Bryden, 1978). Second, various researchers differ in what they consider to be a poor reader. Some simply define a *poor reader* as one who is performing below his or her chronological age level, without regard for any other characteristics. Such a definition lumps together those with specific reading disability and those who are generally intellectually impaired. Other researchers define their *poor readers* as exhibiting specific developmental dyslexia, in that their reading performance is substantially below that which would be predicted on the basis of other measures of intellectual ability, such as a performance IQ measure. Finally, a few workers have taken advantage of some of the more recent concepts of differential classification and have attempted to categorize their *poor readers* into distinct subgroups, such as the dysphonetic and dyseidetic types proposed by Boder (1973). Given the fact that it is unlikely that all poor readers have become so for the same reason, it would appear imperative to use some form of differential classification.

Unfortunately, there are very few studies that combine careful subject selection with good dichotic testing and measurement procedures. Watson and Engle (1982) found signs of weaker lateralization in younger (age 7) developmental dyslexics when a free-recall procedure was used, but not when order of report was controlled. They suggest that recall strategies and memory differences contribute significantly to dichotic laterality differences between good and poor readers. Following a careful analysis of two large-scale longitudinal studies of dichotic performance, Morris, Bakker, Satz, and Van der Vlugt (1984) conclude that so many factors influence the recall of dichotic lists that the data are essentially useless for making any strong statements about cerebral lateralization.

In recent years, a few studies have appeard in which subject selection has been carefully carried out and where good dichotic listening procedures have been employed. However, these studies, like those preceding them, have found differing results, and it would be premature to attempt any general conclusion. Aylward (1984) used dichotic lists, but controlled attentional factors to some extent by employing a postcued partial report procedure. Her subjects were developmental dyslexics subclassified according to Boder's system as dysphonetic, dyseidetic, or nonspecific. She was unable to find any differences among the three subgroups, although the poor readers tended to have *larger* laterality effects than did the control subjects. Relatively few other studies report such a pattèrn (but see Obrzut, Hynd, Obrzut, & Pirozzolo, 1981).

In another study, Prior, Frolley, and Sanson (1983) studied three groups of subjects classified according to the system of Rutter and Yule (1975) as normal, backward readers (or generally backward), and specific reading disability (or developmentally dyslexic). They used the dichotic monitoring system developed by Geffen (Geffen & Caudrey, 1981), a generally unbiased procedure and one demonstrably related to language lateralization. Although Prior et al. reported no significant differences among the three groups, there were only 10 subjects in each group, and it may be worth noting that variance was far higher in the specific reading disability group than in the normal group. Perhaps further subdivision of this group would lead to a clearer pattern of results.

In summary, we must agree with Naylor (1980) that the association between dichotic lateralization and reading disability is not proven. However, it is now clearer just what kind of study needs to be done. Subjects should be carefully selected as developmentally dyslexic rather than simply as poor readers, and should be subclassified by some system such as that proposed by Boder (1973).

The dichotic task should carefully control attentional and memory factors, and thus should involve fused consonant-vowel (CV) pairs (Wellman & Allen, 1983), CV pairs with careful attentional control (Bryden, Munhall, & Allard, 1983), or dichotic monitoring (Geffen & Caudrey, 1981). Finally, the measurement should permit some statistical statement to be made about individual subjects and be independent of overall performance level (Bryden & Sprott, 1981). Given these considerations, it should be possible to provide some clear answers in the near future.

CONCLUSIONS

In this survey, little evidence has been found for any systematic changes in cerebral lateralization after the age of 2 or 3 years. Whether we examine the childhood aphasia literature, the research on perceptual asymmetries, or the handedness literature, there seems to be little evidence for systematic change. Overall, about 92% of the population seems to have left-hemispheric language representation, and about 90% are right-handed. Manifestations of these are observable by the age of 2, and, barring major injury, will remain that way.

In infancy, the situation is somewhat more clouded. While the right-hand and left-hemisphere biases are observable at or soon after birth, the proportions are not as extreme as seen in adults or older children. This may simply indicate that the measures used with infants are crude and variable. Alternatively, it may be that strong right-hand preference induces left-hemisphere language in some, and that strongly lateralized left-hemisphere language induces right-handedness in others. Such a thought is only speculative, and would require better longitudinal studies than are presently available.

Likewise, the association between cerebral lateralization and cognitive abilities remains speculative. We have seen hints of such an association in one area, that of reading disability, but the case remains unproven. Corballis (1983) has also argued for an association between cerebral lateralization and stuttering. Kraft (1983) has studied the relation between dichotic lateralization and general cognitive abilities: If her data are representative, the relation is a very complex one.

There seem to be three major areas in which further research is indicated. First, much of the infant literature indicates that only about 70% of children show anatomical or behavioral asymmetries favoring left-hemisphere language and right-handedness. By the age of 3 years, 90% of children show perceptual and motor laterality effects, albeit on somewhat different measures. Clearly, further research is needed on possible changes in lateralization from infancy to the preschool years.

Second, we now have good techniques for assessing lateralization in school-age children and good techniques for the differential diagnosis of reading disability. These should be combined in careful studies of the relation between language lateralization and reading ability.

Third, the functions of the right hemisphere have been all but ignored in laterality research. Studies of music, visuospatial skills, and affect could all contribute to our understanding of the right hemisphere.

ACKNOWLEDGMENTS

Preparation of this review was aided by a grant from the Natural Sciences and Engineering Research Council of Canada to M.P.B. and by a Leave Fellowship to M.P.B. from the Social Sciences and Humanities Reseach Council of Canada. The authors appreciate the comments of S. J. Segalowitz on an earlier version of the chapter.

REFERENCES

Annett, M. (1970). The growth of manual preference and speed. *British Journal of Psychology, 61*, 545–558.

Annett, M. (1973). Laterality of childhood hemiplegia and the growth of speech and intelligence. *Cortex, 9*, 4–33.

Annett, M., & Turner, A. (1974). Laterality and the growth of intellectual abilities. *British Journal of Educational Psychology, 44*, 37–46.

Aylward, E. H. (1984). Lateral asymmetry in subgroups of dyslexic children. *Brain and Language, 22*, 221–231.

Balow, I. (1963). Lateral dominance characteristics and reading achievement in the first grade. *Journal of Psychology, 55*, 323–328.

Beaumont, J. G. (Ed.). (1982). *Divided visual field studies of cerebral organization*. London: Academic Press.

Belmont, L., & Birch, H. G. (1963). Lateral dominance and right–left awareness in normal children. *Child Development, 34*, 257–270.

Berlin, C. I., Hughes, I. F., Lowe-Bell, S. S., & Berlin, H. L. (1973). Dichotic right ear advantage in children 5 to 13. *Cortex, 9*, 393–401.

Boder, E. (1973). Developmental dyslexia: A diagnostic approach based on three atypical reading patterns. *Developmental Medicine and Child Neurology, 15*, 663–687.

Bradshaw, J. L., & Nettleton, N. C. (1983). *Human cerebral asymmetry*. Englewood Cliffs, NJ: Prentice-Hall.

Bresson, F., Maury, L., Fierault-LeBonniec, G., & de Schonen, S. (1977). Organization and lateralization of reaching in infants: An instance of asymmetric functions in hands collaboration. *Neuropsychologia, 15*, 311–320.

Bryden, M. P. (1965). Tachistoscopic recognition, handedness, and cerebral dominance. *Neuropsychologia, 3*, 1–8.

Bryden, M. P. (1978). Strategy effects in the assessment of hemispheric asymmetry. In G. Underwood (Ed.), *Strategies of information processing*. London: Academic Press.

Bryden, M. P. (1982). *Laterality*. New York: Academic Press.

Bryden, M. P., & Allard, F. A. (1981). Do auditory perceptual asymmetries develop? *Cortex, 17*, 313–318.

Bryden, M. P., Munhall, K., & Allard, F. (1983). Attentional biases and the right-ear effect in dichotic listening. *Brain and Language, 18,* 236–248.

Bryden, M. P., & Sprott, D. A. (1981). Statistical determination of degree of laterality. *Neuropsychologia, 19,* 571–581.

Caplan, P. J., & Kinsbourne, M. (1976). Baby drops the rattle: Asymmetry of duration of grasp by infants. *Child Development, 47,* 532–534.

Carmon, A., Nachshon, I., & Starinsky, R. (1976). Developmental aspects of visual hemifield differences in perception of verbal material. *Brain and Language, 3,* 463–469.

Cioffi, J., & Kandel, G. I. (1979). Laterality of stereognostic accuracy of children for words, shapes, and bigrams. *Science, 204,* 1431–1434.

Corballis, M. C. (1983). *Human laterality.* New York: Academic Press.

Cranney, J., & Ashton, R. (1980). Witelson's dichhaptic task as a measure of hemispheric asymmetry in deaf and hearing populations. *Neuropsychologia, 18,* 95–98.

Dawson, G. L. (1981). Sex differences in dichhaptic processing. *Perceptual and Motor Skills, 53,* 935–944.

Denes, G., & Spinaci, M. P. (1981). Influence of association values in recognition of random shapes under dichhaptic presentation. *Cortex, 17,* 597–602.

Dennis, M., & Whitaker, H. A. (1977). Hemispheric equipotentiality and language acquisition. In S. J. Segalowitz & F. A. Gruber (Eds.), *Language development and neurological theory.* New York: Academic Press.

DeRenzi, E. (1982). *Disorders of space exploration and cognition.* New York: Wiley.

Flanery, R. C., & Balling, J. D. (1979). Developmental changes in hemispheric specialization for tactile spatial ability. *Developmental Psychology, 15,* 364–372.

Forgays, D. G. (1953). The development of differential word recognition. *Journal of Experimental Psychology, 45,* 165–168.

Galaburda, A. (1983). Developmental dyslexia: Current anatomical research. *Annals of Dyslexia, 33,* 41–53.

Geffen, G. (1976). Development of hemispheric specialization for speech perception. *Cortex, 12,* 337–346.

Geffen, G. (1978). The development of the right ear advantage in dichotic listening with focused attention. *Cortex, 14,* 169–177.

Geffen, G., Bradshaw, J. L., & Wallace, G. (1971). Interhemispheric effects on reaction time to verbal and nonverbal visual stimuli. *Journal of Experimental Psychology, 87,* 415–422.

Geffen, G., & Caudrey, D. (1981). Reliability and validity of the dichotic monitoring test for language laterality. *Neuropsychologia, 19,* 413–424.

Gesell, A., & Ames, L. B. (1947). The development of handedness. *Journal of Genetic Psychology, 70,* 155–175.

Gibson, C., & Bryden, M. P. (1983). Dichhaptic recognition of shapes and letters in children. *Canadian Journal of Psychology, 37,* 132–143.

Gibson, J. J. (1962). Observations on active touch. *Psychological Review, 69,* 477–490.

Goodglass, H. (1973). Developmental comparison of vowels and consonants in dichotic listening. *Journal of Speech and Hearing Research, 16,* 744–752.

Hanvik, L. J., & Kaste, C. M. (1973). Mixed cerebral dominance in clinic and school populations. *Perceptual and Motor Skills, 37,* 900–902.

Hardyck, C., Goldman, R., & Petrinovitch, L. (1975). Handedness and sex, race, and age. *Human Biology, 47,* 369–375.

Harris, A. (1957). Lateral dominance, directional confusion, and reading disability. *Journal of Psychology, 44,* 283–294.

Hawn, P. R., & Harris, L. J. (1983). Laterality in manipulatory and cognitive-related activity. In G. Young, S. Segalowitz, C. Corter, & S. Trehub (Eds.), *Manual specialization and the developing brain.* New York: Academic Press.

Hécaen, H., & Sauguet, J. (1971). Cerebral dominance in left-handed subjects. *Cortex, 7,* 19–48.

Heim, A. W., & Watts, K. P. (1976). Handedness and cognitive bias. *Quarterly Journal of Experimental Psychology, 28,* 355–360.

Heir, D. B., LeMay, M., Rosenberger, P. B., & Perlo, V. P. (1978). Developmental dyslexia. *Archives of Neurology, 35,* 90–92.

Hellige, J. B. (Ed.). (1983). *Cerebral hemisphere asymmetry.* New York: Praeger.

Hiscock, M., & Kinsbourne, M. (1977). Selective listening asymmetry in preschool children. *Developmental Psychology, 13,* 217–224.

Hynd, G. W., & Obrzut, J. E. (1977). Effect of grade level and sex on the magnitude of the dichotic ear advantage. *Neuropsychologia, 15,* 689–692.

Ingram, D. (1975). Cerebral speech lateralization in young children. *Neuropsychologia, 13,* 103–105.

Kaufman, A. S., Zelma, R., & Kaufman, N. L. (1978). The relationship of hand dominance to the motor coordination, mental ability and right–left awareness of young normal children. *Child Development, 49,* 885–888.

Kimura, D. (1961). Cerebral dominance and the perception of verbal stimuli. *Canadian Journal of Psychology, 15,* 166–171.

Kimura, D. (1963). Speech lateralization in young children as determined by an auditory test. *Journal of Comparative and Physiological Psychology, 56,* 899–902.

Kimura, D. (1964). Left–right differences in the perception of melodies. *Quarterly Journal of Experimental Psychology, 16,* 355–358.

Kimura, D., & Durnford, M. (1974). Normal studies on the function of the right hemisphere in vision. In S. Dimond & J. G. Beaumont (Eds.), *Hemisphere function in the human brain.* London: Paul Elek Science.

Kirsner, K., & Schwartz, S. (in press). Words and hemifields: Do the hemispheres enjoy equal opportunity? *Brain and Cognition.*

Kraft, R. H. (1983). The effect of sex, laterality, and familial handedness on intellectual abilities. *Neuropsychologia, 21,* 74–89.

Krashen, S. D. (1973). Lateralization, language learning, and the critical period: Some new evidence. *Language Learning, 23,* 63–74.

LaBreche, T. M., Manning, A. A., Goble, W., & Markham, R. (1977). Hemispheric specialization for linguistic and nonlinguistic tactual perception in a congenitally deaf population. *Cortex, 13,* 184–194.

Larsen, S. (1984). Developmental changes in the pattern of ear asymmetry as revealed by a dichotic listening task. *Cortex, 20,* 5–18.

Lenneberg, E. (1967). *Biological foundations of language.* New York: Wiley.

Levy, J. (1972). Lateral specialization of the human brain: Behavioral manifestations and possible evolutionary basis. In J. A. Kiger (Ed.), *The biology of behavior.* Corvallis: Oregon State University Press.

Liederman, J., & Kinsbourne, M. (1980). Rightward motor bias in newborns depends upon parental right-handedness. *Neuropsychologia, 18,* 579–584.

McCormick, D. P. (1978). Right–left orientation and writing hand in children referred for neurodevelopmental assessment. *Perceptual and Motor Skills, 46,* 1175–1180.

Melekian, B. (1981). Lateralization in the human newborn at birth: Asymmetry of the stepping reflex. *Neuropsychologia, 19,* 707–711.

Michel, G. F. (1982). Ontogenetic precursors of infant handedness. *Infant Behavior and Development, 5,* 156.

Miller, L. K., & Turner, S. (1973). Development of hemifield differences in word recognition. *Journal of Educational Psychology, 65,* 172–176.

Morris, R., Bakker, D., Satz, P., & Van der Vlugt, H. (1984). Dichotic listening ear asymmetry: Patterns of longitudinal development. *Brain and Language, 22,* 49–66.

Nagafuchi, M. (1970). Development of dichotic and monaural hearing abilities in young children. *Acta Oto-Laryngologica, 69,* 409–415.

Naylor, H. (1980). Reading disability and lateral asymmetry: An information-processing analysis. *Psychological Bulletin, 87,* 531–545.

Obrzut, J., Hynd, G., Obrzut, A., & Pirozzolo, F. (1981). Effect of directed attention on cerebral asymmetries in normal and learning disabled children. *Developmental Psychology, 17,* 118–125.

O'Connor, C. (1970). Day-to-day difference between dominant and nondominant grip strength in preschool children. *Perceptual and Motor Skills, 30,* 676.

Orton, S. J. (1937). *Reading, writing and speech problems in children.* London: Chapman & Hall.

Palmer, R. D. (1964). Development of differential handedness. *Psychological Bulletin, 62,* 257–272.

Perecman, E. (Ed.). (1983). *Cognitive processing in the right hemisphere.* New York: Academic Press.

Porac, C. & Coren, S. (1976). The dominant eye. *Psychological Bulletin, 83,* 880–897.

Porac, C., & Coran, S. (1981). *Lateral preferences and human behavior.* New York: Springer-Verlag.

Prior, M. R., Frolley, M., & Sanson, A. (1983). Language lateralization in specific reading retarded children and backward readers. *Cortex, 19,* 149–163.

Ramsay, D. (1979). Manual preference for tapping in infants. *Developmental Psychology, 15,* 437–442.

Ramsay, D. (1980). Onset of unimanual handedness in infants. *Infant Behavior and Development, 3,* 377–385.

Ramsay, D. (1983). Unimanual hand preference and duplicated syllable babbling in infants. In G. Young, S. Segalowitz, C. Corter, & S. Trehub (Eds.), *Manual specialization and the developing brain.* New York: Academic Press.

Rasmussen, T., & Milner, B. (1977). The role of early left-brain injury in determining lateralization of cerebral speech functions. *Annals of the New York Academy of Sciences, 299,* 355–369.

Reitsma, P. (1975). Visual asymmetry in children. In *Lateralization of brain function.* Leiden: University of Leiden Press.

Rutter, M., & Yule, W. (1975). The concept of specific reading retardation. *Journal of Child Psychology and Psychiatry, 16,* 181–197.

Sabatino, D. A., & Becker, J. T. (1971). Relationship between lateral preference and selected behavioral variables for children failing academically. *Child Development, 42,* 2055–2063.

Satz, P., Bakker, D. J., Teunissen, J., Goebel, R., & Van der Vlugt, H. (1975). Developmental parameters of the ear asymmetry: A multivariate approach. *Brain and Language, 2,* 171–185.

Satz, P., & Bullard-Bates, C. (1981). Acquired aphasia in children. In M. T. Sarno (Ed.), *Acquired aphasia.* New York: Academic Press.

Saxby, L., & Bryden, M. P. (1984). Left-ear superiority in children for processing auditory emotional material. *Developmental Psychology, 20,* 72–80.

Saxby, L., & Bryden, M. P. (1985). Left visual-field advantage in children for processing visual emotional stimuli. *Developmental Psychology, 21,* 253–261.

Segalowitz, S. J., & Bryden, M. P. (1983). Individual differences in hemispheric representation of language. In S. J. Segalowitz (Ed.), *Language functions and brain organization.* New York: Academic Press.

Sinclair, C. (1971). Dominance patterns of young children: A follow-up study. *Perceptual and Motor Skills, 32,* 142.

Smith, S. D., Pennington, B. F., Kimberling, W. J., & Lubs, H. A. (1983). A genetic analysis of specific reading disability. In C. L. Ludlow & J. A. Cooper (Eds.), *Genetic aspects of speech and language disorders*. New York: Academic Press.

Springer, S., & Deutsch, G. (1981). *Left brain, right brain*. San Francisco: Freeman.

Steingruber, H. J. (1975). Handedness as a function of test complexity. *Perceptual and Motor Skills, 40,* 263–266.

Strauss, E. (1982). Manual persistence in infancy. *Cortex, 18,* 319–322.

Van Camp, S. S., & Bixby, M. B. (1977). Eye and hand dominance in kindergarten and first-grade children. *Merrill-Palmer Quarterly, 23,* 129–139.

Viviani, J., Turkewitz, G., & Karp, E. (1978). A relationship between laterality of functioning at 2 days and at 7 years of age. *Bulletin of the Psychonomic Society, 12,* 189–192.

Wada, J., Clarke, R., & Hamm, A. (1975). Cerebral hemispheric asymmetry in humans. *Archives of Neurology, 32,* 239–246.

Watson, E. S., & Engle, R. W. (1982). Is it lateralization, processing strategies, or both that distinguishes good and poor readers? *Journal of Experimental Child Psychology, 34,* 1–19.

Wellman, M. M., & Allen, M. (1983). Variation in hand position, cerebral lateralization, and reading ability among right-handed children. *Brain and Language, 18,* 277–292.

White, N., & Kinsbourne, M. (1980). Does speech output control lateralize over time? Evidence from verbal–manual time sharing tasks. *Brain and Language, 10,* 215–223.

Witelson, S. F. (1974). Hemispheric specialization for linguistic and nonlinguistic tactual perception using a dichotomous stimulation technique. *Cortex, 10,* 3–17.

Witelson, S. F. (1976). Sex and the single hemisphere? Right hemisphere specialization for spatial processing. *Science, 193,* 425–427.

Witelson, S. F. (1977a). Early hemisphere specialization and interhemispheric plasticity: An empirical and theoretical review. In S. J. Segalowitz & F. A. Gruber (Eds.), *Language development and neurological theory*. New York: Academic Press.

Witelson, S. F. (1977b). Developmental dyslexia: Two right hemispheres and none left. *Science, 195,* 309–311.

Young, A. W. (Ed.). (1983). *Functions of the right cerebral hemisphere*. New York: Academic Press.

Young, A. W., & Ellis, H. D. (1981). Asymmetry of cerebral hemispheric function in normal and poor readers. *Psychological Bulletin, 89,* 183–190.

Young, G., Bowman, J. G., Methot, C., Finlayson, M., Quintal, J., & Boissonneault, P. (1983). Hemispheric specialization development: What (inhibition) and how (parents). In G. Young, S. Segalowitz, C. Corter, & S. Trehub (Eds.), *Manual specialization and the developing brain*. New York: Academic Press.

Young, G., Corter, C., Segalowitz, S., & Trehub, S. (1983). Manual specialization and the developing brain: Overview. In G. Young, S. Segalowitz, C. Corter, & S. Trehub (Eds.), *Manual specialization and the developing brain*. New York: Academic Press.

Chapter 5

Psychophysiological Indices of Early Cognitive Processes and Their Relationship to Language

DENNIS L. MOLFESE
VICTORIA J. MOLFESE

Department of Psychology and School of Medicine
Southern Illinois University at Carbondale
Carbondale, Illinois 62901

INTRODUCTION

Although investigations into the brain's auditory system using auditory evoked responses (AER) have been carried out since the 1930s (Davis, 1939a, 1939b), only since the mid-1970s have researchers used this tool to investigate more-specific brain–language relationships. In fact, it was through the study of *AER*s (the portion of the ongoing electrical activity of the brain that is time-locked to the onset of some external auditory event) that researchers first reported evidence of functional hemispheric asymmetries in human infants (Barnet, de Sotillo, & Campos, 1974; Crowell, Jones, Kapuniai, & Nakagawa, 1973; Molfese, 1972; Molfese, Freeman, & Palermo, 1975; Molfese & Molfese, 1979a, 1979b, 1980; Shucard, Shucard, Cummins, & Campos, 1981).

In recent years, multivariate analyses of data obtained using AER techniques have yielded information concerning the development of hemisphere differences. These procedures have also enabled researchers to isolate and identify those

95

specific components of AER across hemispheres that reflect responses to specific language-relevant acoustic and phonetic cues. Two speech cues that have received considerable attention across different developmental periods are voicing contrasts and place of articulation. This chapter has two sections. The first section contains a review of developmental research involving AERs, hemispheric responses, and speech cues. The second section explores the possible relationship between hemispheric responses to speech cues early in development and later language performance.

VOICING CONTRASTS

Voice onset time (VOT) has been identified as one cue that is particularly important to the perception of speech. VOT refers to the temporal difference between the onset of laryngeal pulsing (e.g., vocal chord vibration) relative to consonant release (e.g., the separation of the lips to release a burst of air from the vocal tract during production of bilabial consonants such as /b/ or /p/). Researchers have noted that when VOT was systematically manipulated, adults can discriminate changes in VOT only to the extent that they can assign unique labels to these sounds (Liberman, Cooper, Shankweiler, & Studdert-Kennedy, 1967).

Listeners generally discriminate consonant sounds with VOT values of 0 and 20 milliseconds (msec) from stimuli with VOT values of 40 and 60 msec. They assign one phonetic label to the first group (0 and 20 msec) and a different label to the second group (40, 60 msec). However, listeners fail to discriminate between the 0- and 20-msec stimuli and identify both stimuli as /ba/. They also fail to discriminate between the 40- and 60-msec stimuli, both of which they identify as /pa/. This ability to assign unique phonetic labels to only those stimuli that could be discriminated has been labeled "categorical perception." Such effects have been replicated with adults (Lisker & Abramson, 1964; Liberman, Delattre, & Cooper, 1958) as well as with young infants in studies that employed high amplitude sucking (HAS) and conditioned head-turning procedures (Eilers, Gavin, & Wilson, 1979; Eimas, 1974; Eimas, Siqueland, Jusczyk, & Vigorito, 1971; Lasky, Syrdal-Lasky, & Klein, 1975; Streeter, 1976; Trehub & Rabinovitch, 1972).

The behavioral studies of infants generally report that VOT category perception is present in infants as young as 1 month of age, long before the emergence of language development. This could suggest that at least some of the mechanisms that subserve language functions are innately specified from birth. However, given the severe limitations of behavioral techniques (such as HAS) with infants less than 1 or 2 months of age, no behavioral studies to date have successfully addressed the question concerning when the mechanisms for VOT perception first appear in development.

Additional questions not directly addressed with behavioral procedures concern the localization of VOT mechanisms in the brain and how such mechanisms change as the child develops into a sophisticated language-user. Because VOT is known to be an important speech cue, and speech processes have generally been thought to be controlled by the language-dominant hemisphere—generally the left hemisphere—most theorists have concluded that VOT category discrimination is controlled by mechanisms within the left hemisphere. However, this question has been experimentally addressed only recently. A final question concerns the nature of the VOT cue itself. Is VOT categorically processed by specialized speech mechanisms or by more basic, acoustically tuned cortical mechanisms (Pisoni, 1977; Stevens & Klatt, 1974)?

Electrophysiological Techniques

Molfese and associates have used electrophysiological recording procedures, as well as behavioral techniques, to address language- and speech-perception issues. Electrophysiological techniques involve the presentation of an auditory stimulus and the recording of the brain's AER that is triggered by this event. Various portions of the AERs have been found to reflect different stimulus properties.

Evoked potential (EP) techniques attempt to establish strict temporal relationships between the onset of some stimulus event and the onset of changes in the various portions of the following EEG pattern. Because of the small size of these electrical patterns (5 to 15 microvolts) relative to other electrical noise sources, researchers must usually repeat the stimuli a number of times in order to evoke further replications of the brain potentials. Next, these replicated evoked potentials are added together and then averaged. Such averaging procedures are used to extract the EP from the background noise of nonreplicable or nonredundant information in the averaged evoked potentials.

The final quotient is then expected to reflect the brain activity elicited by some specific stimulus event. Once the averaged evoked potentials are obtained, a variety of different analyses can be used in order to determine whether changes in stimulus features might produce corresponding changes in various protions of the brain response. In general, analyses focus on certain peaks in the waveforms that occur at certain intervals following the onset of stimulus event (Picton & Strauss, 1980; Vaughan, 1969). Such analyses may be based on procedures as simple as direct time or amplitude measures between two peaks, or they may involve a complex factor analysis to reduce the complex waveform to a smaller set of simpler components.

There is a great deal of evidence that the averaged evoked potential can reflect changes in the neural activity of the brain during sensory (Regan, 1972, pp. 31–116) and cognitive processing (Donchin, Ritter, & McCallum, 1978). In the first case, such exogenous EP components appear to be relatively "impervious to variations of the psychological state of the observer" (Hillyard & Woods, 1979, p. 346). These components (which for the most part occur prior to 100 msec following stimulus onset) seem to be very stable from one individual to the next and are not usually altered by subject state.

Changes in some portion of these waveforms, whether in terms of the amplitude or latency of waveform peaks or the absence of certain waves usually present, signals some problem with a receptor, pathway, or brain area represented by that component (Rockstroh, Elbert, Birbaumer, & Lutzenberger, 1982, p. 3). On the other hand, EP waveforms that are associated with cognitive or perceptual processes of the brain are usually referred to as endogenous components (Hillyard & Woods, 1979, p. 346). In general, the portion of the waveform that occurs after 100 msec following the onset of a stimulus reflects this type of activity. Here, the various characteristics of the EP waveforms, although triggered by some stimulus, are affected by the cognitive–perceptual processes involved in processing the stimulus.

While the exogenous components are relatively stable across different subject states and individuals, the endogenous components can show great intersubject variability and may change across different tasks and subject states. For the research outlined here subsequently, it would appear that the categorical-like effects elicit exogenous types of activity, given the consistent pattern noted across ages and tasks.

In general, two different approaches have been used to study evoked potentials: (1) "defining the neuronal substrates of EPs *and* their relationship to behavioral events" and (2) "a purely empirical relation of EPs and behavior without recourse to neuronal mechanisms" (Purpura, 1978, p. 83). While there are a number of excellent chapters that attempt to identify discrete elements within the brain that are responsible for generating the various components of the EP (Goff, Allison, & Vaughn, 1978; Klee & Rall, 1977), the exact nature of these brain mechanisms remains in doubt and under discussion.

However, at a grosser level, topographic studies of human EPs do indicate that major portions of the EPs originate in the primary and secondary cortical areas that are specific to the modality involved in the detection of the stimuli presented (Vaughan, 1969; Simson, Vaughan, & Ritter, 1977a). In this way, evoked potentials associated with auditory and visual presentations appear to be generated in the secondary cortex of the auditory and visual systems, respectively, as well as in the parietal association cortex (Simson et al., 1977a; Simson, Vaughan, & Ritter, 1977b). At a grosser level, EP activity recorded over the left side of the head originates for the most part in the left hemisphere, whereas EP activity recorded from over the right hemisphere orginiates in the right hemisphere of the brain.

In an early electrophysiology study on adult VOT perception, Molfese (1978a) recorded AERs from the left and right temporal regions of 16 adults during a phonetic identification task. Subjects were presented with a randomly ordered series of synthesized bilabial stop consonants that varied in VOT with values of 0, +20, +40, and +60 msec. The 0- and 20-msec stimuli belong to one phonetic category (/b/) while the 40- and 60-msec belong to a second phonetic category (/p/). Subjects were asked to press one button after each stimulus presentation if they heard a /b/ and a second button if they heard a /p/. Adults identified the consonant–vowel syllables with VOT values of 0 and +20 msec as /ba/ approximately 97% and 93% of the time, respectively, whereas the consonant–vowel syllables with VOT times of +40 and +60 msec were identified 95% and 98% of the time, repsectively, as /pa/.

AERs to each stimulus were recorded during the identification task and then analyzed using standard averaging techniques. Subsequent analyses involving principal-components analysis and analyses of variance (ANOVAs) indicated that two early AER components recorded from electrodes placed over the right hemisphere temporal region varied systematically as a function of the phonetic category of the evoking stimulus. Stimuli with VOT values of 0 and +20 msec elicited a different AER waveform from the right hemisphere site than did the +40- and +60-msec stimuli. No differences in the AER waveforms were found between the VOT values within a phonetic category (i.e., no differences were found between the 0- and +20-msec responses or between the +40- and +60-msec responses).

These AER patterns of responding were comparable to the behavioral responses given by these subjects during the testing session, in that they discriminated between but not within phonetic categories. Components of the left-hemisphere responses reflected an ability of that hemisphere to differentiate between 0- and +60-msec stimuli and to differentiate 0- and +60-msec from +20- and +40-msec stimuli. The left hemisphere appeared responsive to the end boundaries of the VOT stimuli used, but they did not reflect the categorical discriminations shown by the right hemisphere.

Similar effects have also been found with 4-year-old children in a study in which velar stop consonants (/k/, /g/) were presented (Molfese & Hess, 1978). In this study, AERs were recorded from the left and right temporal regions of 12 nursery-school-age children (mean age = 4 years, 5 months) in response to a series of synthesized consonant–vowel syllables that varied in VOT for the initial consonant (0, +20, +40, +60 msec). As with the adults, one AER component from the right-hemisphere electrode site was found to vary systematically as a function of phoneme category, but the AER components did not distinguish between VOT values within a phonetic category. A second and distinct AER component also discriminated VOT values corresponding to the two phonetic categories. However, unlike that found for adults, this component was present in recording sites over both hemispheres.

This work was later extended to include newborns and infants (Molfese &
Molfese, 1979a). In one study, the four consonant–vowel speech syllables used
by Molfese (1978a) were presented to 16 infants 2–5 months old (mean = 3
months, 25 days). AERs to each stimulus were recorded from scalp electrodes
placed over the superior temporal regions of the left and right hemispheres.
Findings were noted that were similar to those noted by Molfese and Hess (1978)
with children.

One component of the cortical AER from the right-hemisphere site discriminated between VOT values from different phonetic categories. A second component of the AER that responded in a similar fashion was present over both
hemispheres. In a related study (Molfese & Molfese, 1979a), 16 newborn infants
were tested in an attempt to determine the developmental onset of VOT discrimination as reflected in AERs. Although the same consonant–vowel speech stimuli
and recording sites just described were used in the newborn study, no evidence of
categorical speech perception was found. Although both hemispheres responded
to all of the VOT stimuli, there was no evidence of any phonetic categorical-like
VOT effect similar to that found with older infants, children, and adults. Given
these data, it appears that the ability to discriminate VOT stimuli along phonetic
boundaries is present in the early months of infancy but may not be present at
birth. Some period of maturation or experience may be required for this ability to
develop or become functional.

Two general findings have emerged from this series of studies: (1) Categorical
discrimination of the VOT cue is controlled by several cortical processes—some
of which are restricted to only the right-hemisphere site and some of which are
common to both hemispheres. (2) There is a developmental pattern to the
emergence of mechanisms related to VOT categorical discrimination—such
mechanisms, not operational at birth, are functioning by 2 months of age; patterns of responding remain very consistent between 2 months and 4 years of age,
but then change again sometime before the adult years.

One question concerning the nature of the VOT cue has focused on the nature
of the stimuli that trigger categorical-like responses. Is VOT discrimination
based on specialized phonetic mechanisms in the brain that are sensitive to
different phonetic categories, or is it due to more acoustically tuned mechanisms
that are sensitive to general timing relationships? Pisoni (1977) suggested that the
ability to discriminate changes in VOT depends on auditory-processing units that
are sensitive to temporal changes in the onset of different events. Such mechanisms would respond to a broad range of stimuli, not just to cues specific to
speech.

As a test of this view, Pisoni (1977) trained 8 adults to discriminate a series of
two-tone stimuli Tone-onset-time (TOT), a −50 msec and a +50 msec tone, that
differed in the onset of tone 1 relative to tone 2. After training, adults were
presented with TOT stimuli that varied in small intermediate steps between the

two training stimuli. Subsequent testing indicated that adults formed two categories of stimuli: They discriminated the -50 to $+10$ msec stimuli from the $+30$ to $+50$ msec stimuli. However, discrimination within these categories was at chance levels. Given that the discrimination boundaries for TOT stimuli closely resembled those for VOT, Pisoni concluded that VOT perception depends on properties of the sensory system that are sensitive to the temporal order between two events. Because of the perceptual salience of such differences, Pisoni went on to suggest, linguistic systems over time have incorporated this temporal cue as important for speech production and perception.

Such similarities in responding to VOT and TOT stimuli have also been noted in a series of papers designed to assess hemisphere involvement in the temporal processing of such information. Molfese (1980a) investigated whether the laterality effects noted with the VOT stimuli were elicited by only speech stimuli or whether similar electrophysiological effects could be found for both speech and nonspeech materials. Molfese used four TOT stimuli with temporal lags similar to the speech materials used in previous electrophysiological studies. The two-tone stimuli differed from each other in the onset time of the lower tone in relation to the higher tone: (1) The lower tone began at the same time as the higher tone for the 0 msec stimulus; (2) the lower tone lagged 20 msec behind the higher tone for the $+20$ msec stimulus; (3) for the $+40$ msec stimulus, the lower tone was delayed 40 msec after the onset of the higher tone; (4) while for the $+60$ msec stimulus, this delay was increased to 60 msec.

AERs from central, temporal, and parietal scalp electrode sites over each hemisphere were recorded from adults in response to a randomly ordered series of TOT stimuli. A number of portions of the brain's response were found to reflect categorical-like discriminations of the TOT stimuli. A large positive wave that categorically discriminated the 0 msec and $+20$ msec TOT stimuli from the $+40$ msec and $+60$ msec TOT stimuli was detected at all four electrode sites over the right hemisphere. No such changes were noted to occur over the left hemisphere electrode sites at this same point in the brain's response (355 msec after the beginning of the stimulus). The left hemisphere electrical activity at this latency did discriminate between TOT stimuli from within a category (e.g., it discriminated 0 from $+20$ msec and $+40$ msec from $+60$ msec). A second AER component with a peak latency of 210 msec reflected the detection of phonetic category-like boundaries over both the left and the right parietal regions (P_3, P_4). A third component that affected the N110–P190 amplitude indicated that categorical-like discrimination of these temporal cues occurred over both hemispheres at the parietal and central electrode sites. AERs to temporal information, then, were characterized both by bilateral component changes in the first half of the ERP that were localized in or near the temporal and parietal regions of both hemispheres and by an additional but later-occurring component present at all right-hemisphere leads.

TABLE 1

Studies using AER techniques, reporting results related to categorical discrimination

Study	Subjects and ages	Stimuli	Electrode sites	Results
Infants:				
Molfese & Molfese (1979b), Study 2	16 newborn infants	Bilabial stop consonants and vowel 0-, 20-, 40-, 60-msec delays	T_3, T_4	No categorical-like effects
Molfese & Molfese (1979a), Study 1	16 infants $\overline{X}$ age = 115 days	Same as above	T_3, T_4	Right hemisphere discriminated between phonetic categories (0-, 20-msec versus 40-, 60-msec) at latency of 920 msec
Children:				
Molfese & Hess (1978)	12 children $\overline{X}$ age = 53 mo.	Velar stop consonants and vowel 0-, 20-, 40-, 60-msec delays	T_3, T_4	Right hemisphere discriminated between phonetic categories at latency of 444 msec Both hemispheres discriminated between phonetic categories at latency of 198 msec

Study	Subjects	Stimuli	Electrode Sites	Results
Molfese & Molfese (1984)	12 children $\overline{X}$ age = 36 mo.	Velar stop consonants and vowel two-formant tone stimuli (TOT) 0-, 20-, 40-, 60-msec delays	T_5, T_4	Right hemisphere discriminated between phonetic categories at latency of 400 msec
Adults: Molfese (1978a)	16 adults $\overline{X}$ age = 27 years	Bilabial stop consonants, 0-, 20-, 40-, 60-msec delays	T_5, T_4	Two right hemisphere responses discriminate between phonetic categories (peak latencies = 135 msec and 300–430 msec)
Molfese (1980a)	16 adults $\overline{X}$ age = 19	Two-formant tone stimuli (TOT) delays: 0-, 20-, 40-, 60-msec	P_3, P_4, T_3, T_4, C_2	Right hemisphere discriminated between phonetic categories at 355 msec Both hemispheres discriminated between phonetic categories at 145 msec and 210 msec

In one study, 3-year-old children participated in an AER study involving both VOT and TOT stimuli (Molfese & Molfese, 1984). While similar patterns of responses have been noted in previous studies for both the VOT and the TOT stimuli, no studies had included both stimulus sets in the same study with the same population. Such comparisons obviously would provide more information concerning the comparability of the mechanisms that subserve the perception of these two types of stimuli and the temporal cues that characterize them. Should brain responses to the VOT and TOT stimuli be identical, one would have a firmer basis for speculating that the mechanisms responsible for processing temporal information in speech materials are in fact comparable to those that process similar temporal delays in nonspeech stimuli.

In this study, a late-occurring component (N400) was found in the right hemisphere that discriminated one category of stimuli (0 and 20 msec) from a second category of stimuli (40 and 60 msec). The peak latency of this component and its ability to discriminate *between,* but not *within* categories is very comparable to the earlier Molfese and Hess (1978) report. Interestingly, this component did not discriminate between the speech (VOT) and nonspeech (TOT) stimuli. Both sets of stimuli contained a comparable temporal delay cue, and both were apparently discriminated along the same temporal boundaries in exactly the same manner. These data support Pisoni's (1977) and Molfese's (1980a) view that perception of the speech-cue VOT is based in part on the ability of the auditory system to discriminate certain temporally based acoustic cues in some fixed manner.

Across these AER studies of voicing contrasts, three general patterns of results have been noted: (1) all subjects older than 2 months of age produce right hemisphere responses that discriminate between stimuli varying in VOT in a categorical-like manner; (2) in response to VOT stimuli, the infants and children produce a second AER response common to both hemispheres that discriminates both within and between phonetic categories; (3) adult and child responses to TOT stimuli also behave in a categorical fashion, and these responses occur over right hemisphere recording sites. A summary of these findings is presented in Table 1.

PLACE OF ARTICULATION

Place of articulation is an important cue for discriminating between consonants such as /b/ and /g/, consonant sounds that are produced in different portions or places of the vocal tract. The consonant /b/ is referred to as a *front consonant* because it is produced in the very front of the vocal tract with the two lips. The consonant /g/, on the other hand, is produced in the back of the vocal tract and is labeled a *back consonant*. When the following vowel sounds are the same, the second formant transition as depicted in a sound spectrograph signals the place of articulation for the consonant. In the case of the syllable /ba/, the second formant transition would be rising to the steady-state vowel formant. This formant transition falls, however, for the initial /g/ of the syllable /ga/. In general, our studies have noted that patterns of electrical activity recorded from different areas of the scalp change as a function of place of articulation. Furthermore, these patterns of discrimination do not appear to change to any great extent from early in infancy (Molfese & Molfese, 1979b, 1980) into adulthood (Molfese, 1978b, 1980b, 1983, 1984; Molfese & Schmidt, 1983).

Studies with adults note that portions of the AER that occur 300 msec after stimulus onset and recorded from electrodes placed over the left hemisphere discriminate between consonants such as /b/ and /g/. That is, the amplitude of this portion of the waveform as measured from the positive peak occurring at 300 msec to the following negative peak at 400 msec is reliably larger for the AERs elicited by the /b/ initial syllables than for the /g/ initial syllables (Molfese, 1978b, 1980b, 1983; Molfese & Schmidt, 1983). In studies with adults in which electrodes are placed at multiple sites over the two hemispheres (Molfese, 1980b, 1983, 1984; Molfese & Schmidt, 1983), a second and earlier occurring portion of the AER located after approximately 100 msec following stimulus onset variables reliably when evoked by a /b/ versus a /g/ initial syllable. This second component behaves in a similar fashion to the one occurring at 300 msec, with the exception that it occurs simultaneously over both hemispheres. In this way, the AERs elicited by speech syllables reliably produce changes in two portions of the waveform in response to the /b/ and /g/ syllables. One area of waveform change discriminates between place differences at one point in time only over the left hemisphere electrode sites, whereas a second portion of the AER changes systematically over both hemispheres in response to place changes.

Building on this work with adults, several papers have reported comparable findings with newborn infants. Molfese and Molfese (1979b), in a report based on tests with 16 newborn infants, reported that the initial large negative deflection or peak of the newborns' AERs that occurred approximately 230 msec following stimulus onset (N230) was larger in size when evoked by /b/ initial syllables than by /g/ initial syllables. This response difference occurred only over the left hemisphere electrode site. As was the case with adults, however, a second portion of the AERs detected at electrodes placed over both hemispheres were also noted to discriminate between the /b/ and /g/ initial syllables. A later study with preterm infants (Molfese & Molfese, 1980) reported comparable lateralized and bilateral responses that discriminated place cues. This pattern of bilateral and lateralized discrimination of the place cue as reflected in different portions of the AERs occurs, then, both in young infants and in adults.

There appear to be some basic differences in the organization and localization of brain activity measured by electrophysiological techniques in response to the

TABLE 2

Studies that have used AER techniques to study place of articulation discrimination

Study	Subjects and ages	Stimuli	Electrode sites	Results
Infants:				
Molfese & Molfese (1980)	11 preterm infants $\overline{X}$ age = 35, 8 wks. conceptional age	/bae, gae/ with phonetic and nonphonetic transitions	T_3, T_4	Left hemisphere (LH) discriminated between consonants at 848 msec. Left hemisphere discriminated between phonetic and nonphonetic transitions at 608 msec.
Molfese & Molfese (1979b)	16 newborn full term infants	/bae, gae/ with speech and nonspeech formants	T_3, T_4	LH at 192 msec discriminates consonants with speech-formant structure. Both hemispheres at 630 msec discriminate consonants with speech-formant structure.
Adults:				
Molfese (1978b)	10 adults $\overline{X}$ age = 19.5 yrs.	/bae, gae/ with phonetic and nonphonetic transitions	T_3, T_4	LH at 300 msec discriminates consonants with phonetic and nonphonetic transitions

Molfese & Schmidt (1983)	20 adults $\overline{X}$ age = 20.1 yrs.	/bi, bae, bo/ and /gi, gae, go/ with speech and nonspeech formants.	$T_3, T_4, T_5, T_6, P_3, P_4$	LH at 290 and 460 msec discriminated between consonants. Both hemispheres at 170 msec discriminated between consonants.
Molfese (1984)	14 adults $\overline{X}$ age = 21.0 yrs.	/bi, di, gi/	$F_3, F_4, F_7, F_8, T_3, T_4, T_5, T_6, P_3, P_4$	LH at 295 msec discriminated between all consonants. Both hemispheres at 100 mec, 155 msec, and 195 msec discriminated /b/ and /d/ from /g/. However, these sites failed to discriminate between /b/ and /d/.
Molfese, Linnville, Wetzel, & Leicht (1985)	18 adults $\overline{X}$ age = 23.8 yrs.	/dae[1], dae[2]/ and /gae[1], gae[2]/	$C_3, C_4, T_3, T_4, T_5, T_6, P_3, P_4$	Both hemispheres at 475 msec discriminated between the two consonants.

temporal information contained in VOT and TOT stimuli and to place-of-artic-ulation contrasts. Although both speech-relevant contrasts elicit simultaneous and identical discrimination responses from both hemispheres (bilateral pro-cesses), they differ in important respects. Voicing contrasts elicit an additional distinction made by right-hemisphere activity, while place-of-articulation con-trasts evoke an additional left-hemisphere response. This pattern of lateralized and bilateralized responses are found in the AER responses of infants, children, and adults. The studies investigating place of articulation are summarized in Table 2.

AUDITORY EVOKED RESPONSES AS PREDICTORS
OF LATER LANGUAGE DEVELOPMENT

One major issue concerns the implications of these lateralized and bilateral patterns of brain responses to speech sounds for later language development (Molfese, 1983; Corballis, 1983). While data have continued to accumulate since the mid-1970s, which support the general view that lateralization of func-tion is present in young infants, the question concerning the relevance of such early patterns of lateralization to later language acquisition has remained un-answered. Do these patterns of responses have any implications for later lan-guage development, or do they reflect some basic patterns of auditory processing in the brain that have little relation to language development?

This interest in the possibility of biological precursors of language can be traced to a number of research findings published since the mid-1960s. Lenne-berg (1967) argued that a biological substrate exists that subserves language abilities. Evidence for such a view, he noted, could be seen at a number of levels in humans. For example, even at the gross morphological level of the vocal tract, humans (unlike other primates) are structured in a certain way to produce a wide variety of speech sounds (Lieberman, 1977). The pinna itself is structured to favor the perception of sound frequencies that characterize the majority of impor-tant speech cues. At the neurological level, Lenneberg argued that language acquisition was linked to brain organization.

For Lenneberg, lateralization of brain functions was a biological sign of lan-guage ability (Lenneberg, 1967, p. 67). In this view, the presence of early lateralized processes for language could influence later language outcomes (Basser, 1962). Children who demonstrated language skills early in development were thought to have language already lateralized to one hemisphere. If the infant should then suffer cerebral damage that affected the language hemisphere, the infant's ability to recover language functions was thought to be more limited than a child whose language system had not yet lateralized. Although investiga-tors have challenged some of Lenneberg's specific hypotheses on lateralization and language development (Molfese, 1972; Molfese et al., 1975), his general view that there are specific biological underpinnings for language that may facilitate language development continues to be supported (Dennis & Whitaker, 1975; Molfese & Molfese, 1979a, 1979b, 1980; Segalowitz, 1983; Segalowitz & Gruber, 1977).

Given Lenneberg's (1967) notion that lateralization is a biological sign of language, could such early patterns of lateralized and bilateral discrimination of speech sounds predict later language outcomes? This was the major aim of a longitudinal study by Molfese and Molfese (1984, in press-a, in press-b). This project attempted to establish the predictive validity of demographic variables, behavior scales, and AEPs for identifying developmental deviations in language abilities. The specific issue addressed concerned whether general hemisphere effects per se or hemisphere differences that interacted with specific stimulus characteristics would discriminate between children who later differed in language skills.

In this longitudinal study, 16 infants were tested at birth. For each subject the following information was obtained: gender, birthweight, length, gestational age; the ages, income level, education, and occupation of both parents; scores on the Obstetric Complications Scale (Littman & Parmelee, 1978); scores on the Brazelton Neonatal Assessment Scale [using scores on each of four a priori dimensions (Als, Tronick, Lester, and Brazelton, 1977) and on the overall profile based on ratings for the 26 items of the scale]; mental subscale scores on the Bayley Scales of Infant Development (Bayley, 1969); and scores on two language tests administered at 36 months of age [the Peabody Picture Vocabulary Test (Dunn, 1965) and the McCarthy Scales of Children's Abilities (McCarthy, 1972)]. AERs were recorded at each testing period, using recording electrodes placed on the scalp over left and right temporal areas. The synthetic speech syllables used by Molfese and Schmidt (1983) were also presented to these babies and children because these materials had been shown to generate both bilateral and lateralized stimulus-related effects, as well as the more general hemisphere non-stimulus-related effects. Eight related stimulus items were added in order to test the generalizability of the findings for consonants across different vowel sounds.

PREDICTING LANGUAGE PERFORMANCE
AT 3 YEARS OF AGE
FROM AERS OBTAINED AT BIRTH

Analyses of the electrophysiological data led to the identification of the electrophysiological response correlates of specific stimulus features that appeared to predict later language performance from brain responses recorded early in development and from behavioral responses. Several portions of the brain response systematically changed across hemispheres and differentiated between specific speech and nonspeech sounds.

One component of the AER that occurred between 88 and 240 msec reliably discriminated between the high- and low-MCVP groups at certain electrode (hemisphere) locations and under certain stimulus conditions. Only the AER waveforms recorded from over the left hemisphere of the high-MCVP group systematically varied as a function of consonant sounds. A right-hemisphere effect was noted for this same group of subjects for nonspeech stimuli. No differences were noted for the low-MCVP group for these electrode sites or stimulus dimensions. One other portion of the brain response that changed across hemispheres approximately 450 msec after the sound began failed to discriminate between the two language groups. No other group-related effects were noted. Thus, it appears that at birth there were hemisphere responses differentially sensitive to specific stimulus characteristics, which discriminated among children at 3 years of age who appeared to have different levels of language skills.

A second portion of the AER (as represented by Factor 7) with a late peak latency of 664 msec also discriminated between the high- and low-MCVP groups. This component was recorded by electrodes placed over both sides of the head and consequently reflected bilateral rather than only lateralized activity that discriminated between the two consonant sounds. This component, however, did not behave in the same manner as that first described here, in that it was not affected by the speech-like quality of the stimuli. Furthermore, the consonant discriminations were dependent on the following vowel sounds. Thus, it appears that lateralized responses alone were not the sole discriminators between children who later differed in language abilities. These data suggest that the AERs are reflecting brain responsiveness to specific language-relevant speech cues rather than readiness of the brain to respond to any general stimulus.

The findings of this last study of a left-hemishpere response that discriminates between the speech consonants /b/ and /g/ replicates an effect reported earlier by Molfese and Molfese (1979a). Both studies note that these left-hemisphere lateralized responses are reflected in amplitude changes for the first large negative deflection in the AER. Furthermore, the bilateral effect that was noted in the present study (peak latency = 664 msec) behaved in a similar fashion in terms of latency and response characteristics to the bilateral response (peak latency = 630 msec) reported earlier in the Molfese and Molfese (1979a) paper. Importantly, these replications hold across changes in the stimulus set, thereby indicating the generalizability of the findings across different vowel sounds.

Hemisphere effects were also noted that did not interact with stimulus or subject variables. The presence of such hemisphere effects, both interacting with stimulus characteristics as well as independent of such variables, suggests that hemisphere effects should be treated as a multidimensional concept when applied to infants (Molfese & Molfese, 1985a; Moscovitch, 1977).

One interpretation for the results of this study is that early discrimination abilities may relate to later language development. The high-MCVP infants in the present study not only discriminated between consonants alone and consonants in different vowel environments, they also discriminated between variants of the speech and the nonspeech stimuli. This pattern of responding could suggest that the high-MCVP infants were advantaged in the process of language development because their nervous systems were either more sensitive to or could make finer discriminations among a variety of auditory events, some of which share some commonality with speech-perception events. Perhaps the earlier an infant can detect and discriminate among patterns of sounds in their language environment, the better able that infant will be to use such information as the extensive process of language acquisition begins.

NONBRAIN MEASURES AS PREDICTORS OF LANGUAGE PERFORMANCE: THE CONTRIBUTION OF PERINATAL AND INFANT VARIABLES

Although the primary focus of this project was to determine the validity of AERs recorded at birth for predicting language performance at age 3 years, the contributions of the behavioral measures were also assessed. As was generally found in the studies reviewed earlier, the correlations between the perinatal variables and the infant and child variables were low. In this case, few of the correlations reached significance. Significant correlations were found between Brazelton Neonatal Assessment Scale scores and 6-month (.41) and 12-month (.53) Bayley mental subscale scores. Obstetric Complication Scale scores were significantly correlated with 6-month Bayley mental subscale scores (.66) but not at other ages. The Bayley mental subscale scores from age 18 months on showed stronger correlations with the 3-year language measures. The 18-month and 24-month Bayley mental subscale scores significantly correlate (.71 and .58, respectively) with the 36-month Peabody score. The 18- and 24-month Bayley scores significantly correlate (.63 and .73, respectively) with the 36-month McCarthy Scale scores. The Peabody scores and the McCarthy Scale scores significantly correlate at .64.

Demographic characteristics were not significant correlates of infant development and langauge performance scores. This may be due to the relatively homogeneous nature of the families and infants involved in the study and the small number of characteristics measured. The families were middle class with average incomes of $20,000 to $25,000, and both parents had at least completed high school.

Regression models were constructed to test hypotheses concerning the usefulness of perinatal, demographic, and infant-development tests to predict language performance at 36 months. The models showed that McCarthy scores can be predicted from individual and from combinations of the following variables: birthweight, length, gestational age, labor length, 18- and 24-month Bayley scores, and Peabody scores (best full model is birthweight, length, gestational age, 18-month Bayley). Peabody scores can be predicted from individual and from combinations of the following variables: labor length, Bayley at 18 and 24 months, McCarthy scales (best models are Bayley-18 and McCarthy, and Bayley-24 and McCarthy). When only birth scores (i.e., BNAS, birthweight, gestational age, length, obstetrical events, and complications) were used to predict language scores at 3 years of age, the regression models were not significant.

Regression models were also constructed to test hypotheses concerning the usefulness of all the independent variables (i.e., perinatal, demographic, infant measures, and AER factor scores) to predict the language performance scores. The only regression model that was significant involved predicting McCarthy scale scores from Brazelton scores, Obstetric Complication Scale scores, and AER factor scores. This regression model accounts for 3% more of the variance using perinatal measures and AER factor scores than was accounted for by using AER factor scores alone. Clearly, the addition of non-brain-related measures did little to improve predictions of language performance based on brainwave data alone.

IMPLICATIONS

It seems clear from these data that brain activity measured at birth can be used with a high degree of accuracy to predict performance on two language tests at age 3 years. Children who later developed into better performers on language tests produced brain responses to speech consonant sounds at birth that were distinctly different from the responses produced by children who did not perform as well. The predictive accuracy achieved using the AER responses exceeds by far the predictive abilities of other perinatal measures used in this study and in other studies (Molfese & Molfese, 1985b).

Although these findings must be viewed as tentative, due to the sample size, the data set on which the findings are based does have good internal consistency. A longitudinal follow-up study involving a larger and more heterogeneous sample currently under way should allow a determination as to whether or not the original AER predictors can generalize their high levels of accuracy to other subjects in identifying later levels of language performance. The AER predictors, plus additional behavioral measures, might form the basis of a new assessment procedure useful in the identification at birth of infants who are at risk for later deviations in language performance.

REFERENCES

Als, H., Tronick, E., Lester, B., & Brazelton, T. (1977). The Brazelton Neonatal Behavioral Assessment Scale (BNAS). *Journal of Abnormal Child Psychology, 5,* 215–231.

Barnet, A., de Sotillo, M., & Campos, M. (1974, November). *EEG sensory evoked potentials in early infancy malnutrition.* Paper presented at the meeting of the Society for Neurosciences, St. Louis.

Basser, L. (1962). Hemiplegia of early onset and the faculty of speech with special reference to the effects of hemispherectomy. *Brain, 85,* 427–460.

Bayley, N. (1969). *Bayley Scales of Infant Development: Birth to two years.* New York: Psychological Corp.

Corballis, M. (1983). *Human laterality.* New York: Academic Press.

Crowell, D. H., Jones, R. H., Kapuniai, L. E., & Nakagawa, J. K. (1973). Unilateral cortical activity in newborn humans: An early index of cerebral dominance? *Science, 180,* 205–208.

Davis, P. A. (1939a). Effects of acoustic stimuli on the waking human brain. *Journal of Neurophysiology, 2,* 494–499.

Davis, P. A. (1939b). The electrical response of the human brain to auditory stimuli. *American Journal of Physiology, 126,* 475–476.

Dennis, M., & Whitaker, H. (1975). Hemispheric equipotentiality and language acquisition. In S. Segalowitz & F. Gruber (Eds.), *Language development and neurological theory.* (pp. 93–106). New York: Academic Press.

Donchin, E., Ritter, W., & McCallum, W. C. (1978). Cognitive psychophysiology: The endogenous components of the ERP. In E. Callaway, P. Teuting, & S. H. Koslow, (Ed.), *Event related potentials in man* (pp. 349–411). New York: Academic Press.

Dunn, L. (1965). *Peabody Picture Vocabulary Test.* Circle Pines, MN: American Guidance Service.

Eilers, R., Gavin, W., & Wilson, W. (1979). Linguistic experience and phonemic perception in infancy: A cross-longitudinal study. *Child Development, 50,* 14–18.

Eimas, P. (1974). Linguistic processing of speech by young infants. In R. Schiefelbusch & L. Lloyd (Eds.), *Language perspectives: Acquisition, retardation and intervention.* (pp. 55–74). Baltimore: University Park Press.

Eimas, P. D., Siqueland, E., Jusczyk, P., & Vigorito, J. (1971). Speech perception in infants. *Science, 171,* 303–306.

Goff, E., Allison, T., & Vaughan, H. (1978). The functional neuroanatomy of event related potentials. In E. Callaway, E. Teuting, & S. Koslow (Eds.), *Event-related brain potentials in man* (pp. 1–79). New York: Academic Press.

Hillyard, S. A., & Woods, D. L. (1979). Electrophysiological analysis of human brain function. In M. S. Gazzaniga (Ed.), *Handbook of behavioral neurobiology* (Vol. 2, pp. 345–378). New York: Plenum.

Klee, M., & Rall, W. (1977). Computed potentials of cortically arranged populations of neurons. *Journal of Neurophysiology, 40,* 647–666.

Lasky, R., Syrdal-Lasky, A., & Klein, D. (1975). VOT discrimination by four- to six-month-old infants from Spanish environments. *Journal of Experimental Child Psychology, 20,* 215–225.

Lenneberg, E. (1967). *Biological foundations of language.* New York: Wiley.

Liberman, A. M., Cooper, F. S., Shankweiler, D., & Studdert-Kennedy, M. (1967). Perception of the speech code. *Psychological Review, 74,* 431–461.

Liberman, A. M., Delattre, P. C., & Cooper, F. S. (1958). Some cues for the distinction between voiced and voiceless tops in initial position. *Language and Speech, 1,* 153–167.

Lieberman, A. (1977). *On the origins of language.* New York: Macmillan.

Lisker, L., & Abramson, A. S. (1964). Across language study of voicing in initial stops: Acoustical measurements. *Word, 20,* 384–422.

Littman, B., and Parmelee, A. (1978). Medical correlates of infant development. *Pediatrics, 61,* 470–474.

McCarthy, D. (1972). *Manual for the McCarthy Scales of Children's Abilities.* New York: Psychological Corporation.

Molfese, D. L. (1972). Cerebral asymmetry in infants, children and adults: Auditory evoked responses to speech and music stimuli. *Dissertation Abstracts International, 33.* (University Microfilms No. 72–48, 394)

Molfese, D. L. (1978a). Neuroelectrical correlates of categorical speech perception in adults. *Brain and Language, 5,* 25–35.

Molfese, D. L. (1978b). Left and right hemisphere involvement in speech perception: Electrophysiological correlates. *Perception & Psychophysics, 28,* 237–243.

Molfese, D. L. (1980a). Hemispheric specialization for temporal information: Implications for the perception of voicing cues during speech perception. *Brain and Language, 11,* 285–299.

Molfese, D. L. (1980b). The phoneme and the engram: Electrophysiological evidence for the acoustic invariant in stop consonants. *Brain and Language, 9,* 372–376.

Molfese, D. L. (1983). Event related potentials and language processes. In A. Guilliard & W. Ritter (Eds.), *Tutorials in ERPs.* Amsterdam: Elsevier.

Molfese, D. L. (1984). Left hemisphere sensitivity to consonant sounds not displayed by the right hemisphere: Electrophysiological correlates. *Brain and Language, 22,* 109–127.

Molfese, D. L., Freeman, R. B., & Palermo, D. S. (1975). The ontogeny of brain lateralization for speech and nonspeech stimuli. *Brain and Language, 2,* 356–368.

Molfese, D. L., & Hess, T. (1978). Hemispheric specialization for VOT perception in the preschool child. *Journal of Experimental Child Psychology, 26,* 71–84.

Molfese, D. L., Linnville, S. E., Wetzel, F., & Leicht, D. (1985). Electrophysiological correlates of handedness and speech perception contrasts. *Neuropsychologia, 23,* 77–86.

Molfese, D. L., & Molfese, V. J. (1979a). VOT distinctions in infants: Learned or innate? In H. A. Whitaker & H. Whitaker (Eds.), *Studies in neurolinguistics* (Vol. 4, pp. 225–240). New York: Academic Press.

Molfese, D. L., & Molfese, V. J. (1979b). Hemisphere and stimulus differences as reflected in the cortical responses of newborn infants to speech stimuli. *Developmental Psychology, 15,* 505–511.

Molfese, D. L., & Molfese, V. J. (1980). Cortical responses of preterm infants to phonetic and nonphonetic speech stimuli. *Developmental Psychology, 16,* 574–581.

Molfese, D. L., & Molfese, V. J. (1984). *Right hemisphere responses from preschool children to temporal cues in speech and nonspeech materials: Electrophysiological correlates.* Manuscript submitted for publication.

Molfese, D. L., & Molfese, V. J. (1985a). Electrophysiological indices of auditory discrimination in newborn infants: The bases for predicting later language development? *Infant Behavior and Development, 8,* 197–211.

Molfese, V. J., & Molfese, D. L. (1985b). Predicting a child's preschool language performance from perinatal variables. In R. Dillon (Ed.), *Individual differences in cognition* (Vol. 2, pp. 95–117). New York: Academic Press.

Molfese, D. L., & Schmidt, A. (1983). An auditory evoked potential study of consonant perception. *Brain and Language, 18,* 57–70.

Moscovitch, L. (1977). The development of lateralization of language functions and its relation to cognitive and linguistic development: A review and some theoretical speculations. In S. Segalowitz and F. Gruber (Eds.), *Language development and neurological theory.* (pp. 194–212). New York: Academic Press.

Picton, T. W., & Strauss, D. T. (1980). The component structure of the human event related potential. In Kornhuber & Deecke, Motivation, Motor and Sensory Processes of the Brain. Electrical Potentials, Behavior, and Clinical Use. (pp. 17–49). Amsterdam: Elsevier.

Pisoni, D. B. (1977). Identification and discrimination of the relative onset time of two component tones: Implications for voicing perception in stops. *Journal of the Acoustical Society of America, 61,* 1352–1361.

Purpura, D. (1978). Commentary. In E. Callaway, P. Tueting, & S. Koslow (Eds.), *Event-related brain potentials in man* (pp. 81–87). New York: Academic Press.

Regan, D. (1972). *Evoked potentials in psychology, sensory physiological, and clinical medicine.* New York: Wiley.

Rockstroh, B., Elbert, T., Birbaumer, N., & Lutzenberger, W. (1982). *Slow brain potentials and behavior.* Baltimore: Urban & Schwarzenberg.

Segalowitz, S. (1983). *Language functions and brain organization.* New York: Academic Press.

Segalowitz, S., & Gruber, F. (1977). *Language development and neurological theory.* New York: Academic Press.

Shucard, J. L., Shucard, D. W., Cummins, K. R., & Campos, J. J. (1981). Auditory evoked potentials and sex related differences in brain development. *Brain and Language, 13,* 91–102.

Simson, R., Vaughan, H. G., Jr., & Ritter, W. (1977a). The scalp topography of potentials in auditory and visual discrimination tasks. *EEG, 42,* 528–535.

Simson, R., Vaughan, H. G., Jr., & Ritter, W. (1977b). The scalp topography of potentials in auditory and visual go/no go tasks. *EEG, 43,* 864–875.

Stevens, K., & Klatt, D. (1974). Role for formant transition in the voiced–voiceless distribution for stops. *Journal of the Acoustical Society of America, 55,* 653–659.

Streeter, L. (1976). Language perception of 2-month-old infants shows effects of both innate mechanisms and experience. *Nature (London) 259,* 39–41.

Trehub, S., & Rabinovitch, S. (1972). Auditory–linguistic sensitivity in early infancy. *Developmental Psychology, 6,* 74–77.

Vaughan, H. G., Jr. (1969). The analysis of brain activity to scalp recordings of event-related potentials. In E. Donchin & D. B. Lindsley (Eds.), *Averaged evoked potentials: Methods, results, evaluations* (pp. 45–94). Washington, DC: U.S. National Aeronautics and Space Administration.

Chapter 6

Neuropsychological Functioning and Cognitive Processing

J. P. DAS
CONNIE K. VARNHAGEN

Centre for the Study of Mental Retardation
The University of Alberta
Edmonton, Alberta, Canada T6G 2G5

INTRODUCTION

This chapter examines a model of information processing that has as its roots both neurological and cognitive-psychological principles. Because the model relies heavily on Luria's neuropsychological research, one of the major goals is a presentation of Luria's basic concepts relating to brain functions. The supporting evidence for the model is provided by factor-analytic and experimental research, primarily on children. A second goal of the chapter is the delineation of developmental changes in cognitive processes, with a view to understanding them in the theoretical context of the model. In order to achieve this objective, normal as well as exceptional children have been considered. Cognitive tasks that are indicative of development have been analyzed in terms of the processes involved in information integration. A final goal of the chapter is to describe how the critical components of cognitive or neuropsychological tasks can be identified in order to better understand the processes that may be used in performing the task.

CHILD NEUROPSYCHOLOGY, VOL. 1
Copyright © 1986 by Academic Press, Inc.

A HISTORICAL PERSPECTIVE OF THE SEARCH
FOR BRAIN–BEHAVIOR CONNECTIONS

The search for brain–behavior relationships can be traced to the very roots of psychology. Aristotle's struggle to unify body and soul in order to understand how function follows from form still predominates in modern neuropsychological research. Although the original concepts of brain–behavior relationships stem from philosophy, more-modern developments have resulted from animal experimentation and, more importantly, from clinical investigations of brain damaged humans.

Localization of Behavior within
Particular Brain Structures

As early as 1809, Gall identified the location in the brain of approximately 30 different intellectual and personality traits. The locations were marked according to a pattern of indentations and prominences in the skull. Gall's phrenological map lacked any empirical base and was poorly received by the scientific community. The general notion of cerebral localization of human behavior persisted, however. In his handbook on physiology, Muller (1833–1840) speculated about the localization of function within specialized brain tissues. The first *scientific* investigation of brain–behavior relationships was pursued by Broca, who in 1861 described a case in which a cerebral lesion was associated with a disturbance in speech production. Additional cases led Broca to conclude that the motor aspects of speech are localized in a small area of the left frontal lobe. Wernicke, in 1874, described cases in which left-temporal-lobe lesions were associated with disturbances in speech understanding.

These findings stimulated the identification of numerous structural centers, which, when destroyed, lead to the disturbance of particular, narrowly defined behaviors. Similar centers were identified in other mammals (Ferrier, 1876; Fritsch & Hitzig, 1870). Very little attempt was made to provide a complete psychological analysis of the functional disturbances associated with lesions in these various parts of the brain, however. Narrow localization became such a popular undertaking that by 1934, Kleist's elaborate functional map of the cerebral cortex looked very much like Gall's phrenological map, including such functional centers as tone sense, sense of place, memory of place, etc. Regardless of its lack of scope, strict localization of narrowly defined functions has retained a certain amount of popularity (Geschwind, 1965), especially as a framework by which to characterize different types of aphasias, agnosias, etc.

Opposition to Strict Localization:
The Antilocalization Position

Even while new functional centers were being identified through animal experimentation and clinical examination, opponents began to argue against the
notion of localization of brain function. One of the original skeptics, Jackson
(1874, cited in Taylor, 1958), suggested that complex mental processes are
organized and reorganized within different levels of the brain—from the brainstem, vertically through to the cortex—not merely localized in circumscribed
areas of the cerebral cortex. This early hypothesis eventually led to the antilocalizationist position that the neurological organization of complex functioning
cannot be localized within single small segments of the cortex but require the
integration of many different brain structures (Goldstein, 1936, 1948).

Some antilocalizationists (see, e.g., Head, 1923; Lashley, 1929) went to the
extreme of considering the brain as an essentially undifferentiated entity. In
Lashley's (1929) conceptualization, the brain is equipotential; that is, each portion of brain tissue is capable of performing almost any function. In addition, he
argued that the complexity of functioning determines the mass of brain tissue
required. These laws of equipotentiality and mass action were supported by
numerous animal lesion studies in which Lashley trained animals, excised different amounts of different parts of their brains, and examined their retention as a
function of type and degree of tissue damage.

Thus, at one extreme, behavior has been considered a function of particular
brain structures, with different activities localized within circumscribed areas of
the brain. At the other extreme, behavior has been considered to be a function of
undifferentiated, holistic neurological activity. It is obvious, however, that neither extreme position provides a completely feasible explanation for the results of
animal experimentation and clinical investigations. For example, the localizationist position cannot explain general cognitive deficits that often accompany
specific brain lesions. On the other hand, the antilocalizationist position cannot
account for the common finding of pervasive disruption of even simple functioning from minimal brain damage.

Luria's Reformulation
of Brain–Behavior Relationships

Luria (1973, 1980) has re-examined the basic concepts underlying both positions and has developed a more-complete model of brain function in terms of
accounting for clinical and experimental findings. In Luria's working-brain
model, functions are not conceptualized in terms of individual end-products of
mental activity, such as speech perception, which is either narrowly localized
within specialized regions of the brain, as in Wernicke's area in the left temporal

lobe, or require the undifferentiated pulsing of the entire brain. Rather, function is conceptualized as a complete system of coordinated behavioral and neurological activities. Speech perception, for example, requires neurological activities associated with arousal and attention, auditory perception, phonological and linguistic analysis, etc. These activities require the optimal operation of portions of the lower brain stem, reticular formation, thalamus, and cortex. Thus, even so simple a function as speech perception is *"organized in systems of concertedly working zones, each of which performs its role in complex functional system(sic),* and which may be located in completely different and often far distant areas of the brain" (Luria, 1973, p. 31).

Luria's conceptualization of brain–behavior relationships explains both the findings of general cognitive deficits and the disruption of multiple functions. Because the brain operates as an integrated functional system, damage to even a small area causes disorganization within the entire working system, which depending on the level at which the disorganization occurs, may lead to symptoms of a general cognitive deficit or multiple specific disabilities.

An additional aspect of Luria's working-brain model, essential to describing recovery (or lack of recovery) of function and prescribing remediation for different disabilities, concerns the development of complex behaviors and their concomitant neurological development. Just as complex behaviors do not occur from birth, the concertedly working functional systems underlying complex behavior are also not present at birth. Systematic behavioral and neurological reorganization takes place throughout development and/or the learning of a new behavior.

For example, learning to add two numbers depends on the integration of a great number of cognitive and motor activities. The child likely will be initially unable to mentally add two numbers. He or she may require physical objects to manipulate as an aid to solving the problem. At this early stage, the child is likely to count out the number of objects corresponding to the first number to be added, set these aside, count out the number of objects corresponding to the second number, combine the two sets of objects, then count the total number of items in order to determine the result.

With much practice, the child begins to internalize this physical process, counting or setting a mental counter, incrementing the counter the required number of times, then reading out the result. These activities, which at first require a great deal of concentration, goal setting, physical and mental activity, eventually become automatic. Eventually, the child can be presented with an addition problem and immediately visualize the result, without performing all the component activities necessary during the developmental stages of learning to add.

As these behavioral processes change, so does the concomitant neurological organization underlying the processes. The participation of planning, motor, and visual areas of the cortex, as well as underlying midbrain structures, so essential for early solution of the addition task, are no longer necessary for the final stages of learning to add. Conversely, other cortical areas, primarily the left parietooccipital area (Luria, 1966), increasingly become critical to the functional system as mature addition skills are acquired. Thus, multiple behavioral and underlying neurological systems are capable of attaining the same end product. Similarly, especially at lower levels of behavior, it appears that functional systems give rise to very different end-product behaviors.

In summary, a predominant concern in neuropsychology has been to specify how neurological structure and function relate to motoric and cognitive behavior. Two opposing early positions conceptualized very specific, circumscribed areas of the brain as responsible for particular behaviors—the localizationist view—or defined the brain as an essentially undifferentiated mass that operated holistically to govern behavior—the antilocalizationist view. Luria reformulated the relationship between the brain and behavior in terms of functional systems in which concertedly working brain structures contribute to governing behavior.

Luria's model of the working brain provides great explanatory power to integrating and understanding experimental and clinical findings about the relationship between the brain and behavior. The following section examines Luria's conceptualization of brain function in greater detail and uses the neurological model of the working brain as the framework for a psychological model of cognitive processing.

THE INFORMATION–INTEGRATION MODEL

Few attempts have been made to develop a comphrehensive theory of cognitive processing based on findings from neurological and psychological research. Although modern conceptualizations of cognitive processing do have their roots in sensory-motor experimentation and neurological functioning, the advent of intelligence testing and associated statistical techniques focused attention on the concept of abilities rather than processes (Brody & Brody, 1976; Vernon, 1979). Abilities were conceptualized as discrete causative agents underlying behavior. Attempts to isolate and examine these abilities have resulted in their static nature.

However, there has been a shift away from the identification of cognitive abilities toward examining cognitive processes—that is, how cognitive functioning gives rise to behavior (Glaser, 1972; Messick, 1973; Pellegrino & Glaser, 1979). Although occurring decades later, this shift from studying discrete, static abilities to examining integrated, dynamic processes in psychological research parallels the shift in neurological research from isolating discrete functional centers to understanding integrated brain functions.

In response to this shift in attention from ability to process, some psychologists have turned to neurological research to support their notions about cognitive processes. The information-integration model, although still in its formative stage, has been developed by Das (1972, 1973a; Das, Kirby, & Jarman, 1975, 1979) to provide one of the most comprehensive accounts of behavior based on psychological and neurological theory. Specifically, the Das model of cognitive functioning expands on Luria's (1966, 1970, 1973) model of neuropsychological functioning to include concepts from cognitive psychology (see, e.g., Atkinson & Shiffrin, 1968).

Roots of the Model: Luria's Three Functional Units

The Three Functional Units Defined

Luria (1970, 1973) details groups of concertedly working zones of the brain, each of which makes its own contribution within the functional system of complex behavior. He distinguishes three functional units of the brain, defined in terms of their responsibilities within the functional systems. They are (1) the arousal and attention unit, involving the brainstem, reticular formation, and areas of the limbic system and hippocampus; (2) the information reception, analysis, and storage unit, involving the occipital, parietal, and temporal regions of the cortex and their underlying structures radiating from the thalamus; and (3) the programming, regulation, and verification of activity unit, involving the frontal lobe and its projections from the remainder of the cortex.

Each of these three functional units is hierarchically organized according to three functions they perform within their particular realm of responsibilities. These functions are (1) receiving and transmitting neural impulses from other areas of the brain, located in primary or projection areas; (2) processing and programming the information received or transmitted, respectively, as neural impulses, located in projection-association areas; and (3) complex mental activity requiring the integration of different information, located in overlapping tertiary zones along the cortex.

Any cognitive or motoric behavior is thus considered by Luria to be a complex functional system, requiring the coordinated operation of all three hierarchically organized functional structures within each of the functional units of the brain. Furthermore, behavior requires combined, integrated processing within the three functional units. The first functional unit provides the necessary degree of arousal for information processing and behavioral regulation. Inappropriate arousal (in either direction) interferes with attention and can disrupt the information-processing functions of the second unit and the regulation processes of the third functional unit. The second functional unit is responsible for information processing. Disruptions within the operation of this unit may affect or be affected by attention and arousal, processes controlled by the first functional unit. Similarly, information processing affects the operation of the third functional unit, responsible for planning and the regulation of mental and motoric activities. In turn, the planning and decision-making responsibilities of the third functional unit directly influence arousal and attention, responsibilities of the first functional unit, and information processing by the second functional unit.

Control of Behavior

In order to better describe how cognitive and motoric behaviors require the coordination and integration of the three hierarchical functions within the three functional units of the brain, one may consider voluntary movement and planful behavior involved in drawing a circle. Soviet physiological studies (Bernstein, 1967) have shown that even involuntary movement cannot be accomplished merely by activation of efferent nerves in the cerebral cortex. Thus, drawing behavior cannot be accomplished merely by stimulating some cortical drawing center. Voluntary movement requires the coordinated operation of many areas of the brain, jointly responsible for the entire functional system of drawing.

A certain degree of arousal is necessary for voluntary movement to occur. This arousal allows for attention to muscle contraction and associated sensory feedback and provides the cortical tone necessary for the voluntary regulation of the muscle contractions leading to arm, wrist, and finger movement. Quite simply, without appropriate arousal—a responsibility of the first functional unit of the brain—voluntary movement can be neither planned nor carried out. In the example of drawing a circle, insufficient arousal could lead to an inability to even hold a pencil, much less draw a circle. Conversely, too much arousal could result in gripping the pencil so tightly that it breaks or may lead to an inability to concentrate on the drawing behavior to the exclusion of other, disrupting behaviors.

Information processing comprises an additional integral component of voluntary movement. Sensory feedback and spatial analysis are necessary in order for precise, appropriately oriented movement. Soviet physiological studies (Luria, 1970) have shown that when sensory areas of the cortex are destroyed, the voluntary efferent impulses are uncontrolled and are equally distributed between extensor and flexor muscles, essentially blocking any attempt at movement. Spatial disruptions, on the other hand, caused by tertiary-zone lesions in cortical areas associated with the second functional unit, result in movement that is disorganized in terms of precise spatial orientation. Voluntary attempts to move a pencil in a circular pattern may actually result in movement in a square or triangular pattern in cases of spatial disorientation.

Finally, every voluntary movement requires a precise, stable plan or intention. The formulation of such a plan and the regulation of arm, wrist, and finger movement behavior according to the plan of drawing a circular figure is the responsibility of the third functional unit of the brain. The lack of an appropriate plan may result in a lack of voluntary movement. Similarly, a disruption in the regulation of the behavior according to the plan specifications may result in aimless repetitions of the circle or misdirected movement such as squiggles and straight lines due to distractions from nonessential stimuli (Pribram & Luria, 1973).

Thus, even so simple a behavior as drawing a circle can only result from the coordinated, joint operation of the three functional units of the brain. Disruption of any one of these functions due to a lesion of some brain area may result in, at least, uncoordinated or incomplete behavior or, at worst, a total absence of voluntary, conscious behavior. In addition, disruption of function may prevent an individual from ever learning how to coordinate these functions as a single, automatic kinetic melody (Luria, 1973).

Central to coordinating behavior and developing automaticity is the role of the second functional unit, which is responsible for information processing. Luria (1966, 1973, 1980) has further distinguished two general modes of information processing that are accomplished by the second functional unit and are also jointly coordinated by the first and third functional units. These two modes of processing—simultaneous and successive integration—are detailed in the following section.

Two Forms of Information Processing: Simultaneous and Successive Syntheses

Luria's (1966, 1980) analysis of information processing in terms of simultaneous and successive syntheses is derived from Sechenov's (1878) original hypotheses about perception. Sechenov distinguished two principles guiding the perceptual analysis of different types of incoming sensations. Auditory perception, according to Sechenov, involves the integration of individual sound signals into a successive, temporal series. Visual and tactile analyses, on the other hand, involve the integration of complexes of visual and tactile signals into a simultaneous spatial combination.

Luria (1966) expanded on Sechenov's (1878) conceptualizations, examining simultaneous and successive forms of information synthesis across different modes of processing—that is, verbal and nonverbal modes—and across different levels of processing—that is, perception, memory, and complex intellectual levels of processing. Thus, according to Luria, both verbal and nonverbal information can be synthesized according to a simultaneous or a successive organization. In addition, these forms of information integration are common to all types of mental activity. What distinguishes these two types of information integration in Luria's model, then, is the way in which information is organized. Simultaneous synthesis involves the organization of information into a quasi-spatial scheme. Each unit of information is immediately accessible in relation to other units in the simultaneous organization. Successive synthesis, on the other hand, involves the organization of information into a sequential, temporally based scheme. An individual unit of information is accessible only in a linear manner and can be surveyed only in relation to its serial position within the sequence.

Luria (1966, 1973, 1980) reviewed clinical investigations that link simultaneous synthesis to regions of the parietooccipital cortex and successive synthesis to frontotemporal regions, regardless of the type of information being processed and the level at which it is analyzed. He developed tests for the assessment of simultaneous and successive information syntheses involved in various perceptual, memorial, and conceptual processing tasks. Simultaneous synthesis assessment included copying figures, reproducing maps from memory, and performing numerical operations as perceptual, memorial, and conceptual processing tasks, respectively. Successive synthesis assessment included reproducing auditory signals, digit span tests, and speech-pattern analysis as perceptual, memorial, and conceptual tasks. Luria's concept of developing tasks that are specifically designed to assess a particular type of information integration within a particular level of mental processing has a very important role in Das (Das, Kirby, & Jarman, 1979) model and tasks for the assessment of cognitive processing.

In summary, Luria's (1966, 1970, 1973, 1980) theory of the working brain conceptualizes three concertedly working functional units of the brain. The first unit is responsible for arousal and attention, the second is responsible for information processing, and the third functional unit is responsible for planning and regulation of behavior. These three units are highly interrelated; their coordinated operation is essential to all forms of complex mental activity and behavior.

Luria's model provides a process approach to studying the underlying neurology of cognitive and motoric behavior. This contrasts with the specific-abilities approach to understanding behavior advocated by the localizationist position. According to the model of the working brain, any complex behavior can be examined in terms of its underlying functional system and the attentional, information integration, and planning processes that it comprises. These processes are linked, in a very broad sense, to different brain structures. Unlike the localizationist position, however, these brain structures are not specific to particular behaviors; rather, according to Luria's model, they accomodate a variety of processes underlying different cognitive and motoric behaviors.

The Model

Because of its process orientation, Luria's theory of the working brain provides an ideal neuropsychological framework for developing a model by which to describe cognitive processes. It is not surprising, then, that the model of information integration developed by Das (1972, 1973a, 1980; Das, Kirby, & Jarman, 1975, 1979) has as its roots Luria's (1966, 1970, 1973, 1980) theory about the working brain. Whereas the Luria model is quite specific for describing

neuropsychological functioning, the information-integration model is more specific for describing cognitive processing. As such, although the model is dependent on Luria's neuropsychological concepts, it goes beyond neuropsychology to
include psychological principles of information processing.

Basic Principles

Das (Das, Kirby, and Jarman, 1975, 1979) described four basic components
of information integration. They are (1) sensory input; (2) a sensory register; (3)
a central processing unit; and (4) behavioral output. These components and their
relationships are shown in Figure 1.

The first component of the information-integration model is sensory input.
Sensory input may be presented to any of the sensory receptors. This input may
be presented in a parallel, simultaneous manner or in a sequential, successive
manner. For example, a chord played on a piano represents an auditory stimulus
presented in a simultaneous manner. Watching a jet stream form in the sky
represents a visual stimulus presented in a successive manner.

The sensory register acts essentially as a buffer; it receives sensory information in the form initially coded by the sensory receptors and transmits the information to the central processing unit. This transmission occurs in a serial fashion
regardless of the mode and manner of stimulus presentation. Not all information
received by the sensory register is automatically transmitted to the central processor, however. A complex interaction between states of arousal and attention,
information processing, and planning—Luria's three functional units—determines which information is transmitted by the sensory register to the central
processing unit.

The central processing unit comprises two major components: (1) simultaneous and successive processes; and (2) planning and decision-making processes. Simultaneous processes synthesize separate units of information into a
quasi-spatial, relational organization. Successive processes synthesize separate
units of information into a temporally organized sequence.

The type of processing that occurs in the central processing unit is not affected
by either the mode or the manner in which the sensory information was originally
received by the sensory receptor. For example, a chord may be processed as a
simultaneous set of notes, or it may be processed as a sequential series of
segregated tones. Similarly, a jet stream may be processed sequentially in terms
of a temporal series of events, or it may be processed simultaneously in terms of
the relationships between the location of the stream and other points in the sky.

The actual type of information processing selected depends on the individual's
preferred mode of processing (which is influenced by experiential, sociocultural,
and genetic factors), the task demands, and the interaction between preferred
mode and task demands. For example, a child who has memorized his or her
addition facts using a number table may process a verbally presented addition

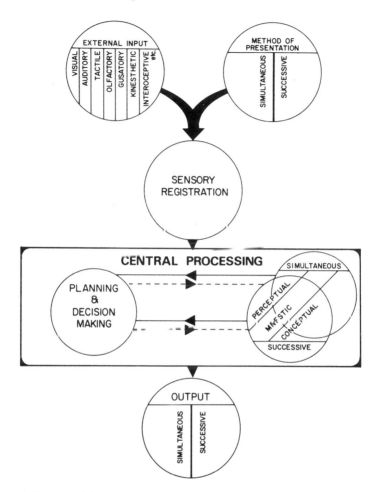

Figure 1. Diagram of the components of the information-integration model. (From Das, Kirby, & Jarman, 1975. Copyright 1975 by the American Psychological Association. Reprinted by permission.)

problem simultaneously, examining a mnemonic number table and selecting the correct answer. A child who has learned addition facts through flashcard practice may, on the other hand, process the same addition problem sequentially, sorting through serially ordered memory traces for the correct problem and answer. Each child, when presented with the same addition problem printed on a worksheet containing a number line, may process the problem sequentially, using the number line to manually add the numbers.

The final component of the information-integration model is responsible for behavioral output. The output unit determines and organizes cognitive or motoric behavior as a function of task demands and planning processes. Output can be simultaneous or successive in nature and is independent of both input mode and manner of presentation and of manner of processing. For example, recalling a series of words according to semantic categories requires simultaneous processing at output, even though the words were presented successively and may have been processed successively. On the other hand, recalling the same list in correct serial order requires successive processing at output.

Empirical Evidence

The bulk of the empirical evaluation of the information-integration model has concerned simultaneous and successive processes and planning—components of the central processor unit. A battery of tasks aimed at eliciting and assessing these theoretical cognitive processes has been developed (Das, 1984a, 1984b; Das, Kirby, & Jarman, 1975, 1979). The tasks have been adapted from various sources, including Luria (1966, 1980).

Research methods used with the information-integration model have been of two types, namely confirmatory factor analysis and experimental analysis of groups of individuals differing in terms of their processing skills. The initial studies have mainly employed factor-analytic techniques in order to verify the model and distinguish simultaneous, successive, and planning processes. More-recent research has been concerned with detailing the interactions between different modes of processing and various cognitive behaviors relating to a variety of abilities, such as language, reading, writing, and mathematics, and with developing a better understanding of the processes themselves. Some of these experimental, manipulative studies will be detailed later.

The factor-analytic method employed by Das and colleagues (Das, Kirby, & Jarman, 1975, 1979) to initially evaluate the information-integration model is distinct from, but complementary to, Luria's method of syndrome analysis (Luria & Artem'eva, 1970). Luria identified simultaneous and successive modes of processing on the basis of in-depth clinical assessment of a small number of individuals exhibiting behavioral symptoms characteristic of various brain lesions. Luria used tests that appear, theoretically, to have similar task demands. Similarities in performance across these tests were used to diagnose a deficient cognitive process or identify individual differences in processing. Das, on the other hand, has identified simultaneous and successive modes of information processing and planning processes on the basis of factor-analytic comparisons of the performance of a relatively large number of individuals drawn from a variety of populations, including normal and mentally retarded children and adults, and various cultural and ethnic groups. Individual differences in performance across the tests are used, through factor analysis, to confirm the theoretically defined cognitive processes. Thus, whereas the clinical method uses individual differences to determine some deficit in cognitive processing, the factor-analytic method uses individual differences to determine the reliable existence of some form of cognitive processing. The many factor-analytic studies of performance on various tests of simultaneous and successive processing and planning provide strong evidence for the existence of these cognitive processes across age, IQ, and different cultural groups. Representative studies are briefly described in this section. However, the interested reader is referred to Das, Kirby, and Jarman (1975, 1979) and the appropriate references for more-detailed reviews of the factor-analytic research pertaining to simultaneous–successive processes and to Das (1980) for research on planning.

The relative invariance of simultaneous and successive modes of processing across age groups was first examined by Das and Molloy (1975). First- and fourth-graders were administered a series of marker tasks for simultaneous and successive modes of information processing. Separate factor analyses revealed remarkable consistency in loadings of the different tests on factors identified as representing simultaneous and successive processing across the two age groups. Slight variations were related to developmental differences, primarily in terms of speed of processing differences between the younger and older children, limiting information-processing abilities in the younger children.

Simultaneous and successive processes have similarly been identified across different IQ groups, in studies by Das (1972), Jarman and Das (1977), and Jarman (1978), using factor analysis of performance on various tests designed to tap these theoretical modes of processing. Although the first study (Das, 1972) revealed apparently different factor patterns for average intelligence and mentally retarded children, replications (Jarman, 1978) pointed out extraneous methodological considerations contributing to the variance; subsequent studies (Jarman & Das, 1977; Snart, O'Grady, & Das, 1982) indicate comparable factor patterns across normal intelligence, mildly and moderately mentally retarded children and adolescents. On more-complex tasks, such as syllogistic reasoning, however, mentally retarded individuals demonstrate different patterns of cognitive processing (Das, Kirby, & Jarman, 1979). These findings indicate that although simultaneous and successive processes can be identified in normal and mentally retarded individuals, the two populations do not necessarily use them in the same manner while processing and solving complex tasks. Similar findings have been obtained in studies comparing normal and reading-disabled children (Leong, 1974).

Ashman and Das (1980) adapted and added tasks designed to measure planning processes to the simultaneous–successive battery. These tasks loaded heavily on a separate planning factor, revealing the independence of simultaneous, successive, and planning processes. Subsequent factor-analytic studies have demonstrated three distinct factors corresponding to simultaneous and successive processing and planning, using normal children (Das, 1984a), adolescents (Ashman & Das, 1980), and college students (Das & Heemsbergen, 1983); mildly and moderately retarded children (Snart et al., 1982) and adults (Snart & Swann, 1982).

Many cross-cultural studies have been conducted to examine the universality of the principles represented in the information-integration model. Black and native Canadian Indian children, and children from various regions in India, differing in socioeconomic status and caste, have been examined (Das, 1973b; Das, Kirby, & Jarman, 1979). Distinctive factors relating to the information integration and planning processes can be identified in most cases; variability in processing, as anticipated, is generally related to cultural factors influencing preferred modes of processing.

Summary

Das (Das, 1972, 1973a, 1984a, 1984b; Das, Kirby, & Jarman, 1975, 1979) has developed a model of cognitive processing that merges essential principles from neuropsychological and cognitive theory. Critical to the information-integration model is the notion of a central processing unit in which information is analyzed and integrated through simultaneous and successive processing modes; this information processing is strongly influenced by attentional and planning processes.

Das and colleagues (Das, Kirby, & Jarman, 1975, 1979; Ashman & Das, 1980) have developed numerous tests aimed at assessing and examining simultaneous and successive information processing and planning. These test batteries have been administered to various subject populations in order to evaluate the efficacy with which the information-integration model can be used to describe cognitive processing. These studies have provided new insight into developmental, individual, and cultural differences in intellectual and academic behavior. Current research has employed the information-integration model in more thorough investigations of cognitive processes, which is discussed below.

APPLICATION OF THE INFORMATION–INTEGRATION MODEL TO STUDYING COGNITIVE PROCESSES

The information-integration model may have its roots in neuropsychology, but its branches are spread over developmental and educational psychology.

Any theory of development has implications for education, in as much as mental growth is fostered and accelerated by formal or informal learning. The information-integration model should be useful in understanding children's learning and learning problems. Thus, as an example, reading is considered in terms of the basic cognitive processes of simultaneous, successive, and planning. Also, reading disability can be examined in an attempt to identify processing deficiencies peculiar to disabled children. In this research, we have just begun to unscramble the various components that make up successive processing tasks. Similar analyses are needed for the simultaneous and planning tasks.

Relationship to Piagetian Theory

Two studies have shown that simultaneous, but not successive, processing is related to Piagetian tasks requiring concrete operations. These experiments are summarized for two reasons: (1) to define the information-integration model according to an existing theory; and (2) to discover cultural universals using the paradigm dictated by the information-integration model. These studies complement and extend the aforementioned factor-analytic studies in terms of providing evidence for the information-integration model and for using the model to better understand cognitive processing.

The first study, by Mwamwenda, Dash, and Das (1984), reports data from Canadian children as well as children from India. It was observed that children who prefer simultaneous to successive processing did better in the Piagetian tasks of conservation, transitive inference, and class inclusion. Each of these Piagetian tasks can be reinterpreted in terms of simultaneous processing. A simultaneous processor can decenter attention when looking at a number of given objects, such as may be the case in conservation. In other words, the child is able to conceptualize relations between objects and among the different dimensions of the same object. For example, in conservation of liquids, the child may argue that although beaker A is thin, it is nevertheless compensated for by its height, or given that beaker B is short, it is compensated for by its width. Such reasoning is likely to lead to the attainment of the concept of conservation.

Similarly, for transitive inference, a simultaneous processor looks at objects symmetrically, rather than asymmetrically. That is, a simultaneous processor is able to examine each object in the light of both a direct and an inverse relational operation. He or she is able to perceive that an object can be related to another object in more than one way at the same time. In class inclusion, the adoption of simultaneous coding should enable the child to decompose classes from a superordinate level to a subordinate class. This happens when the child can grasp the relation between subclasses and their superordinate class. In other words, an understanding of part–whole relations is essential for the attainment of a class-inclusion concept; this is achieved with the help of simultaneous processing. However, in class inclusion, some amount of verbal sequential processing is required to understand the information in the propositions (e.g., "Are there more cows or animals?"). Therefore, one is likely to find that successive processing, as well as simultaneous processing, may be involved in solving class-inclusion problems.

Carlson and Wiedl (1977) have found support for considering concrete operational tasks as instances of simultaneous processing. Their results showed that Piagetian tasks require a mode of information integration that could be labeled as simultaneous. However, class inclusion, in their study, was also related primarily to simultaneous and, to a lesser extent, to successive processes. In the Mwamwenda et al. (1984) study, conservation and transitive inference were very closely related to simultaneous processing both in the Canadian group and in the sample collected from India. In the Canadian sample, class inclusion was also exclusively related to simultaneous processing, whereas in the sample from India, it was influenced by simultaneous as well as successive processing.

It was concluded by Mwamwenda et al. (1984) that although a relationship between Piaget's concrete operational tasks and simultaneous processing has been established, it is not clear how simultaneous processing is specifically used when children are engaged in solving the concrete operational tasks. Children who process information simultaneously are apparently capable of achieving a simultaneous grasp of the whole, so that they recall the past, represent the present, and at the same time, anticipate the future. This is in contrast to preoperational thought, which is characterized by a successive approach, in as much as it links actions to perceptual states in a sequential manner. However, such a strategy is inappropriate for concrete operational tasks, and therefore the utilization of a successive processing strategy leads to poor performance.

A complementary study (Dash & Das, 1984) examined the relative contributions of development and schooling to performance in simultaneous and successive tasks in India. Children were given a set of concrete operational tasks, as well as simultaneous and successive tasks. The findings of the study were very clear. A general improvement over age for the Piagetian tasks for both schooled and unschooled children was observed. Schooling did not accelerate the rate of improvement in the Piagetian tasks of concrete operations, but years of schooling resulted in a superior competence in schooled compared to unschooled children with regard to simultaenous and successive processing. Furthermore, school children performed better than unschooled children on simultaneous and successive tasks, but not in the Piagetian tasks. Schooling was more advantageous for older children, so that as children grew older, there was a divergence in information processing competence between schooled and unschooled children.

These two studies, taken together, warrant the following conclusions: The salient process involved in tasks of concrete operational thought is simultaneous processing. However, the simultaneous processing tasks used are distinctively sensitive to the effects of schooling, in that skills learned in school help develop information processing skills. This is in contrast to the Piagetian tasks; in Dash and Das's study, the Piagetian tasks were shown to be unrelated to skills learned at school.

Understanding Language and Reading Skills

Cummins and Das (1978) have argued that studies of aphasia provide a basis for generating hypotheses regarding the relation between simultaneous and successive processing, on the one hand, and several aspects of linguistic performance on the other. Luria (1966, 1973, 1980) remarked that individuals who have lesions of the frontotemporal area experience difficulties in successively automacized and organized speech. Such individuals have difficulty in evaluating the correctness of grammatical structures that link together different statements into a single concrete whole. For instance, they would not always be able to say which one of the following two sentences is correct: 'The steamer is going along the river.'/'The steamers is going along the river.' This problem is indicative of a difficulty in receptive speech. The patients also experience difficulties in producing successively automacized, organized speech, which is essential when the individual is called on to explain something at length.

While successive processing clearly underlies the understanding and production of contextual grammatical structures, as in the preceding example, simultaneous processing is involved in processing the other aspect of grammatical structure, which Luria calls "the communication of relationships." Patients with lesions in the parietooccipital sections of the speech area experience no impairment in the predicative functions of inner speech; nor do they have any difficulty in the linear pattern of the sentence. This is so because they understand the syntax quite well. However, they are unable to comprehend some kinds of logical grammatical constructions. For example, comprehending sentences that involve comparison, such as *taller than,* or spatial prepositional constructions, such as *above, below,* or *inside,* are difficult for these brain-damaged patients.

Thus, on the basis of Luria's neuropsycholinguistic research, it can be predicted that successive processing is involved in analyzing syntax and the linear structure of a sentence. On the other hand, simultaneous processing is required in understanding spatial–conceptual relationships. Indeed, numerous studies (Luria, 1966, 1980; Das, Cummins, Kirby, & Jarman, 1979; Das, Kirby, & Jarman, 1979) have demonstrated the importance of successive processing for the contextual grammatical aspects of language and simultaneous processing for the logical grammatical aspects of language.

In addition, these distinctions provide an essential framework for understanding reading ability. Cummins and Das (1977) review research implicating successive processing in the development of initial reading skills such as word decoding and vocabulary comprehension. On the other hand, simultaneous processing appears to be critical for the development of advanced levels of reading skills such as narrative and expository prose comprehension.

Given this framework, reading disability can be examined in terms of component information-integration processes. Several studies have implicated successive processing as a critical factor in reading disability. Doehring (1968), for example, has reported that reading disability is highly correlated with performance on tasks requiring sequential processing. Several studies conducted by Das and colleagues (Das, Kirby, & Jarman, 1979) outline the relationship between reading and successive processing quite clearly. In one study, for example, carried out on low achieving high school students, reading achievement was significantly related to successive, but not simultaneous tasks. Das, Manos, and Kanungo (1975) compared the contributions of simultaneous and successive processing to reading achievement of children from high and low socioeconomic classes. They found that success in reading was related to successive processing in the low socioeconomic class, but to both simultaneous and successive processing in children from the high socioeconomic class.

Other studies have implicated *both* modes of information integration in reading disability. For example, Leong (1974) found reading-disabled children attending special classes to be inferior to average-reading children in both simultaneous and successive processing. Subsequently, the early work of Leong has been more or less supported. In a study by Das, Snart, and Mulcahy (1982), disabled readers attending special classes were observed to score significantly lower than average readers in both simultaneous and successive tasks, as well as in planning tasks. In that study, however, it was obvious that the disabled readers were particularly backward in successive tasks. In another study (Das, Bisanz, & Mancini, 1984), average and disabled readers from elementary schools were compared on various span tasks, representing successive processing. A test for simultaneous processing and one test for planning were also used. The results showed that, in general, the disabled readers performed more poorly than average readers, but unlike the earlier studies with more severely disabled readers, there was no generalized deficiency noticed for the successive tasks. Specifically, the disabled readers performed more poorly on the nonconfusable letter-span task in which proficient phonological coding appears to enhance performance but not on the confusable letter-span task in which phonological coding actually detracts from performance.

Taking the results of studies on reading disability and information-integration and planning processes, it is concluded that when specific reading disability is severe (more than 2 years delay in reading), the children are found to be clearly behind the average readers both in successive tasks and in simultaneous and planning tasks. However, when children who are less severely disabled in reading are chosen, they are found to be poor in some (e.g., those that require proficient phonological coding), but not all, successive processing tasks.

Furthermore, although psychometric examinations demonstrate deficiencies in simultaneous and successive processes in reading-disabled children, research suggests that these children may suffer more from deficient planning processes for applying information-integration processes to reading tasks. Robinson (1983) examined specific relationships between simultaneous and successive processes, syntactic and semantic language skills, and the use of these grammatical relations in word-attack and comprehension tasks. Robinson confirmed the predicted finding of an association between simultaneous processing and semantic skills. No confirmation of the relationship between successive processing and syntactic skills was obtained, however. On the other hand, Robinson observed that the reading-disabled children tended to use simultaneous modes of processing where successive modes would have been more appropriate. Das and Snart (1982) also report a study that confirms the relationship between information-integration and planning processes in reading disability. Thus, reading disability may result from a combination of deficient information-processing skills *and* inappropriate selection of modes of information processing (i.e., planning).

Cognitive Processes: A Closer Look

The information-integration model provides not only a framework for describing cognitive processes and characterizing intellectual abilities, but also an essential theoretical framework for investigating cognitive processes themselves. Research (Das, 1985; Das, Varnhagen, & Luettgen, 1984; Varnhagen & Das, in preparation) has employed the information-integration model in the investigation of the cognitive-processing components of memory span and their relationship to reading.

Successive Processing, Memory Span, and Reading Ability

Individual and developmental differences in working-memory capacity have long been associated with individual and developmental differences in intellectual and academic abilities (Dempster, 1981). For example, Lesgold and Perfetti (1978) have discussed the relationship between working-memory capacity and reading. They argue that because important information can be held in memory for only a short period of time, the speed with which this information is processed determines the capacity left over in working memory for comprehension. What this implies is that fast and automatic decoding of letters or words leaves a greater capacity in working memory for other processing requirements involved in reading.

Tests of memory span—commonly used as successive processing marker tasks—have traditionally been used to obtain a measure reflecting working-memory capacity (Dempster, 1981) and as well consistently correlates with reading ability (Jorm, 1983). At least two processes have been implicated in memory-span performance (Dempster, 1981): (1) identification of the name or label for each presented item; and (2) a successive component that is involved in the processing of the order in which the items are presented. Given these hypotheses about the components of memory span, systematic research into the processes involved in successive tasks in relation to reading, therefore, seems urgent to further understanding of why individual differences in successive processing contribute to reading competence.

To date, four experiments looking at the relationship between successive processing and reading have been conducted. In terms of the components that make up successive processing itself, the following question has been asked: If the disabled reader has a poor memory span, which indicates incompetence in successive coding, is it due to a relatively slower rate of identification of the items, or is it because of a defect in recalling the order of the items? In light of the preceding discussion, it is conceivable that item memory and order memory may not be independent variables. Order memory, indeed, may be determined by item identification time in some populations.

Gajraj (1983) observed that by using naming time as an index of speed of item identification, sight words can be named faster by children who have higher memory spans. The relationship between naming time and memory span was predicted from the assumptions regarding working memory. In addition, naming time, or reading time for a set of words, has been shown to be positively correlated with memory span for words (Baddeley, 1981; Nicoloson, 1981). Gajraj (1983) further showed that the relationship was a linear one; in other words, as naming time increased, word span decreased among disabled children.

In another study (Das, 1985), normal fourth grade readers were compared with educable mentally retarded children of similar chronological age. The children were given three tasks: memory for the order of digits to be remembered, naming time for the digits, and digit span. Again, a linear equation could be constructed to describe the relationship between reading time and span for digits, but only for the educable mentally retarded children. The normal children in both studies did not show any correlation between reading time and memory span, probably because the items that were to be read were quite simple (in Gajraj's study, they were sight words; in Das's study, they were single digits).

In a subsequent study (Das, Varnhagen, & Luettgen, 1984), the subjects had still lower IQs—they were trainable mentally retarded individuals. Path analysis of performance on naming time, free recall, memory for order, and tasks of memory span for words and objects revealed the combined importance of three component processes for determining memory span, namely accessing a memory code for item identification, memory for the actual items, and memory for the serial order of the items. An additional study (Varnhagen, Das, & Varnhagen, in preparation), designed to provide more pure measures of item identification, supports these component processes in the memory span of trainable mentally retarded individuals.

In summarizing the implications of the research on successive processing and reading time, it is observed that a thorough understanding of successive processes depends on research on how items are remembered versus on the order of items. Encoding the item involves several processes, such as lexical accessing time and attentional factors. One can argue that the basic component in speed of encoding is to be found in the mobilization of attention. The allocation of attentional resources is certainly involved in determining the capacity of working memory. Thus, a basic process that should be investigated is the manner in which an individual, such as a reading-disabled child, decides when to allocate attention, the amount of allocation, and the target that should be attended to. Salient to all this is the notion of automaticity. An *automatic process* does not require attentional resources or reduce capacity (Shiffrin, Dumais, & Schneider, 1981). Attentional resources are conserved and their use extended by automatic encoding, which requires little central processing time. An investigation of successive processing, then, brings us face to face with research in cognitive psychology; most of this research is in the frontier of that scientific field.

Future Directions

Simultaneous tasks and tasks in planning should also be analyzed in terms of the basic cognitive processes that make up such tasks. This requires that researchers consider concepts derived from neuropsychology to have their roots in cognitive psychology. The neuropsychological findings first prompted us to hypothesize about general cognitive processes and to engage in researching the notions from neuropsychology; these notions are then heuristically tested on samples of children with varying competencies in learning. Research in cognitive psychology itself, in its turn, enhances the understanding of the processes of integrating information, which were initially suggested by neuropsychological studies.

SUMMARY

Cognitive processes have a structural base in the central nervous system, particularly in cortical and subcortical structures. The relationship between behavior that is cognitive and its base is, as yet, not clearly understood. However, attempts at constructing models of intellectual behavior by referring to neurological research have continued. This chapter reviewed one of these efforts, mostly derived from Luria's (1966, 1973, 1980) clinical investigations. The historical context of the brain–behavior relationship in order to evaluate Luria's unique contribution was reviewed. Then, a model of how information is integrated was described. Factor-analytic research on various tasks used to operationalize Luria's concepts regarding the organization of brain functions was also presented. The model was then applied to understanding cognitive activities such as reading and linguistic functions. Finally, experiments on the cognitive processes themselves were presented.

This chapter attempted to focus on the developmental aspects of cognitive processes. It examined both typical and atypical children, on general as well as specific patterns of cognitive functioning. Derived from Luria's neuropsychological notions, the model provides a framework for considering intellectual behavior of normal children as well as those with learning disability and mental retardation.

REFERENCES

Ashman, A. F., & Das, J. P. (1980). Relation between planning and simultaneous–successive processing. *Perceptual and Motor Skills, 51,* 371–382.

Atkinson, R. C., & Shriffrin, R. M. (1968). Human memory. In K. W. Spence & J. T. Spence (Eds.), *Advances in the psychology of learning and motivation research and theory* (Vol. 2). New York: Academic Press.

Baddeley, A. D. (1981). Cognitive psychology and psychometric theory. In M. P. Friedman, J. P. Das, & N. O'Connor (Eds.), *Intelligence and learning.* New York: Plenum.

Bernstein, N. A. (1967). *The coordination and regulation of movements.* Oxford: Pergamon Press.

Broca, P. (1861). Remarques sur le siege de la faculté du langage articule, suivi d'une observation d'aphemie. *Bulletin de la Société Anatomique de Paris, Series 2, 6,* 330–357.

Brody, E. B., & Brody, N. (1976). *Intelligence: Nature, determinants, and consequences.* New York: Academic Press.

Carlson, J. S., & Wiedl, K. H. (1977). Modes of information integration and Piagetian measures of concrete operational thought. *Intelligence, 1,* 335–343.

Cummins, J. P., & Das, J. P. (1977). Cognitive processing and reading difficulties: A framework for research. *Alberta Journal of Educational Research, 23,* 245–256.

Cummins, J. P., & Das, J. P. (1978). Simultaneous and successive syntheses and linguistic processes. *International Journal of Psychology, 13,* 129–138.

Das, J. P. (1972). Patterns of cognitive ability in nonretarded and retarded children. *American Journal of Mental Deficiency, 77,* 6–12.

Das, J. P. (1973a). Structure of cognitive abilities: Evidence for simultaneous and successive processing. *Journal of Educational Psychology, 65,* 103–108.

Das, J. P. (1973b). Cultural deprivation and cognitive competence. In N. R. Ellis (Ed.), *International review of research in mental retardation* (Vol. 6). New York: Academic Press.

Das, J. P. (1980). Planning: Theoretical considerations and empirical evidence. *Psychological Research, 41,* 141–151.

Das, J. P. (1984a). Aspects of planning. In J. Kirby (Ed.), *Cognitive strategies and educational performance.* New York: Academic Press.

Das, J. P. (1984b). Intelligence and information integration. In J. Kirby (Ed.), *Cognitive strategies and educational performance.* New York: Academic Press.

Das, J. P. (1985). Aspects of digit span performance: Objects, words and light sequences. *American Journal of Mental Deficiency, 70,* 78–82.

Das, J. P., Bisanz, G. L., & Mancini, G. (1984). Performance of good and poor readers on cognitive tasks: Changes due to development and reading competence. *Journal of Learning Disabilities, 17,* 549–555.

Das, J. P., Cummins, J., Kirby, J. R., & Jarman, R. F. (1979). Simultaneous and successive processes, language, and mental abilities. *Canadian Psychological Review, 20,* 1–11.

Das, J. P., & Heemsbergen, D. B. (1983). Planning as a factor in the assessment of cognitive processes. *Journal of Psychoeducational Assessment, 1,* 1–15.

Das, J. P., Kirby, J. R., & Jarman, R. F. (1975). Simultaneous and successive synthesis: An alternative model for cognitive abilities. *Psychological Bulletin, 82,* 87–103.

Das, J. P., & Kirby, J. R., & Jarman, R. F. (1979). *Simultaneous and successive cognitive processes.* New York: Academic Press.

Das, J. P., Manos, J., & Kanungo, R. N. (1975). Performance of Canadian Native, Black and White children on some cognitive and personality tests. *Alberta Journal of Educational Research, 21*(3), 183–195.

Das, J. P., & Molloy, G. N. (1975). Varieties of simultaneous and successive processing in children. *Journal of Educational Psychology, 67,* 213–230.

Das, J. P., & Snart, F. (1982, June). *Coding and planning functions of normal and disabled readers.* Paper presented at the annual meeting of the Canadian Psychological Association.

Das, J. P., Snart, F., & Mulcahy, R. F. (1982). Reading disability and its relation to information-integration. In J. P Das, R. F. Mulcahy, & A. E. Wall (Eds.), *Theory and research in learning disabilities.* New York: Plenum.

Das, J. P., Varnhagen, C. K., & Luettgen, J. (1984). *Memory for order: Objects, words and light sequences.* Centre for the Study of Mental Retardation, University of Alberta. Unpublished manuscript.

Dash, U. N., & Das, J. P. (1984). Development of concrete operational thought and information coding in schooled and unschooled children. *British Journal of Developmental Psychology, 2,* 63–72.

Dempster, F. N. (1981). Memory span: Sources of individual differences. *Psychological Bulletin, 89,* 63–100.

Doehring, D. G. (1968). *Patterns of impairment in specific reading disability.* Bloomington: Indiana University Press.

Ferrier, D. (1876). *The functions of the brain.* London: Smith, Elder.

Fritsch, G., & Hitzig, E. (1870). Uber die elektrische Erregbarkeit des Grosshirns. *Archiv für Anatomie und Physiologie, 37,* 300–332.

Gajraj, I. (1983). *The relationship between memory span and reading achievement.* Unpublished doctoral dissertation, University of Alberta, Edmonton.

Gall, F. J.(1809). *Recherches sur le système nerveux en général, et sur celui sur cerveaux en particular.* Paris: Schoell.

Geschwind, N. (1965). Disconnexion syndromes in animals and man. *Brain, 88,* Part I, 237–294; Part II, 585–644.

Glaser, R. (1972). The new aptitudes. *Educational Researcher, 1,* 5–13.

Goldstein, K. (1936). The mental changes due to frontal lobe damage. *Journal of Psychology, Neurology and Psychiatry, 17,* 27–56.

Goldstein, K. (1948). *Language and language disorders.* New York: Grune & Stratton.

Head, H. (1923). *Aphasia and kindred disorders of speech* (2 vols.). Cambridge, England: Cambridge University Press.

Jarman, R. F. (1978). Patterns of cognitive ability in retarded children: A reexamination. *American Journal of Mental Deficiency, 82,* 344–348.

Jarman, R. F., & Das, J. P. (1977). Simultaneous and successive synthesis and intelligence. *Intelligence, 1,* 151–169.

Jorm, A. F. (1983). Specific reading retardation and working memory: A review. *British Journal of Psychology, 74,* 311–342.

Kleist, D. (1934). *Gehirn pathologie.* Leipzig: Barth.

Lashley, K. S. (1929). *Brain mechanisms and intelligence.* Chicago: University of Chicago Press.
Leong, C. K. (1974). *An investigation of spatial–temporal information processing in children with specific reading disability.* Unpublished doctoral dissertation, University of Alberta, Edmonton.
Lesgold, A. M., & Perfetti, C. A. (1978). Interactive processes in reading comprehension. *Discourse Processes, 1,* 323–336.
Luria, A. R. (1966). *Human brain and psychological processes.* New York: Harper & Row.
Luria, A. R. (1970). The functional organization of the brain. *Scientific American, 222*(3), 66–78.
Luria, A. R. (1973). *The working brain.* New York: Basic Books.
Luria, A. R. (1980). *Higher cortical functions in man* (2nd ed.). New York: Basic Books.
Luria, A. R., & Artem'eva, E. Y. (1970). Two approaches to an evaluation of the reliability of psychological investigations. *Soviet Psychology, 8,* 271–282.
Messick, S. (1973). Multivariate models of cognition and personality: The need for both process and structure in psychological theory and measurement. In J. Royce (Ed.), *Contributions of multivariate analysis to theoretical psychology.* New York: Academic Press.
Muller, J. (1833–1840). *Handbuch der physiologie des menschen* (3 vols.). Coblenz: Holscher.
Mwamwenda, T., Dash, U. N., & Das, J. P. (1984). A relationship between simultaneous–successive synthesis and concrete operational thought. *International Journal of Psychology, 19,* 547–563.
Nicolson, R. (1981). The relationship between memory, span and processing speed. In M. Friedman, J. P. Das, & N. O'Connor (Eds.), *Intelligence and learning.* New York: Plenum.
Pellegrino, J. W., & Glaser, R. (1979). Cognitive correlates and components in the analysis of individual differences. *Intelligence, 3,* 187–214.
Pribram, K. H., & Luria, A. R. (1973). *Psychophysiology of the frontal lobes.* New York: Academic Press.
Robinson, G. L. W. (1983). *Simultaneous and successive information processing, language, and reading processes in reading disabled children.* Unpublished doctoral dissertation, University of Newcastle, Newcastle, Australia.
Sechenov, I. (1878). *Selected physiological and psychological work.* Moscow: Foreign Languages Publishing House.
Shiffrin, R. M., Dumais, S. T., & Schneider, W. (1981). Characteristics of automatism. In J. Long & A. Baddeley (Eds.), *Attention and performance, IX.* Hillsdale, NJ: Lawrence Erlbaum Associates.
Snart, F. D., O'Grady, M., & Das, J. P. (1982). Cognitive processing by subgroups of moderately mentally retarded children. *American Journal of Mental Deficiency, 86,* 465–472.
Snart, F. D., & Swann, V. (1982). Assessment of intellectually handicapped adults: A cognitive processing model. *Applied Research in Mental Retardation, 3,* 201–212.
Taylor, J. (Ed.). (1958). *Selected writings of John Hughlings Jackson.* New York: Basic Books.
Varnhagen, C. K., & Das, J. P. (1986). *Information processing components of memory span in TMRs.* Manuscript in preparation.
Varnhagen, C. K., Das, J. P., Varnhagen, S. Auditory and Visual Memory Span: Cognitive Processing by Down's Syndrome and Other Etiology TMH Individuals. Manuscript submitted for publication.
Vernon, P. E. (1979). *Intelligence: Heredity and environment.* San Francisco: Freeman.
Wernicke, C. (1874). *Der aphasische symtomenkomplex.* Breslau: Cohn & Weigart.

Chapter 7

Plasticity and Recovery of Function in the Central Nervous System*

FRANCIS J. PIROZZOLO

Department of Neurology
Baylor College of Medicine
Houston, Texas, 77030

ANDREW C. PAPANICOLAOU

Department of Neurosurgery
University of Texas Medical Branch
Galveston, Texas 77550

INTRODUCTION

Not so many years ago, neuroscientists had come to accept several basic rules about the mammalian central nervous system (CNS), including both the fact that degenerating and necrotic nerve cells do not regenerate and the principle that recovery from brain injury is more rapid and more successful in the young animal. Since then, however, exceptions to these rules have been discovered. Graziadei and colleagues (see, e.g., Graziadei, 1973; Graziadei & DeHan, 1973; Graziadei, Levine, & Montigraziadei, 1979) have discovered a remarkable property of mammalian olfactory receptor cells: These cells have a relatively brief life span (approximately 1 month) during which they differentiate, mature, and establish new synaptic connections within the CNS. At a critical stage, these cells degenerate and are replaced by newly formed neurons. While this property seems

*This work was supported in part by a grant from NIH-NIA (#1 R01-AG05680-01) to Francis J. Pirozzolo and by a grant from the Department of Education (#G 008435031) and a grant from the Dallas Rehabilitation Foundation to Andrew C. Papanicolaou.

to be confined to the olfactory-receptor-cell population, it nevertheless violates the concept that nerve cells cannot be replaced in the adult mammalian animal.

Exceptions to the so-called *Kennard principle* (Kennard, 1936; Schneider, 1979; Teuber, 1974), that the greatest functional sparing after brain injuries occurs in young animals, have also been found, illustrating how deceptively simple rules for plasticity, recovery, and reorganization of function are violated. Research has demonstrated that recovery is dependent not only on age but also on the neural site and the behavioral function involved. Indeed, in some cases it is not "better to have your brain lesion early," as Teuber implied, because there are many examples of how young animals, including humans, sustaining early damage to the CNS are more impaired by lesions that, in the adult, manifest themselves only in specific, circumscribed sensory or motor defects whereas in childhood cause more-global cognitive retardation. Many studies (reviewed in Pirozzolo & Lawson-Kerr, 1981) have shown that infant animals recover some functions more slowly than older animals. Indeed, some studies of recovery from aphasia have shown that age is not a statistically significant factor in recovery (Culton, 1969; Sarno, Sarno, & Levita, 1971). This chapter focuses on the basic principles of plasticity and recovery of function. Because the present volume is devoted to pediatric neuropsychological issues, the emphasis is on the subject of language and linguistic recovery.

There is great confusion in the neuropsychologic literature over the issues of plasticity and recovery of function. Because many of the studies in this area were also tests of the cerebral-dominance idea, even further confusion was introduced by abuses of these terms. It would not be inaccurate to state that the prototypical experiment in the human neuropsychological literature before 1970 investigated these interrelated issues by documenting that young children seem to recovery well from early brain lesions that produce aphasia. Unfortunately, the conclusions drawn from these observations were that the young child's brain is more plastic than the adult's, that language is probably not very hard-wired to the left hemisphere in the first place, and that the right hemisphere must have taken over the functions of the left hemisphere in order for linguistic competence to be attained. It is highly plausible that all three results are incorrect. More-recent research, which has taken advantage of tremendous strides in the basic sciences and has been more appropriately designed to fully evaluate these issues clearly, shows exceptions to these simple (and probably incorrect) rules of brain function.

It seems important, therefore, to describe at the outset what is meant by the various terms to be employed in this chapter. Plasticity is a concept that can be used to refer to either or both neural and behavioral resilience—that is, the ability to reorganize: neurally through neuron proliferation, migration, and increased cell synaptic interactions; and behaviorally through altered behavioral strategies. Recovery of function implies a return to a premorbid level of competence in a certain skill, without prejudice for the structural mechanisms that accounts for this recovery to the baseline state.

CORTICOGENESIS: DEVELOPMENT
OF THE CYTOARCHITECTONICS
OF THE CENTRAL CORTEX

Modern methods of neuroanatomy and neurophysiology have enabled a better understanding of the establishment of cytoarchitectonic boundaries of the cortex and the patterns of convolutional development. Advances in techniques of pre-natal neurosurgery have allowed researchers to remove selected cortical regions at critical early ages and observe the development of the brain. Studies em-ploying these methods allow specification of the approximate timetables for corticogenesis, in order to learn how the normal brain develops neuronal inter-connections and to observe how the surgically altered fetal brain responds to cerebral injury. These studies have great implications for an understanding of normal development, for the development of hemispheric asymmetries of struc-ture and function, and for the pathogenesis of neonatal cerebral injury (Goldman-Rakic & Rakic, 1984).

In normal human development, the cerebral cortex has a smooth appearance well into the midgestational period. The Sylvian, Rolandic, and calcarine fis-sures are visible, but secondary fissures do not appear until later, with the most rapid development of gyri in the gestational period of fetal weeks 26 and 35 (Chi, Dooling, & Gilles, 1977). The gyration process increases the surface area of the cortex dramatically. By the time the cortex is undergoing this convolutional development, all or nearly all cortical neurons have been generated (Sidman & Rakic, 1982). Thus, the notion that the neocortical surface develops convolu-tions from buckling under the pressure of expansive neuronal growth in a space-limited cranial vault (Papez, 1929) is incorrect. Similarly, attempts to explain all structural and functional aberrations of cortical development (dysgenesis syn-dromes) by the mechanism of defective cell migration may also be inaccurate (Pirozzolo, 1985).

The work of Rakic and Goldman-Rakic (1982, 1983) has examined the re-sponse of the immature nervous system to cerebral insult. In a series of studies, these investigators have systematically ablated certain regions of the fetal brain and compared the consequences to those observed in identically neurosurgically treated postnatal and adult animals. Their results stand in dramatic contradiction to the Kennard principle. Prenatal lesions directly or indirectly cause a variety of disturbances ranging from gross morphologic distortions of the convolutional pattern to cellular and subcellular modifications of synaptic contacts and cytoplasmic organelles. The cerebral surfaces in these animals were altered not only in the areas bordering the surgical lesion but also in remote cortical regions.

There is growing evidence that certain developmental disorders of higher cognitive function, such as developmental dyslexia and developmental aphasia, may result from subtle cortical dysgenesis. Pathological studies of single cases have shown that dyslexics have aberrations of cortical development, such as atypical gyral configuration, ectopic neurons in the white matter, poorly differentiated columnar organization and polymicrogyria (Drake, 1968; Galaburda & Kemper, 1979). Radiological studies with computerized tomography (CT) (Hier, LeMay, Rosenberg, & Perlo, 1978) and magnetic resonance imaging (Pirozzolo et al., 1985) have also shown atypical cortical appearance, suggesting cortical dysgenesis, in children with developmental oral language disturbances. If the neonatal brain possessed as much plasticity as assumed, then these apparently minor malformations would not cause the major disruptions of function that they do.

Discussions of plasticity generally focus on the other side of the issue: subtle (and sometimes not so subtle) structural alterations can be obscured by the brain's ability to reorganize itself so that disturbances of function are not apparent. Indeed, there are hundreds of cases in the literature of asymptomatic dysgenesis syndromes. Saul and Sperry (1968) reported a case of callosal agenesis in a college student who did not manifest the disconnection symptomatology. Numerous other examples exist (Pirozzolo, Pirozzolo, & Ziman, 1979), with the more spectacular ones being cases of cerebellar agenesis and temporal lobe agenesis—such as the case of a gifted child (Pirozzolo, Selnes, Whitaker, & Horner, 1977) who had neurosurgically and neuroradiologically confirmed left-temporal-lobe agenesis. Clearly, perturbations of cerebral development can give rise to very significant neuropsychological disturbances, and in other instances, these anomalies can be completely masked by reorganization of neural mechanisms.

Studies of diffusely brain-injured children also show that, in some cases, cognitive deficits secondary to early insults are greater than those observed after later-occurring cerebral insults (Davidson, Willoughby, O'Tauma, Swisher, & Benjamins, 1978). Plasticity in infancy and early childhood is obviously a much more complex matter than assumed by Kennard. Early studies of children who had undergone left hemispherectomy showed complete recovery of language function in later life (see, e.g., Basser, 1962). Smith and Sugar (1975) have even described the acquisition of superior verbal skills in a patient who underwent left hemispherectomy at age 5 years. More-recent studies of Dennis and Whitaker (1976) and Woods and Carey (1979) have modified early notions about plasticity and linguistic recovery in childhood by showing (1) that residual deficits do occur in left-hemispherectomized and left-hemisphere-damaged children and (2) that the left hemisphere may be biologically committed to carry out language functions, as is suggested by studies showing anatomical asymmetries in language regions (reviewed in Galaburda, LeMay, Kemper, & Geschwind, 1978).

As mentioned previously, the concept of plasticity is inevitably linked to concepts about so-called cerebral dominance, or hemispheric specialization. There is growing acceptance of the concept that language is preprogrammed for the left hemisphere in most people. Indeed, there is even evidence of dominance for vocalization in certain birds.

Nottebohm and colleagues have carried out a series of experiments that demonstrated asymmetries in the vocalization of canaries. They lesioned the tracheosyringealis branch of the right and left hypoglossus nerve and found differential effects on sound-spectrographic studies of canaries' song (Nottebohm & Nottebohm, 1976). Lesions involving the right hypoglossus modified or eliminated only one-tenth of the syllables in the song repertoire of the canaries. Lesions in the left tracheosyringealis nerve dramatically affected all syllables in the vocal repertoire. These studies suggested an asymmetry for efferent control of vocalization in the canary. Central asymmetries were also demonstrated by this group (Nottebohm, Stokes, & Leonard, 1976). Unilateral lesions involving the hyperstriatum ventricle also showed differential effects; i.e., left-sided lesions disturbed the quality of canary song, whereas right-sided lesions did not. These data argue in favor of left-hemisphere specialization for song control.

Song recovery in these unilaterally lesioned animals showed that the song repertoire of right-hyperstriatum ventrale-lesioned birds were equivalent to or superior to premorbid song characteristics. Left-lesioned animals' song included only a small number of syllables from premorbid songs and the repertoire was, in general, smaller than that observed before surgery in these animals. These results suggest a certain amount of preprogramming of song control by the left hemisphere and, perhaps, that recovery is associated with a change in dominance to the right side when the left side is damaged. Interestingly, in birds that have had left-hemisphere lesions early in life, subsequent lesions have the same effect as right-sided lesions in the intact birds (Nottebohm, 1984).

Simlarly, one of the mechanisms postulated to account for restitution of human language is the functional reorganization of the brain whereby homotopic structures in the intact nondominant hemisphere (usually the right hemisphere) are utilized to a greater or less extent, depending on particular circumstances, for language processing. The idea of shift of hemispheric dominance is attributed to Wernicke (1874) and was extended by Henschen (1922), Geschwind (1970), and Kinsbourne (1971). The possibility that the right hemisphere can, in fact, mediate language is supported by studies of commissurotomy (split-brain) patients, showing that the right hemisphere possesses some language-processing capabilities. However, direct evidence for right-hemisphere involvement in recovery from aphasia derives mainly from the study of children with extensive left-hemisphere damage and from clinical observations of adult aphasics. As early as the 1880s, Gowers observed that recovered aphasics who had sustained left-hemisphere injuries relapsed following new lesions in the right hemisphere.

Kinsbourne (1971) has studied the effect of intracarotid injection of barbiturates in three aphasics with left-hemisphere lesions. He found that injection into the left carotid artery did not affect residual speech in these patients, but injection into the right carotid resulted in arrest of speech of two of the three patients. More recently, Cummings, Benson, Walsh, and Levine (1979) reported recovery of language in a 54-year-old patient who was rendered globally aphasic due to extensive damage of his dominant left hemisphere after an embolic infarction. CT scans showed total destruction of the temporoparietal area of the dominant hemisphere. Therefore, the observed partial recovery of language in that patient was attributed to increased participation of his right hemisphere.

The performance of recovering aphasics on dichotic listening also suggests possible hemispheric reorganization. Dobie and Simmons (1971), Pettit (1970, 1976), Schulhoff and Goodglass (1969), Shanks and Ryan (1976), Sparks, Goodglass, and Nickel (1970) have reported that unlike normal subjects typically showing right-ear advantage for verbal material, many aphasics display a left-ear preference, indicating predominant right-hemisphere language processing.

The role of the right hemisphere in restitution of language has also been inferred from the study of left hemidecortication, and hemispherectomy in infants and very young children who, despite total or nearly total incapacitation of their dominant hemisphere, develop apparently normal language. Investigators have reported, however, that the remaining intact hemisphere shows a generalized depression of both verbal and visuospatial abilities and no superiority of visuospatial over verbal skills. In contrast, following hemispherectomy in adults (Levin, Ewing-Cobbs, & Benton, 1984), the intact right hemisphere exhibits superior visuospatial ability in comparison with verbal skills. This apparent crowding phenomenon in the developing hemisphere after infantile hemispherectomy has not been carefully studied in adult recovered aphasics.

The relative scarcity of unequivocal observations pertaining to shift of hemispheric dominance as one mechanism of language recovery after injury (e.g., infarct), as opposed to hemispherectomy, can be partly attributed to technical difficulties in directly establishing patterns of hemispheric asymmetries for language in the normal and injured brain. Recently, however, the establishment of patterns of hemispheric activity during a variety of linguistic and nonlinguistic cognitive tasks has become feasible through the use of cortical evoked potentials (EPs) and regional cerebral blow flow (rCBF).

Patterns of task-specific differential hemispheric activation have been obtained with the use of cortical EPs, especially in the context of the probe paradigm (Papanicolaou & Johnstone, 1985). This paradigm entails recording of EPs to an irrelevant probe stimulus (a tone or a flash of light) from left- and right-hemisphere sites during the performance of various cognitive tasks. When the task is purely linguistic, the amplitude of the probe EPs is attenuated significantly more over left-hemisphere sites, whereas when the task involves nonlinguistic processing (e.g., visuospatial), the probe EPs show greater attenuation over the right-hemisphere sites. It has been proposed that this task- and hemisphere-specific attenuation is due to the limitation of neuronal pools in the engaged hemisphere to process simultaneously the relevant task and the irrelevant probe stimulus (see, e.g., Papanicolaou, Levin, & Eisenberg, 1984).

Consistent patterns of regional brain activation indicating predominant left-hemisphere involvement in language and predominant right-hemisphere engagement in nonlinguistic tasks have been repeatedly obtained from normal dextral adult subjects. Significantly greater left-hemisphere engagement has been observed during perception of speech; specifically, detection of phonetic and semantic targets embedded in the speech stream (Papanicolaou, 1980), perception and memorization of speech passages (Shucard, Shucard, & Thomas, in press), performance of mental arithmetic tasks (Papanicolaou, Levin, Eisenberg, & Moore, 1983), production of covert speech (Papanicolaou, Eisenberg, & Levy, 1983), and writing (Galin & Ellis, 1975). Significantly greater right-hemisphere activation has similarly been observed during perception of musical passages (Thomas & Shucard, 1983), perception of the emotional content of speech conveyed by intonation (Papanicolaou, Levin, Eisenberg, Moore, 1983), and performance in a block-design task (Galin & Ellis, 1975).

The reliability of the probe EP paradigm in revealing task-specific patterns of hemispheric asymmetries in normal subjects has encouraged its application to the study of development of hemispheric asymmetries in infants (Shucard, Shucard, & Thomas, 1977) and to the study of aberrant patterns of brain activation in children with developmental abilities (Papanicolaou, Levin, Eisenberg, & Moore, 1983). Moreover, the paradigm has been applied to the study of hemispheric activation in aphasic patients. Probe EP data (Selinger, Shucard, & Prescott, 1980) from five left-hemisphere-injured patients with varying degrees of linguistic impairment were collected during processing of verbal material. It was found that patients with mild language impairment displayed hemispheric activation patterns similar to those of normal subjects, but severely impaired patients displayed greater right-hemispheric involvement. These preliminary data point to a shift of hemispheric control for language following injury to the language-dominant hemisphere.

Probe EP evidence of hemispheric-dominance shift was also obtained in a recent study by Papanicolaou et al. (1984) of six recovered aphasics with CT-scan-verified lesions in the left hemisphere, of six nonaphasic diffuse injury patients, and of eight normal controls, during a verbal perception and memorization task. Both the nonaphasic patients and the normal controls displayed the normal pattern of greater left-hemisphere activation, whereas all the recovered aphasics displayed the opposite pattern of greater right-hemisphere engagement. These data also support the notion that the intact right hemisphere is implicated in the spontaneous restitution of language.

Another potential contribution to this differential hemispheric activation problem in recovery from aphasia may come from studies of rCBF. The rCBF can be measured noninvasively by monitoring the buildup and washout of inhaled [133]Xenon gas in cerebral tissue with external scintillation detectors. Analysis of the xenon-desaturation curves yields values for gray matter flow in the cortical convexity, as well as several other indices of cerebral flow and tissue distribution (see, e.g., Obrist & Wilkinson, 1979). New programs have been developed to reduce artifactual problems and thus enhance the sensitivity and reliability of the technique (see, e.g., Risberg & Prohovnik, 1981). The interpretation of rCBF patterns as estimates of cortical activity levels is an accepted practice in normal subjects and most stabilized patients (Risberg, 1980) and is based on the fact that brain tissue regulates its blood supply in accordance with its metabolic demands (Sokoloff, 1977).

Studies of rCBF using the [133]Xenon inhalation technique have repeatedly shown differential hemispheric involvement in specific language-related (verbal) and nonlanguage (visuospatial) tasks performed by normal volunteers. The xenon-inhalation method allows for simultaneous bilateral measurement of rCBF. The nontraumatic nature of the technique furthermore allows a much greater use of normal volunteers for research purposes than that possible with earlier intra-arterial methods of rCBF measurement. The first major report of task-dependent asymmetries in hemispheric blood flow in right-handed male subject was published by Risberg, Ali, Wilson, Wills, and Halsey (1975). The investigators showed greater increases of activity in the right hemisphere for a test of perceptual closure (visual task) and greater increase in the left hemisphere for a verbal reasoning test. Another study (Gur & Reivich, 1980) found similar results for the verbal test but reported greater right-hemisphere increases during a perceptual-closure task only in the subjects who were most skilled on the test. These authors suggested that processing of verbal tasks may be more hard-wired to the left hemisphere, while spatial cognition is more affected by individual differences and situational variables.

Simple auditory stimulation has also been shown to result in hemispheric-flow asymmetries in normal subjects. One study (Knopman, Rubens, Klassen, Meyer, & Niccum, 1980) reported highly significant increases in rCBF in the posterior region of the left Sylvian fissure during listening for word meaning. Another study reported left-right asymmetries in the rCBF in temporoparietal regions during listening to wood strings presented to one ear (Maximillian, 1982). Either left- or right-ear stimulation resulted in higher flows in these regions of the left hemisphere.

Behavioral-activation studies with stroke patients have shown an increase in rCBF, usually outside the lesion site, under several task conditions (Ingvar & Risberg, 1967). Gur et al. have more-recently reported that cognitive activation of patients with CT-scan-documented infarcts resulted in improved detection of these lesion sites by the rCBF technique—that is, the activation-accentuated abnormalities as recorded by rCBF (Gur et al., 1980). Also important is a study indicating there may be compensatory increases in right-hemisphere flow in patients who recover from aphasia (Meyer, Sakai, Yamaguchi, & Shaw, 1980).

The concurrence of rCBF and electrophysiological measures in demonstrating task-specific differences in hemispheric activation in normal subjects may be expected to allow assessment with greater precision of the nature and degree of long-term reorganization of brain function following injury to the dominant hemisphere.

Functional reorganization of the brain involving shift of hemispheric dominance is considered to be one of the basic mechanisms of recovery of lateralized cognitive functions, particularly language. However, the conditions necessary for reorganization, such as extent of damage to the areas normally mediating language, the precise location of lesions, and the associated particular language deficits, have not been studied systematically. Moreover, the consequences of such reorganization, when, or if, it occurs, for the mediation of nonlinguistic functions normally lateralized in the intact nondominant hemisphere have also not been investigated.

Numerous important questions remain to be answered. For example: (1) Does hemispheric dominance shift underlie recovery from all three basic types of aphasia, namely global, expressive (nonfluent), and receptive (fluent)? (2) Is occurrence of dominance contingent on the size of lesion? (3) Is the occurrence of dominance-shift contingent on the initial severity of the aphasic deficit? (4) Is the probability of dominance-shift different for recovery from aphasia due to cortical and subcortical lesions? (5) Is cerebral reorganization an incremental process covarying with the gradual process of language recovery? (6) Is hemispheric dominance shift for language related to the integrity of nonlinguistic functions normally lateralized in the nondominant hemisphere? (7) Is the frequency of occurrence of hemispheric dominance shift different for male and female patients? (8) Does the age of the patient determine the occurrence of hemispheric dominance shift?

We are currently engaged in a study involving EPs, rCBF, and dichotic listening measures of a large sample of recovering aphasics, directed toward a resolution of some of the aforementioned issues.

NONLINGUISTIC RECOVERY

At the present, a strong case for homotopic structures in the intact hemisphere taking over the functions of the injured hemisphere's motor functions cannot be made on the basis of the data available. Most experimental evidence with animals suggests that functional reorganization is related to collateral sprouting in adjacent neural tissue rather than in the contralateral hemisphere or other distant brain region. The classic study carried out by Glees and Cole (1950) examined the recovery of fine-motor function (opposition of the thumb and forefinger) after ablation of sections of the motor cortex in monkeys. These investigators observed that the animals could regain, within a few weeks, the use of their thumbs (after extirpation of the thumb area on the motor cortex). After the initial period of recovery, the motor cortex was exposed and electrocorticographically mapped. Results showed that the new thumb area was adjacent to the old, ablated thumb region on the motor cortex. Subsequent lesions of this new zone resulted in the deficits seen after the first lesions, and recovery of function after the second extirpation was much slower than after the first surgery.

This pattern of structural plasticity and recovery can be seen after lesions in subcortical areas and functions as different from language and motor functions as appetitive behaviors. Results of studies investigating these limbic needs show that fibers grow around a brain lesion and make synaptic contact with axon terminals of other cells. Teitelbaum and Epstein (1962) produced the lateral hypothalamic syndrome in rats, with bilateral lesions of this region, in order to study recovery of feeding and drinking behavior. When these animals had recovered from aphasia and adapsia, second lesions were made in the area adjacent to the initial lesions. This subsequent destruction of the hypothalamic appetitive centers caused a reappearance of the lateral hypothalamic syndrome, suggesting that plasticity may have been related to reorganization of the adjacent tissue.

Recovery of function is dependent on factors other than those that have been discussed here, such as the nature, locus, extent, and progression of lesions. Many subject factors are also known to affect sparing of functions, as well as recovery. These factors, in addition to age, include education, premorbid status, and immunity. Only recently have scientists begun to consider in this connection the immune system and its unique ability to communicate with the brain. It is known that the brain's ability to withstand insult is related in an as-yet-obscure manner to the activity of T cells. T cells probably interact with the endorphins to stimulate the activity of macrophages, which in turn aid in the healing and recovery process. Neuroscientists have begun to realize that organisms have two mechanisms for the reception, registration, and storage of information about the status of itself—the brain and the immune system. Clues to how these two information-processing systems interact are beginning to be revealed, and progress is being made in understanding how these two windows to the outside world respond to what they perceive. Many of the factors that influence the sparing and recovery of functions may simply be manifestations of the activity of the immune system.

REFERENCES

Basser, L. S. (1962). Hemiplegia of early onset and the faculty of speech with reference to the effects of hemispherectomy. *Brain, 85,* 427–460.

Chi, J. G., Dooling, E., & Gilles, F. H. (1977). Gyral development of the human brain. *Annals of Neurology, 1,* 86–93.

Culton, G. L. (1969). Spontaneous recovery from aphasia. *Journal of Speech and Hearing Research, 12,* 825–832.

Cummings, J. L., Benson, D. F., Walsh, M. J., & Levine, H. L. (1979). Left-to-right transfer of language dominance: A case study. *Neurology, 29,* 1547–1550.

Davidson, P. W., Willoughby, R. H., O'Tauma, L. A., Swisher, L., & Benjamins, D. (1978). Neurological and intellectual sequelae of Reye's syndrome. *American Journal of Mental Deficiency, 82,* 535–541.

Dennis, M., & Whitaker, H. A. (1976). Language acquisition following hemidecortication: Linguistic superiority of the left over the right hemisphere. *Brain and Language, 3,* 404–433.

Dobie, R., & Simmons, B. (1971). A dichotic threshold test: Normal and brain damaged subjects. *Journal of Speech and Hearing Research, 14,* 71–81.

Drake, W. E. (1968). Clinical and pathological findings in a child with a developmental learning disability. *Journal of Learning Disabilities, 1,* 486–502.

Galaburda, A. M., & Kemper, T. L. (1979). Cytoarchitectonic abnormalities in developmental dyslexia: A case study. *Annals of Neurology, 6,* 94–100.

Galaburda, A. M., LeMay, M., Kemper, T., & Geschwind, N. (1978). Right–left asymmetries in the brain. *Science, 199,* 852–856.

Galin, D., & Ellis, R. (1975). Asymmetry in evoked potentials as an index of lateralized cognitive processes: Relation to EEG alpha symmetry. *Neuropsychologia, 1,* 45–50.

Geschwind, N. (1970). The organization of language in the brain. *Science, 170,* 940–944.

Glees, P., & Cole, J. (1950). Recovery of skilled motor functions after small repeated lesions of the motor cortex in the *Macaque. Journal of Neurophysiology, 13,* 137–148.

Goldman-Rakic, P., & Rakic, P. (1984). Experimental modification of gyral patterns. In A. Galaburda & N. Geschwind (Eds.), *Cerebral dominance.*

Graziadei, P. P. C. (1973). Cell dynamics in the olfactory mucosa. *Tissue and Cell, 5,* 113–131.

Graziadei, P. P. C., & DeHan, R. S. (1973). Neuronal regeneration in frog olfactory system. *Journal of Cell Biology, 59,* 525–530.

Graziadei, P. P. C., Levine, R. R., & Montigraziadei, G. A. (1979). Regeneration of olfactory neurons of the olfactory sensory neuron: Regeneration into the forebrain following bulbectomy in the neonated mouse. *Neuroscience, 4,* 713–727.

Gur, R. C., Gur, R. E., Obrist, W. D., Hungerbuhler, J. P., Younkin, D., Rosen, A. D., Skolnick, B. E., & Reivich, M. (1980). Sex and handedness differences in cerebral bloodflow during rest and cognitive activity. *Science, 217,* 659–661.

Gur, R. C., & Reivich, M. (1980). Cognitive task effects on hemispheric bloodflow in humans: Evidence for individual differences in hemispheric activation. *Brain and Language, 9,* 78–92.

Halsey, J., Nakai, K., & Wariyar, B. (1981). The sensitivity of rCBF to focal lesions. *Stroke, 12,* 631–635.

Henschen, S. E. (1922). *Klinische und anatomishe beitrage zur pathologie des gehirns* (Vols. 5–7). Stockholm: Nordiska Bokhandelin.

Hier, D. B., LeMay, M., Rosenberg, P. B., & Perlo, V. P. (1978). Developmental dyslexia: Evidence for a subgroup with reverse asymmetry. *Archives of Neurology, 35,* 90–92.

Ingvar, D. H., & Risberg, J. (1967). Increase of regional cerebral bloodflow during mental effort in normals and in patients with focal brain disorders. *Experimental Brain Research, 3,* 195–211.

Kennard, M. A. (1936). Age and other factors in motor recovery from precentral lesions in monkeys. *American Journal of Physiology, 115,* 138–146.

Kinsbourne, M. (1971). The minor cerebral hemispheres as a source of aphasic speech. *Archives of Neurology, 25,* 302–306.

Knopman, D. S., Rubens, A. B., Klassen, A. C., Meyer, M. W., & Niccum, N. (1980). Regional cerebral bloodflow patterns during verbal and nonverbal auditory activation. *Brain and Language, 9,* 93–112.

Levin, H. S., Ewing-Cobbs, L., & Benton, A. L. (1984). Age and recovery from brain damage. A review of clinical studies. In S. W. Scheff (Ed.), *Aging and recovery of function in the central nervous system.* New York: Plenum.

Maximilian, V. A. (1982). Cortical bloodflow asymmetries during monaural verbal stimulation. *Brain and Language, 15,* 1–11.

Meyer, J. S. (1978). Improved method for non-invasive measurement of regional cerebral bloodflow by [133]Xenon inhalation. II: Measurements in health and disease. *Stroke, 9,* 205–210.

Meyer, J. S., Sakai, F., Yamaguchi, F., Yamamoto, M., & Shaw, T. (1980). Regional changes in cerebral bloodflow during standard behavioral activation in patients with disorders of speech and mentation compared to normal volunteers. *Brain and Language, 9,* 61–77.

Nottebohm, F. (1984). Learning, forgetting and brain repair. In A. M. Galaburda & N. Geschwind (Eds.), *Cerebral dominance.*

Nottebohm, F., & Nottebohm, M. (1976). Left hypoglossus dominance in the control of canary and white-crowned sparrow song. *Journal of Comparative and Physiological Psychology, 108,* 171–192.

Nottebohm, F., Stokes, T., & Leonard, C. (1976). Central control of song in the canary, *Serinus canarius. Journal of Comparative Neurology, 165,* 457–486.

Obrist, W. D., & Wilkinson, W. E. (1979). The noninvasive xe-133 method: Evaluation of CBF indices. *Cerebral Circulation 507,* 119–124.

Papanicolaou, A. C. (1980). Cerebral profiles in language processing: The photic probe paradigm. *Brain and Language, 9,* 269–280.

Papanicolaou, A. C., Eisenberg, H. M., & Levy, R. (1983). Evoked potential correlates of left hemisphere dominance in covert articulation. *International Journal of Neuroscience, 20,* 289–294.

Papanicolaou, A. C., & Johnstone, J. (1985). Probe evoked potentials: theory, methods, and applications. *International Journal of Neuroscience, 24,* 107–131.

Papanicolaou, A. C., Levin, H. S., & Eisenberg, H. M. (1984). Evoked potential correlates of recovery from aphasia after focal left hemisphere injury in adults. *Neurosurgery, 14,* 412–415.

Papanicolaou, A. C., Levin, H. S., Eisenberg, H. M., & Moore, B. D. (1983). Evoked potential indices of selective hemispheric engagement in affective and phonetic tasks. *Neuropsychologia, 21,* 401–405.

Papez, J. W. (1929). *Comparative neurology.* New York: Crowell.

Pettit, J. (1970). Cerebral dominance and the process of language recovery in aphasia. *Dissertation Abstracts International,* 5278-B.

Pettit, J. (1976). *Cerebral processing of non-verbal stimuli during recovery in adult aphasics.* Paper presented at the American Speech and Hearing Association Convention, Houston.

Pirozzolo, F. J. (1985). Mental retardation: An introduction. In P. Vinken & G. Bruhn (Eds.), *Handbook of clinical neurology* (Vol. 2). Amsterdam: North-Holland.

Pirozzolo, F. J., Jerger, J., Jerger, S., Morris, G., Levy, J., Goldman, A., & Handel, S. (1985). Neuropsychologial electrophysiological and NRM studies of developmental aphasia. *International Neuropsychological Society Bulletin, 15,* 16.

Pirozzolo, F. J., & Lawson-Kerr, K. (1981). Recovery from alexia: Factors influencing restoration of function after focal cerebral damage. In F. J. Pirozzolo & M. C. Wittrock (Eds.), *Neuropsychological and cognitive processes in reading.* New York: Academic Press.

Pirozzolo, F. J., Pirozzolo, P. H., & Ziman, R. (1979). Neuropsychological assessment of callosal agenesis. *Clinical Neuropsychology 1,* 15–21.

Pirozzolo, F. J., Selnes, O. A., Whitaker, H. A., & Horner, F. (1977). Left temporal lobe agenesis. *Neuroscience Abstracts 1*, 273.

Rakic, P., & Rakic-Goldman, P. S. (1982). *Development and modifiability of the cerebral cortex* (Neurosciences Research Program Bulletin, Vol. 20, pp. 429–611). Cambridge, MA: MIT Press.

Rakic, P., & Rakic-Goldman, P. (1983). Use of fetal neurosurgery for experimental studies of structural and functional brain development. In R. T. Thompson & O. R. Green (Eds.), *Prenatal neurology and neurosurgery*. Hampton, VA: Spectrum.

Risberg, J. (1980). Regional cerebral bloodflow measurements by ^{133}xenon-inhalation: Methodology and applications in neuropsychology and psychiatry. *Brain and Language, 9*, 9–34.

Risberg, J., Ali, Z., Wilson, E., Wills, E., & Halsey, J. (1975). Regional cerebral blood flow by ^{133}xenon inhalation: Preliminary evaluation of an initial slope index in patients with unstable flow compartments. *Stroke, 6*, 142–148.

Risberg, J , Halsey, J. H., Wills, E. L., & Wilson, E. M. (1975). Hemispheric specialization in normal man studied by bilateral measurement of the regional cerebral bloodflow—a study with the ^{133}-Xe inhalation technique. *Brain, 98*, 511–524.

Risberg, J., & Prohovnik, I. (1981). rCBF measurements by ^{133}Xe inhalation: Recent methodological advances. In O. Juge & A. Donath (Eds.), *Progress in nuclear medicine* (Vol. 7). Basel: Karger.

Sarno, J. E., Sarno, M. T., & Levita, E. (1971). Evaluating language improvement after completed stroke. *Archives of Physical Medicine and Rehabilitation, 52*, 73–78.

Saul, R. E., & Sperry, R. W. (1968). Absence of commissurotomy symptoms with agenesis of the corpus callosum. *Neurology, 18*, 307–315.

Schneider, G. E. (1979). Is it really better to have your brain lesion early? A revision of the Kennard principle. *Neuropsychologia, 17*, 557–584.

Schulhoff, C., & Goodglass, H. (1969). Dichotic listening, side of brain injury, and cerebral dominance. *Neuropsychologia, 7*, 149–160.

Selinger, M., Shucard, D. W., & Prescott, T. E. (1980). Relationships between behavioral and electrophysiological measures of auditory comprehension. In R. H. Brookshire (Ed.), *Clinical aphasiology: Conference proceedings*. Minneapolis: BRK Publishers.

Shanks, J., & Ryan, W. (1976). A comparison of aphasic and non-brain-injured adults on a dichotic CV-syllable listening task. *Cortex, 12*, 100–112.

Shucard, D. W., Cummins, D. R., Thomas, D. G., & Shucard, J. L. (1981). Evoked potentials to auditory probes as indices of cerebral specialization of function—replication and extension. *Electroencephalography and Clinical Neurophysiology, 52*, 389–393.

Shucard, D. W., Shucard, J. L., & Thomas, D. G. (1977). Auditory evoked potentials as probes of hemispheric differences in cognitive processing. *Science, 197*, 1295–1298.

Shucard, D. W., Shucard, J. L., & Thomas, D. G. (in press). The development of cerebral specialization in infants. In R. N. Emole & R. J. Harmon (Eds.), *Continuities and discontinuities in development*. New York: Plenum.

Sidman, R. L., & Rakic, P. (1982). Development of the central nervous system. In W. Haymaker & R. D. Adams (Eds.), *Cytology and cellular neuropathology* (2nd ed.). Springfield, IL: Charles C. Thomas.

Smith, A., & Sugar, O. (1975). Development of above normal language and intelligence 21 years after left hemispherectomy. *Neurology, 25*, 813–818.

Sokoloff, L. (1977). Local cerebral energy metabolism: Its relationship to local functional activity and bloodflow. In *Cerebral vascular smooth muscle and its control* (Ciba Foundation Symposium, Vol. 56). Amsterdam: Elsevier.

Sparks, G., Goodglass, H., & Nickel, B. (1970). Ipsilateral versus contralateral extinction in dichotic listening resulting from hemispheric lesions. *Cortex, 6*, 249–260.

Teitelbaum, P., & Epstein, A. (1962). The lateral hypothalamic syndrome: Recovery of feeding and drinking after lateral hypothalamic lesions. *Psychological Review, 69,* 74–90.

Teuber, H. L. (1974). Recovery of function following lesions of the central nervous system: History and prospects. *Neurosciences Research Program Bulletin, 12,* 197–209.

Thomas, D. G., & Shucard, D. W. (1983). Changes in patterns of hemispheric electrophysiological activity as a function of instructional set. *International Journal of Neuroscience, 18,* 11–20.

Wernicke, C. (1874). *Der aphasische symptomenkomplex.* Breslau: Cohn & Weigart.

Woods, B. T., & Carey, S. (1979). Language deficits after apparent clinical recovery from childhood aphasia. *Annals of Neurology, 6,* 405–409.

Chapter 8

Biological Interactions in Dyslexia*

GLENN D. ROSEN
GORDON F. SHERMAN
ALBERT M. GALABURDA

*Charles A. Dana Research Institute
and the Dyslexia Research Laboratory,
and Department of Neurology
Beth Israel Hospital and Harvard Medical School,
Boston, Massachusetts 02215*

INTRODUCTION

In this chapter it is suggested that there is a neuroanatomical substrate for dyslexia. Five consecutive cases are presented (4 in our laboratory) of dyslexic individuals who share similar neuroanatomical anomalies. Evidence is presented to support the notion that these anomalies develop during gestation and can be traced to the period of neuronal migration to the cortex. An animal model for dyslexia is presented that provides the opportunity of studying the neuroanatomical mechanisms of these anomalies. The authors conclude by speculating about the future direction of research on the neural and behavioral bases of dyslexia.

Before presenting the findings in the dyslexic brain, it is useful to briefly discuss the anatomy of language in the brain.

*This research was supported, in part, by NIH grants 14018 and 02711, and grants from Beth Israel Hospital, the Wm. Underwood Co., The Powder River Co., The Essel Foundation, and the Orton Dyslexia Society. We gratefully acknowledge Loraine Karol for secretarial assistance.

155

LANGUAGE AND THE LEFT HEMISPHERE

Adult

Functional Asymmetries

It has been generally accepted for more than a century that language in the adult brain is lateralized (Broca, 1865; Wernicke, 1874). In the majority of dextral individuals, lesions of Broca's or of Wernicke's area in the left hemisphere can result in severe language disturbances, whereas lesions in analogous locations of the right hemisphere produce such aphasias much less frequently. This lateralization has also been confirmed in a variety of physiological and psychological studies (Anderson, 1977; Kimura, 1961; Larson, Skinhoj, & Lassen, 1978; Penfield & Roberts, 1959; Sperry, 1974; Springer, 1977). Thus, language mechanisms in most right-handed individuals tend to be lateralized to the left hemisphere.

Anatomical Asymmetries

Anatomical asymmetries in the brain had long been known (Eberstaller, 1884), yet these findings were largely ignored until Geschwind and Levitsky (1968) demonstrated anatomical asymmetries in the planum temporale (an area containing auditory cortices and lying on the superior temporal surface). They found that 65% of the brains had a longer left planum, whereas the right was longer in only 11% of the cases. The remaining 24% had symmetrical plana. This finding has been replicated in a number of other studies. Wada, Clarke, and Hamm (1975) found that the left planum was larger in 85% of the cases examined; Witelson and Pallie (1973) found that 69% of the adult brains they studied had a larger left planum.

Additional investigators have confirmed the presence of planum asymmetry and have extended our knowledge of the asymmetry in the Sylvian fissure as well. The Sylvian fissure is the deep furrow on the lateral convexity of the brain, which, on the left side, contains the standard language areas in its banks. Direct observation of histological material (Chi, Dooling, & Gilles, 1977; Rubens, Mahowald, & Hutton, 1976; Teszner, Tzavaras, Gruner, & Hecaen, 1972), measurements of intact brains through computerized axial tomography (CAT) and other radiological techniques have demonstrated consistent asymmetries in the Sylvian fissures, frontal and occipital lobes, and cerebral ventricles (Hochberg & LeMay, 1975; LeMay & Culebras, 1972; LeMay & Kido, 1978; McRae, Branch, & Milner, 1968; Rubens et al., 1976; Yeni-Komshian & Benson, 1976). In general, there is agreement that the left planum temporale tends to be larger, and the left Sylvian fissure longer and more horizontally placed, thus accommodating larger temporal and parietal opercula.

Asymmetries also have been shown in the volume of auditory cytoarchitectonic areas (Galaburda, LeMay, Kemper, & Geschwind, 1978; Galaburda, Sanides, & Geschwind, 1978). The planum temporale and cytoarchitectonic area Tpt (an auditory-association field likely to comprise a major component of Wernicke's area) were measured in four serially sectioned brains. Striking asymmetries were seen in area Tpt, with the left up to 620% larger than the right. Moreover, the degree of cytoarchitectonic asymmetry correlated perfectly with the degree of planum asymmetry. This work indicates that there is (1) a demonstrable asymmetry in volume in a language-related auditory association area and (2) a direct relationship between cytoarchitectonic and planum temporale asymmetries.

Children

The Theory of Equipotentiality

The question of the development of lateralization of function is controversial. One school of thought, based on the work of Basser (1962), contends that the two hemispheres of the brain are equipotential for language during the first 6 years of life. Basser found that (1) lesions of the right hemisphere in early life resulted in language deficits much more often than comparable lesions in adulthood, (2) as the infant matured, the incidence of aphasia following right-hemisphere lesions decreased, (3) the aphasia seen in these children was much less severe than that of adults, and (4) aphasia acquired sometime after the eighth year of life approached the severity of aphasia acquired in adulthood. These findings led Lenneberg (1967) to conclude that the hemispheres were equipotential for language at birth and that this equipotentiality diminished as the infant matured. By 6 years of age, speech and language processes become more lateralized until the individual acquires the adult pattern between 10 and 12 years of age.

Lateralization at Birth

There are a number of problems with accepting the theory of equipotentiality. First, left-hemisphere lesions in young children still dominate in the production of aphasia. There are other problems, and these relate to the more-general difficulty of comparing data from brain damage in childhood to brain damage in adulthood. It is difficult to confirm discretely lateralized brain damage in children. Three of the most common causes of brain damage in children (trauma, tumor, and localized infection) often result in bilateral damage or, at the very least, bilateral mass effect. In addition, tumors, as well as strokes in childhood, commonly occur in the face of existing developmental anomalies such as arteriovenous malformations (AVMs) or glial/neuronal remnants. These anomalies have their origin early during brain development and thus allow for significant restructuring of the brain, thereby rendering any conclusions based on standard structure–function relationships difficult to accept. Thus issues of plasticity and recovery play a much larger role in childhood lesions than in adulthood lesions. It is clear that brain damage at critical stages of brain development results in significant restructuring of the cellular architecture of the cortex as well as the architecture of its connections (Goldman, 1978; Innocenti & Frost, 1980; Schneider, 1981). It is reasonable to suspect that with such a degree of structural reorganization there will be accompanying changes in function. As strategies of similar magnitude are not available in the adult brain, direct comparisons should be handled cautiously.

Because the theory of equipotentiality is predicated on the notion of bilateral representation of skills at birth, it must therefore be critically viewed in the light of demonstrable functional lateralization in early life. Eimas, Siqueland, Jusczyk, and Vigorito (1971) found that 1- to 4-month-old infants perceive and distinguish various speech sounds—a finding that has since been replicated by Moffit (1971) and Morse (1972). Molfese, Freeman, and Palermo (1975; see also Molfese & Molfese, chap. 5, this volume) recorded auditory evoked potentials over homologous areas of the left and right hemispheres of infants during presentation respectively of speech and musical stimuli. They found that the left hemisphere was more active during the presentation of speech stimuli, and that the right hemisphere was more active during musical stimuli. Dichotic listening procedures have demonstrated that infants have a left-ear advantage for music and nonspeech sounds and a right-ear advantage for speech sounds (Entus, 1977). This is the same pattern of ear advantage that is seen in the adult. Vargha-Khadem and Corbalis (1979) failed to replicate these results; however, there are still other investigations suggesting a right-ear superiority for linguistic-like stimuli (Mehler, 1985).

There is evidence to indicate that lesions sustained in the left hemisphere early in development may, in fact, have profound effects on later language abilities. Dennis (1983) examined young children who underwent either left or right hemispherectomy early in life. Those children with left hemispherectomies showed deficits in the verbal section of the Illinois Test for Psycholinguistic Abilities (ITPA), whereas the right hemispherectomized child was deficient in spatial aspects of the test. This suggested that hemispheric specialization was present at 1 year of age and that the right and left hemispheres were organized differently at that early age. Again, however, these data must be considered with caution because children undergoing hemispherectomy are also likely to have dramatic reorganization of brain structure and function, as a result of the congenital lesions or tumors that lead to that type of surgical remedy.

Finally, it is well documented that the infant brain is structurally asymmetrical. Anatomical asymmetries at birth have been reported in several studies. Witelson and Pallie (1973) found that the left planum temporale was larger than the right in the majority of the infants they studied. Wada et al. (1975) described similar asymmetries as early as the 29th week of gestation.

In addition to the finding of static asymmetries in the fetal brain akin to those seen in the adults, there are also dynamic asymmetries in the rate of development of the two sides. It has been demonstrated that the right hemisphere structurally matures earlier than the left hemisphere. Hervé (1888) pointed out that the gyri of Broca's area on the right side appeared earlier than those on the left. Fontes (1944) demonstrated that in general the gyri and sulci surrounding the Sylvian fissure appear earlier on the right. More recently, Chi et al. (1977) showed that the development of convolutions around the Sylvian fissure occurs earlier on the right side, and pointed out that structures surrounding the planum temporale may be recognizable on the right side as much as 2 weeks earlier than on the left. Therefore, certain language areas of the brain are visibly larger on the left side as early as the 29th week of gestation, although they develop more slowly than their mates in the nondominant hemisphere.

Thus, it would appear that portions of the right hemisphere develop earlier in utero but the left hemisphere eventually surpasses the right in size and complexity of development vis à vis language. There are several possible explanations for this. It may be that the right hemisphere develops faster than the left, but the left grows for a longer period of time and eventually surpasses the right. Scheibel's (1981) observations on the later dendritic development of Broca's area as compared to its homologue in the right hemisphere appears to support this possibility. Alternatively, the rate of development may be faster in the right during the early period of gestation and faster on the left during the later period, without having to implicate an arrest of the development on the right side. A third possibility implicates an altogether different mechanism. Thus the earlier forming of the right perisylvian structures may reflect histoclastic processes involving programmed cell death that occur to a greater extent in that side and lead to asymmetry by selection within the smaller side rather than by addition to the larger side. In any case, the observation invites the notion that the left and right hemispheres receive different instructions during development and that this difference contributes to the formation of asymmetrical hemispheres capable of asymmetrical function.

Furthermore, the possible difference in the developmental rate of the two hemispheres provides the opportunity for the formation of asymmetry in the size of equivalent architectonic areas on the two hemispheres as well as the numbers and types of connections they achieve. During development, the number of surviving neurons depends, to an extent, on the availability of synaptic relationships. Neurons that do not connect die (Gluckmann, 1965; Hamburger & Levi-Montalcini, 1949), and the size of given cortical areas is affected. Developing neurons compete for synaptic contacts, and it quite possible that rates of development affect the outcome of this competition. It is likely, therefore, that a rate difference between the two hemispheres can at least partially determine the connections achieved by cells on either side, as well as the survival of these cells and the sizes of the architectonic areas to which they belong.

Summary

Language lateralization to the left hemisphere is related to asymmetrical neural substrates. These anatomical asymmetries are already present early in life, and may be the result of lateralized differences in developmental rates, which in turn determine hemispheric size of equivalent architectonic areas and their connectional patterns.

It is possible that biological factors rendering the two hemispheres asymmetric also could explain asymmetry of vulnerability and attack by pathological agents. Dyslexia may be an example of such an asymmetrical pathology. Next, five consecutive brain studies of dyslexia are presented in which predominantly asymmetrical pathology is evident.

NEUROPATHOLOGICAL ANOMALIES IN DEVELOPMENTAL DYSLEXIA

Summary of Cases

1. Drake (1968)

The first case of neuropathology associated with developmental dyslexia reported in the literature was that of Drake (1968), who examined the brain of a 12-year old boy who, despite normal intelligence, exhibited marked difficulty with reading, writing, and spelling, as well as some trouble with arithmetic. He had difficulty in telling time, and complained of dizzy spells, blackouts, and unilateral headaches. He was said to have mixed handedness, many members of his family were left-handed, and there was a positive family history of learning disabilities, migraines, and vascular malformations. The boy also had an intestinal allergy and was asthmatic. He died of a cerebral hemorrhage into the cerebellum due to an AVM. The autopsy revealed abnormal gyral configurations consisting of many small gyri, as well as a thin corpus callosum. Ectopic, that is, misplaced, neurons were found in the subcortical white matter. It was not stated whether these anomalies were asymmetrically distributed.

2. MU-157

The second case (the first in our laboratory) was a 20-year-old left-handed male who had been a clumsy child, had delayed speech, had difficulties in reading and spelling in grade school, and was diagnosed as having developmental dyslexia. He had a normal IQ, but language testing in adulthood showed a fourth-grade level of ability for reading, spelling, and comprehension of the written word. Mild cognitive problems were present in adulthood, which included a problem in finger recognition and right–left orientation. At the age of 16, he developed nocturnal seizures that were controlled by drug therapy. He died as a result of a fall.

Gross examination of the brain revealed no abnormalities. The brain (as well as all dyslexic and control brains analyzed in our laboratory) was then processed in whole-brain serial sections and stained for cell bodies and myelin. Microscopic analysis of the brain revealed that the planum temporale of the left side contained a region of microgyric cortex. The region was characterized by fused molecular layers, incomplete lamination and excessive folding. In addition, collections of ectopic neurons and multiple examples of mild dysplasia were present in the left auditory regions (e.g., see Figure 1), throughout the left hemisphere, and near the area of microgyria. The cortex of the right hemisphere, on the other hand, contained few dysplasias or ectopias and bilateral abnormalities were present in the posterior thalamus (Galaburda & Eidelberg, 1982). The planum temporale was symmetrical (Galaburda & Kemper, 1979).

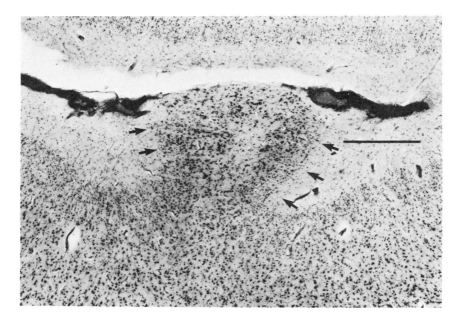

Figure 1. Photomicrograph of ectopic collections of cells in layer I of the cerebral cortex of a dyslexic man (ORT-5). Bar = 500 μm.

3. ORT-1

This was a 14-year-old right-handed boy with a positive family history of dyslexia and thyroid disorder. He was ambidextrous in early life, and he had a dyslexic brother with mixed dominance. He was diagnosed in the second grade as being dyslexic and in the seventh grade entered a boarding school for the learning disabled, where he died of viral myocarditis. His IQ scores were in the normal range although his reading ability was at grade-school level.

Gross examination of the brain revealed no abnormalities. Upon microscopic examination, numerous instances of ectopias and dysplasias were present throughout the left hemisphere. Some of the ectopias formed warty excrescences on the cortical surface. The anomalies were located predominantly in the frontal, temporoparietal, and superior temporal regions of the brain. The brain differed from MU-157 in severity of the anomalies. In general, the dysplasias in ORT-1 were less severe than those of MU-157 (e.g., no micropolygyria were seen). There were a few anomalies in the right hemisphere, although far fewer than in the left. The planum temporale was again symmetrical (Galaburda, 1983).

4. ORT-2

This was a 20-year-old right-handed male who had left-handed twin brothers and whose youngest brother was left-handed and dyslexic. At the age of 5 years, he was noted to be slightly behind his peers in reading ability, and was noted at age 8 to have a significant verbal–performance discrepancy in the ITPA in favor of performance. At 14 years of age, he fell 8 feet onto concrete and fractured the left temporal bone. At 15 he was evaluated for daytime drowsiness and vertigo. An EEG diagnosed a dysrhythmia over the right hemisphere. At 19, he was evaluated for dyslexia and was again noted to have a significant verbal–performance discrepancy, although his full-scale intelligence score was in the normal range. He was found at that time to be reading at approximately the second-grade level. He died in a car accident of multiple internal injuries.

Gross examination of the brain indicated some signs of recent trauma consisting of subarachnoid and intraventricular blood and cortical contusions, as well as scarring and cystic degeneration at the site of the old trauma. Upon microscopic examination, numerous ectopias, dysplasias, and brain warts were noted in the left hemisphere, especially in the perisylvian region. There were, in addition, a few instances of these anomalies in the right hemisphere concentrated mostly in the frontal lobes. The planum temporale was symmetrical (Galaburda, Rosen, Sherman, & Aboitiz, 1984).

5. ORT-5

This was a 32-year-old ambidextrous male who died suddenly of a massive subarachnoid hemorrhage. His mother had lost 33 pounds during her pregnancy

With him, due to tuberculosis, and she had abdominal surgery 1 month prior to delivery, at which time her pregnancy was discovered. There is a family history of left-handedness and ambidexterity. He was noted to be a late talker and repeated a number of grades during his educational career despite higher-than-average intelligence. His reading and writing skills were consistently noted to be inferior, although when tests were administered orally he did well. He was diagnosed as dyslexic at an early age, but very little special education was offered.

Gross examination of the brain revealed the planum temporale to be symmetrical. Histological examination disclosed ectopias, dysplasias, and brain warts bilaterally although predominently in the left hemisphere (Galaburda, Sherman, Rosen, Aboitiz, & Geschwind, 1985).

Summary

In five consecutive cases, neuroanatomical anomalies have been seen in the brains of dyslexics. In our laboratory, we have seen anomalies bilaterally, although most were located in the left hemisphere. In the following section, evidence is presented to indicate that these types of anomalies have their origin during gestation—specifically during the fifth to sixth months. Also discussed is the prevalence of these types of anomalies in unselected autopsy brains and how that might relate to our findings in the dyslexic brain. Finally, possible etiologies are suggested for these anomalies and their relationship to the subsequent language disturbance of these individuals.

Neuronal Ectopia and Dysplasia

The types of neuroanatomical abnormalities seen in the dyslexic brain are not unique to this behavioral disorder. Micropolygyria, for example, has been associated with *porencephaly,* or cystic degeneration of the hemisphere (Levine, Fisher, & Caviness, 1974), and psychomotor retardation (McBride & Kemper, 1982). In the former case, the authors believe that microgyria represents a mild degree of the pathophysiology of porencephaly. Neuronal ectopias have been associated with cases of profound psychomotor retardation (Caviness, Evrard, & Lyon, 1978) and are seen in 5–30% of normal brains at autopsy (Brun, 1975; Veith & Schwindt, 1976). It should be noted, however, that what are termed normal brains at autopsy refers to a situation where little or no detailed history relating to the cognitive, perceptual, or motor abilities of the individual is available. It simply refers to subjects with no *known* neurological diseases. Thus, it is possible that many of those individuals thought to be normal may have had varying degrees of cognitive deficits not documented in life. It is, therefore, very difficult to get a true picture of the actual incidence of these types of brain anomalies in the control population. Brain warts have been reported in as many as 26% of brains (Schulze & Braak, 1976) although, again, there is little information as to the subject pool from which these brains were derived and as to the topography and lateralization of the anomalies.

Etiology of Neuropathology in the Dyslexic Brain

The etiology of micropolygyria and associated ectopias remains uncertain, but strong evidence points toward an insult to the forebrain during the later part of the period of neuronal migration to the cortical plate (McBride & Kemper, 1982)—that is, from 20 to 24 weeks of gestation. The abnormal location of neurons in the involved areas serves as evidence that the disruptions occurred near the end of the migrational period. In laboratory animals, similar alterations can be produced experimentally only during the period before neuronal migration to the cortical plate is complete (Dvorak & Feit, 1977; Dvorak, Feit, & Jurankova, 1978). Because the cytoarchitectonic areas in which the most striking alterations are seen in the dyslexic brain are the last neocortical areas to complete neuronal migration (Chatel, 1976), we can ostensibly narrow down the time of insult to around the sixth month of gestational age.

Questions can now be raised as to why the left hemisphere is preferentially affected in the dyslexic brain. The knowledge about differential rates and/or patterns of growth of the two hemispheres provides a springboard from which to consider a number of possible mechanisms: It may be that any given cerebral insult presented at random acts preferentially on the side developing more slowly, in that it may be easier to have an effect on more slowly developing areas. Another possibility is that the anomalies seen in the dyslexic brain result from the more prolonged exposure of the left hemisphere to an etiologic agent than the right. Thus, an etiologic agent would act only during critical periods that last longer on the left side. Another possibility would argue that the injurious agent does not occur at random, but is specifically directed at a particular biological feature present primarily in the left hemisphere and less so in the right. The production of an antibody against an antigenic component of cells present asymmetrically could be an instance of this type of mechanism. Chemical (Oke, Keller, Mefford, & Adams, 1978) and immunological (Renoux, Biziere, Renoux, Guillaumin, & Degenne, 1983) asymmetries argue for nonrandom mechanisms for unilateral damage. Yet another mechanism would implicate differential survival of lesions on the two sides. Thus ectopias on the right might be preferentially eliminated.

Another group of explanations would contend that the left lateralized abnormalities occur as the result of random insults to the left and right hemisphere, irrespective of their distinct biological properties, and are found as a result of a bias that selects for left-hemisphere behavioral deficits. The behavioral consequences of the insult would be expected to be dependent on the time of the insult, the hemisphere affected, and the location within the hemisphere. In the five cases described, therefore, the patients might have been dyslexic because the insult occurred in the left hemisphere late in the stage of cortical migration coincidental with the period during which areas crucial to language are at a critical period of development. Furthermore, anomalies could occur in the left hemispheres of subjects who exhibited no signs of dyslexia. These anomalies would be localized to areas of the brain not essential for language organization, or at a time when unlesioned areas could better compensate for the lesioned areas. Likewise, similar distortions in development might be seen to affect the right hemisphere preferentially. These alterations might produce clinically recognizable right-hemisphere disturbances (akin in severity to the dyslexia of the left hemisphere) or simply subclinical manifestations. In short, a set of random insults could affect various locations in either developing hemisphere, and the presence or absence of clinical manifestations would depend entirely on whether the regions involved handle everyday functions and whether uninvolved areas can compensate. Thus, it is quite possible that in our society the right hemisphere anomalies escape notice because the associated cognitive deficits may not be as obvious as language disturbances, or because functions can be carried out by other parts of the brain.

Summary

The neuropathological anomalies seen in the dyslexic brain are not unique to dyslexia, although their timing and location may be. They are present in a variety of normal and abnormal brains; the exact percentage is in question due to the difficulty in determining exactly what is normal at autopsy from a neurological perspective. It appears that the anomalies are formed sometime around the fifth to sixth month of gestation. The etiologic agent (or agents) that cause these anomalies is, at present, unknown, as is the mechanism whereby these anomalies preferentially affect the left hemisphere. What is required in order to elucidate these questions is an animal model. In the following section, therefore, we discuss findings that link dyslexia to left-handedness and autoimmune disease and ways by which this link can point the way to an animal model for the neuropathological anomalies in the dyslexic brain.

AUTOIMMUNITY, LEFT-HANDEDNESS, AND DEVELOPMENTAL DISABILITIES

Humans

While anecdotal information linking dyslexia, left-handedness, and allergies had been around for some time (Geschwind & Behan, 1984), the first systematic examination of this relation was undertaken only a few years ago. Geschwind and Behan (1982) in two studies examined a total of 500 strong left-handers and 900 strong right-handers to see if there was any relation among handedness, autoimmune disease, and learning disabilities. They found that left-handers had a higher incidence of autoimmune disease and developmental learning disabilities than right-handers. This was also found to be the case in the first- and second-degree relatives. In a subsequent study (Geschwind & Behan, 1984), left-handers had significantly greater or higher incidences of migraine, allergies, dyslexia, stuttering, skeletal malformations, and thyroid disorders than right-handers. Approaching the same question from a different perspective, Geschwind and Behan examined a population of subjects with well-documented auto-immune disease and then administered a handedness questionnaire. They found that there were significantly more left-handed subjects among patients with Crohn's disease, celiac disease, thyroid disorders, ulcerative colitis, and myasthenia gravis than would be predicted from the incidence of left-handedness in the general population. These studies, then, convincingly demonstrated a link between left-handedness and developmental learning disabilities and autoimmune disease.

Animal Model—The New Zealand Mouse

Based on the link of left-handedness with both learning disorders and immune disease, Geschwind and Behan suggested that alterations in the development of the dyslexic brain and the occurrence of immune disorders might reflect a common influence that alters both brain and immune development. Thus, they suggested an in utero role for testosterone, which is postulated to decrease the development of the left hemisphere and alter the development of the thymus and other immune-related processes. One way to test this hypothesis is to examine brains of animals that develop immune disorders to see whether similar anomalies to those seen in the dyslexic brains are present. Therefore, we examined the brains of New Zealand Black (NZB) mice and hybrids with the nonimmune disordered New Zealand White. The NZB mouse was originally bred for cancer research, but subsequently it was seen that these mice died prematurely, with the primary cause of death being autoimmune hemolytic anemia. The hybrid (NZB/W) develops antinuclear antibodies, lupus erythematosus cells, and severe renal disease. Because the immune problems in New Zealand mice develop spontaneously, these strains are considered useful models of human immune disorders (e.g., systemic lupus erythematosus (SLE)).

The brains of a total of 56 male and female New Zealand mice were examined in serial sections (Sherman, Galaburda, & Geschwind, 1983, 1985). Thirty micron sections throughout the entirety of the brain were stained for nerve cell bodies and examined under the light microscope. Eighteen percent of the brains had ectopic neurons in layer I of the cerebral cortex with dysplasias of the underlying layers (Figure 2). The anomalies generally consisted of groups of neurons located in the usually cell-free layer I and distortion of layers II–IV. The anomalies were (1) unilateral except in one case, (2) slightly more prevalent on the right side, (3) present always in the sensorimotor cortex, and (4) seen more often in males. Ninety-six control mice (C57BL/6 and 6J, CFW, DBA/2) have been examined and a small number of anomalies were seen in the cortex, although the frequency of occurrence in the latter group is significantly lower than that in the New Zealand strains. The majority of the anomalies seen in control mice were present in C57BL/6J females—a finding that must be examined further.

In a subsequent study (Sherman, Behan, & Galaburda, 1985), similar anomalies were seen in 32% of brains from the BXSB autoimmune strain. Most of the anomalies were present in frontal-motor cortices and were unilateral although no overall lateral bias was seen in the population. An additional autoimmune strain (MRL), which differs from the NZB and BXSB in the type of autoimmune disorder (Talal, 1983), did not have brain anomalies. It is reasonable to suggest that the New Zealand mouse and other autoimmune strains of mice may be

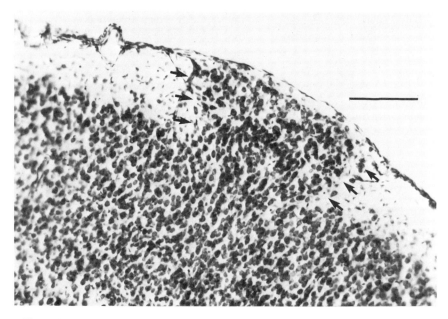

Figure 2. Photomicrograph of ectopic collections of cells in layer I of an autoimmune mouse (New Zealand Black). Bar = 10 μm.

appropriate animal models for study of the relationship between immune disorders and developmental brain anomalies. The NZB is also interesting from a behavioral perspective, in that they are significantly impaired in the acquisition of a task that has a strong temporal ordering component. Nandy, Lal, Bennett, and Bennett (1983) found that while 33 out of 55 control C57BL/6 female mice were able to learn a conditioned avoidance task in 30 trials or less, only 1 NZB mouse out of 33 was able to acquire the appropriate response. In addition, Spencer and Lal (1983) found that NZB mice were less active than controls during the first 4 minutes of open field testing, which indicates that NZB mice may be more emotional than controls (Whimbey & Denenberg, 1967). Thus, not only do these immune-disordered mice exhibit brain anomalies, but they may also express learning difficulties. The mouse model now offers an opportunity for studying the relationship between immune and cortical development, sex-steroid influences, and resulting behavioral consequences.

DISCUSSION

Planum Symmetry and Dyslexia

Samuel Orton suspected that the difficulty in dyslexia arises from the unresolved competition for language control by the two hemispheres (Orton, 1937). Interestingly, the four brains of dyslexic persons studied in our laboratory have had symmetrical planum temporale. Most studies of the planum have reported roughly a 25% incidence of symmetrical plana in the standard autopsy population. The finding of four consecutive brains with symmetrical plana is therefore well beyond a random sampling artifact.

Whether symmetry in this language area is etiologically related to dyslexia is more difficult to assess, because by the most liberal estimates only 10% of the population is dyslexic. This observation, however, does not exclude the possibility that symmetry and dyslexia are causally related, because there may be additional factors that determine the final expression of the dyslexic phenotype. It is quite possible that in some percentage of this symmetrical population there are compensatory mechanisms. Females, for instance, may comprise a significant portion of those individuals that are able to compensate. Levy (1984) has reported that dyslexic girls carry out certain compensatory language functions with the right hemisphere—an ability that is apparently not demonstrated in dyslexic boys. It has been argued that the structure of the language used by the dyslexic may affect the ability to compensate. Thus, some redundancies present in one language and not in another may permit partial compensation.

Additionally, there may be extralinguistic mechanisms available to both boys and girls. For example, some dyslexic subjects with very superior nonlinguistic skills may have escaped detection because they may be able to learn to read by unusual strategies. Work by Kean (1984) has shown that in tests dealing with spoken language, adult dyslexics demonstrate anomalous grammars, yet in standard discourse these anomalies are not detectable, probably because redundancy of information is obtained from context. When the grammatical knowledge is tested out of context, however, the problems appear. It is conceivable, therefore, that extralinguistic contextual strategies can be employed by some dyslexics (even in written language) and that these mechanisms are capable of hiding the dyslexic tendencies. The documentation of the existence of these mechanisms could lead to new forms of remediation. It may be, therefore, that the expression of the deficits of dyslexics may be diminished if one were able to harvest these compensatory mechanisms and offer them to those who do not compensate on their own.

Relevance of the NZB Mouse to the Study of Dyslexia

It is important to stress that the brain findings in the immune-deficient mice did not come about by random search, but resulted instead from the hypothesis that immune-disordered animals, by virtue of their similarity to immune-disordered human patients, might be expected to show comparable brain lesions to those seen in the dyslexic brains. Although the hypothesis has proven to be correct, much work needs be done on the suitability of these animals as experimental models. Factors in support of this suitability include the presence of strikingly asymmetrical anomalies, similarity of morphology of lesions under light microscopy, and the demonstration that these mice may exhibit learning disabilities.

One important difference between the mouse anomalies and the findings in the dyslexic brain concerns the presence in the former of ambilateral lesions—that is, lesions may be severe in either hemisphere. In the dyslexic, the lesions have all thus far been more severe on the left. Possible explanations for this difference may relate to the possibility that populations of mice are less biased in their population pattern of lateralization—that is, roughly 50% are right-pawed, and 50% are left-pawed (Collins, 1968). Human populations, as previously discussed, tend to show biased lateralization—for example, more people are right-handed than left-handed.

Another possibility may relate to issues of selection. Mouse brains have been studied because they come from an immune-disordered strain, without consideration to behavior, whereas the dyslexic brains are selected by virtue of their predominantly left-hemisphere disabilities. Thus, just as we find mice with either right- or left-hemisphere lesions, there may be a subpopulation of human subjects with right-hemisphere anomalies accompanying right-hemisphere learning problems—for example, attentional and/or some visuospatial deficits. The study of brains of individuals with other learning disabilities, as well as brains of immune-disordered humans, could help resolve this issue.

The finding of developmental lesions in the immune mice raises the possibility that the lesions are immunologically mediated. It is conceivable that immune-mediated attacks on the migration apparatus disrupt the glial–neural architecture needed for proper migration of the cells. This would be true for any patient with autoimmune problems, irrespective of the presence of dyslexia. It would be important, therefore, to look at brains of nondyslexic relatives of dyslexic individuals. It may be that there is a proportion of those relatives who have the lesions, yet no dyslexia. Again compensatory strategies may be available to them and not to their affected relatives, and it is important to find out what those strategies might be. Or it may be simply a quantitative issue, with the unaffected relative showing fewer or less-severe anomalies. The distribution and timing of the lesions would undoubtedly also play a role.

Finally, there is the issue of the special skills in dyslexics and their families. This ties into the issue of symmetry. It has been shown that early unilateral experimental lesions produce significant readjustment of architecture and connections in the cortex and subcortical structures, capable even of changing the patterns of asymmetry (Goldman, 1978; Schneider, 1981). It is possible, therefore, that the spontaneous lesions in the dyslexic brains have a similar effect, and that this may account, in some, for the better development of areas of the brain handling nonlinguistic cognitive functions. The ability to manipulate the number of lesions in an experimental animal like the immune-mouse offers the possibility for studying the relationship between lesions, architecture, connectivity, and behavior as it applies to dyslexia and also to the issue of normal individual variability of behavioral attributes.

REFERENCES

Anderson, S. W. (1977). Language-related asymmetries of eye-movement and evoked potentials. In S. Harnad, R. W. Doty, L. Goldstein, J. Jaynes, & G. Krauthamer (Eds.), *Lateralization in the central nervous system* (pp. 403–428). New York: Academic Press.

Basser, L. S. (1962). Hemiplegia of early onset and faculty of speech with special reference to the effects of hemispherectomy. *Brain, 85,* 427–460.

Broca, P. (1865). Sur la faculté de langage articule. *Bulletin de la Société de Anthropologie, Paris, 6,* 337–393.

Brun, A. (1975). The subpial granular layer of the foetal cerebral cortex in man. *Acta Pathologica et Microbiologica Scandinavica, Supplement, 179,* 40.

Caviness, V. S., Evrard, P., & Lyon, G. (1978). Radial neuronal assemblies, ectopia and necrosis of developing cortex: A case analysis. *Acta Neuropathologica, 41,* 67–72.

Chatel, M. (1976). Développement de l'isocortex au cerveau humain pendant les periodes embryon-naires et foetales jusque la 24eme semaine de gestation. *Journal für Hirnforschung, 17,* 189–212.

Chi, J. G., Dooling, E. C., & Gilles, F. H. (1977). Gyral development of the human brain. *Annals of Neurology, 1,* 86–93.

Collins, R. L. (1968). On the inheritance of handedness: I. Laterality in inbred mice. *Journal of Heredity, 59,* 9–12.

Dennis, M. (1983). The developmentally dyslexic brain and the written language skills of children with one hemisphere. In O. Kirk (Ed.), *Neuropsychology of language, reading, and spelling* (pp. 185–208). New York: Academic Press.

Drake, W. E. (1968). Clinical and pathological findings in a child with a developmental learning disability. *Journal of Learning Disorders, 1,* 486–502.

Dvorak, K., & Feit, J. (1977). Migration of neuroblasts through partial necrosis of the cerebral cortex in newborn rats—contribution to the problems of morphological development and developmental period of cerebral microgyria. *Acta Neuropathologica, 38,* 203–212.

Dvorak, K., Feit, J., & Jurankova, Z. (1978). Experimentally induced focal microgyria and status verrucosus deformis in rats—pathogenesis and interrelation histological and auto-radiographical study. *Acta Neuropathologica, 44,* 121–129.

Eberstaller, D. (1884). Zur oberfachen Anatomie des Grosshirn Hemisphären. *Wiener Medizinische Blaetr, 7,* 479–642.

Eimas, P. D., Siqueland, E. R., Jusczyk, P., & Vigorito, J. (1971). Speech perception in infants. *Science, 171,* 303–306.

Entus, A. K. (1977). Hemispheric asymmetry in processing of dichotically presented speech and nonspeech stimuli by infants. In S. J. Segalowitz & F. A. Gruber (Eds.), *Language development and neurological theory* (pp. 64–74). New York: Academic Press.

Fontes, V. (1944). *Morfologia do cortex cerebral.* Lisbon: Boletim do Instituto de Antonio Aurelio da Costa Ferreira.

Galaburda, A. M. (1983). Developmental dyslexia: Current anatomical research. *Annals of Dyslexia, 13,* 41–53.

Galaburda, A. M., & Eidelberg, D. (1982). Symmetry and asymmetry in the human posterior thalamus. II. Thalamic lesions in a case of developmental dyslexia. *Archives of Neurology, 39,* 333–336.

Galaburda, A. M., & Kemper, T. L. (1979). Cytoarchitectonic abnormalities in developmental dyslexia: A case study. *Annals of Neurology, 6,* 94–100.

Galaburda, A. M., LeMay, M., Kemper, T. L., & Geschwind, N. (1978). Right–left asymmetries in the brain *Science, 199,* 852–856.

Galaburda, A. M., Rosen, G. D., Sherman, G. F., & Aboitiz, F. (1984). Developmental dyslexia: Fourth consecutive case with cortical anomalies. *Society for Neuroscience Abstracts, 10,* 957.

Galaburda, A. M., Sanides, F., & Geschwind, N. (1978). Human brain: Cytoarchitectonic left–right asymmetries in the temporal speech region. *Archives of Neurology, 35,* 812–817.

Galaburda, A. M., Sherman, G. F., Rosen, G. D., Aboitiz, F., & Geschwind, N. (1985). Develop-mental dyslexia: Four consecutive patients with cortical anomalies. *Annals of Neurology, 18,* 222–233.

Geschwind, N., & Behan, P. (1982). Left-handedness: Association with immune disease, migraine, and developmental learning disorder. *Proceedings of the National Academy of Sciences U.S.A., 79,* 5097–5100.

Geschwind, N., & Behan, P. (1984). Laterality, hormones and immunity. In N. Geschwind & A. M. Galaburda (Eds.), *Biological foundations of cerebral dominance.* (pp. 211–224). Cambridge, MA: Harvard University Press.

Geschwind, N., & Levitsky, W. (1968). Human brain: left right asymmetries in temporal speech region. *Science, 161,* 186–187.

Glucksmann, A. (1965). Cell death in normal development. *Archives de Biologie, 76,* 419–437.

Goldman, P. S. (1978). Neuronal plasticity in primate telencephalon: Anomalous crossed cortico-caudate projections induced by prenatal removal of frontal association cortex. *Science, 202,* 768–776.

Hamburger, V., & Levi-Montalcini, R. (1949). Proliferation, differentiation, and degeneration in the spinal ganglia of the chick embryo under normal and experimental conditions. *Journal of Experimental Zoology, 111,* 457–501.

Hervé, G. (1888). *La circonvolution de Broca.* Paris: Delahage & Lecrosnier.

Hochberg, F. H., & LeMay, M. (1975). Arteriographic correlates of handedness. *Neurology, 25,* 218–222.

Innocenti, G. M., & Frost, D. O. (1980). The postnatal development of visual callosal connections in the absence of visual experience or of the eyes. *Experimental Brain Research, 39,* 365–375.

Kean, M.-L. (1984). The question of linguistic anomaly in developmental dyslexia. *Annals of Dyslexia.* 34, 137–151.

Kimura, D. (1961). Cerebral dominance and the perception of verbal stimuli. *Canadian Journal of Psychology, 15,* 166–171.

Larson, B., Skinhoj, E., & Lassen, N. A. (1978). Variation in regional cortical blood flow in the right and left hemispheres during automatic speech. *Brain, 101,* 193–209.

LeMay, M., & Culebras, A. (1972). Human brain morphological differences in the hemispheres demonstrable by carotid arteriography. *New England Journal of Medicine, 287,* 168–170.

LeMay, M., & Kido, D. K. (1978). Asymmetries of the cerebral hemispheres on computed tomograms. *Journal of Computer Assisted Tomography, 2,* 471–476.

Lenneberg, E. (1967). *Biological foundations of language.* New York: Wiley.

Levine, D. N., Fisher, M. A., & Caviness, V. S. (1974). Porencephaly with microgyria: A pathologic study. *Acta Neuropathologica, 29,* 99–113.

Levy, J. (1984, April). *Sex differences in dyslexia.* Paper presented at the 36th annual meeting of the American Academy of Neurology, Boston.

McBride, M. C., & Kemper, T. L. (1982). Pathogenesis of four-layers microgyric cortex in man. *Acta Neuropathologica, 57,* 93–98.

McRae, D., Branch, C., & Milner, B. (1968). The occipital horns and cerebral dominance. *Neurology, 18,* 95–98.

Mehler, J. (1985). Language related dispositions in early infancy. In J. Mehler & R. Fox (Eds.), *Neonate cognition: Beyond the blooming buzzing confusion* (pp. 7–28). Hillsdale, NJ: Lawrence Ehrlbaum Associates.

Moffit, A. R. (1971). Consonant cue perception by 20–24 week old infants. *Child Development, 42,* 717–731.

Molfese, D. L., Freeman, R. B., & Palermo, D. S. (1975). The ontogeny of brain lateralization for speech and nonspeech stimuli. *Brain and Language, 2,* 356–368.

Morse, P. A. (1972). The discrimination of speech and nonspeech stimuli in early infancy. *Journal of Experimental Child Psychology, 14,* 447–492.

Nandy, K., Lal, H., Bennett, M., & Bennett, D. (1983). Correlation between a learning disorder and elevated brain-reactive antibodies in agd C57BL/6 and young NZB mice. *Life Sciences, 33,* 1499–1503.

Oke, A., Keller, R., Mefford, I., & Adams, R. N. (1978). Lateralization of norepinephrine in the human thalamus. *Science, 200,* 1411–1413.

Orton, S. T. (1937). *Reading, writing and speech problems in children.* London: Chapman & Hall.

Penfield, W., & Roberts, L. (1959). *Speech and brain mechanisms*. Princeton, NJ: Princeton University Press.

Renoux, G., Biziere, K., Renoux, M., Guillaumin, J.-M., & Degenne, D. (1983). A balanced brain asymmetry modulates T cell mediated events. *Journal of Neuroimmunology, 5*, 227–238.

Rubens, A. B., Mahowald, M. W., & Hutton, J. T. (1976). Asymmetry of lateral (sylvian) fissures in man. *Neurology, 26,* 320–324.

Scheibel, A. B. (1981, January). The emergent capabilities of the aging forebrain. Paper presented at the 14th annual winter conference on Brain Research, Keystone, CO.

Schneider, G. E. (1981). Early lesions and abnormal neuronal connections. *Trends in Neuroscience, 4,* 187–192.

Schulze, K.-D., & Braak, H. (1976). Hirnwarzen. *Zeitschrft für Mikroskopisch-Anatomische Forschung, 92,* 609–623.

Sherman, G. F., Galaburda, A. M., & Geschwind, N. (1983). Ectopic neurons in the brain of the autoimmune mouse: a neuropathological model of dyslexia? *Society for Neuroscience Abstracts, 9,* 939.

Sherman, G. F., Dehan, P. O., & Galaburda, A. M. (1985). Brain anomalies and autoimmunity in mice. *Society for Neuroscience Abstracts, 11,* 400.

Sherman, G. F., Galaburda, A. M., & Geschwind, N. (1985). Cortical anomalies in brains of New Zealand mice: A neuropathologic model of dyslexia. *Proceedings of the National Academy of Sciences (U.S.A.), 82,* 8072–8074.

Spencer, D. G., & Lal, H. (1983). Specific behavioral impairments in associational tasks with an autoimmune mouse. *Society for Neuroscience Abstracts, 9,* 96.

Sperry, R. W. (1974). Lateral specialization in the surgically separated hemispheres. In B. Milner (Ed.), *Hemispheric specialization and interaction* (pp. 5–19). Cambridge, MA: MIT Press.

Springer, S. P. (1977). Tachistoscopic and dichotic-listening investigations of laterality in normal and human subjects. In S. Harnad, R. W. Doty, L. Goldstein, J. Jaynes, & G. Krauthamer (Eds.), *Lateralization in the nervous system* (pp. 325–336). New York: Academic Press.

Talal, N. (1983). Immune response disorders. In H. L. Foster, J. D. Small, & J. G. Fox (Eds.), *The Mouse in Biomedical Research. Volume III. Normative Biology, Immunology, and Husbandry* (pp. 391–401). New York: Academic Press.

Teszner, P. A., Tzavaras, A., Gruner, J., & Hecaen, H. (1972). L'asymétrie droite–gauche du planum temporale: À-propos de l'étude anatomique de 100 cerveaux. *Revue Neurologique, 126,* 444–449.

Vargha-Khadem, F., & Corbalis, M. C. (1979). Cerebral asymmetry in infants. *Brain and Language, 8,* 1–9.

Veith, G., & Schwindt, W. (1976). Pathologisch-anatomischer Beitrag zum Problem "Nichtsesshaftigkeit". *Fortschritte der Neurologie, Psychiatrie und Ihrer Grenzgebiete, 44,* 1–21.

Wada, J. A., Clarke, R., & Hamm, A. (1975). Cerebral hemispheric asymmetry in humans. *Archives of Neurology, 32,* 239–246.

Wernicke, C. (1874). *Der aphasische symptomen Komplex*. Breslav, Poland: Cohn & Weigart.

Whimbey, A. E., & Denenberg, V. H. (1967). Two independent behavioral dimensions in open-field performance. *Journal of Comparative and Physiological Psychology, 63,* 500–504.

Witelson, S. F., & Pallie, W. (1973). Left hemisphere specialization for language in the newborn: Neuroanatomical evidence of asymmetry. *Brain, 96,* 641–646.

Yeni-Komshian, G. H., & Benson, D. A. (1976). Anatomical study of cerebral asymmetry in the temporal lobe of humans, chimpanzees, and rhesus monkeys. *Science, 192,* 387–389.

Chapter 9

Dementia in Infantile and Childhood Neurological Disease

PAUL RICHARD DYKEN
GERALD E. McCLEARY

Department of Neurology
University of South Alabama
College of Medicine
Mobile, Alabama 36617

INTRODUCTION

There has been a chauvinistic tendency in some circles to consider dementia as a problem that occurs only in adults. In fact, limiting categories to senile and presenile forms of dementia, a medical classification in use only a few years ago, tends to obscure the fact that dementia is found across the lifespan. The emphasis on the dementias that occur in the middle-aged and older population is more than likely due to their prevalence in contrast to dementias that occur in younger individuals, children and infants.

Dementia (*de*=decreased; *ment*=mental; *ia*=condition of) is a term practically defined in different fashions. As Wells (1977) points out, a problem in defining dementia exists because the term is used in both lay and medical communications. Webster derives the term from the Latin *dement*, from *demens* (mad) and defines it as "a condition of deteriorated mentality that is charac-

CHILD NEUROPSYCHOLOGY, VOL. 1

terized by marked decline from the individual's former intellectual level and often by emotional apathy." Dorland defines it as "a general designation for mental deterioration." Wells (1977) uses it only to refer to the deterioration of mental function due to diffuse or disseminated organic disease of the cerebral hemisphere, differentiating it from focal cerebral diseases presenting as isolated defects like aphasia. Furthermore, it is common practice to use *dementia* in referring to chronic mental dysfunction, while designating acute forms of dysfunction as *delirium*. Obviously, admixtures of dementia and delirium are also possible. Wells (1977) adds two other essentials to the definition of dementia which are not universally accepted. First, that *dementia* shows demonstrable pathological changes, whereas *delirium* does not, and secondly, that dementia is not reversible. He also states, "dementia is considered here as a spectrum of mental states resulting from disease of the cerebral hemisphere in adult life" (p. 11).

Cummings and Benson (1983) have offered a different definition of dementia. They operationally define it "as an acquired persistent impairment of intellectual function with compromise in at least three of the following spheres of mental activity: language, memory, visuospatial skills, emotion or personality, and cognition (abstraction, calculation, judgment, etc.)" (p. 1). They stress the acquired nature of dementia to discriminate it from the congenital mental retardation syndromes, and they also admit that their definition is applicable to reversible and irreversible changes in mental status. Cummings and Benson (1983) eschew the often synonomously used terms acute or chronic organic brain syndrome and primary degenerative dementia (PDD).

The present authors propose to define the term in the broadest sense as a general designation for chronic deterioration in multiple mental functions. No restrictions are established for age, for demonstrable pathological lesions, or for irreversibility of the disorder that produces the dementia. *Dementia* represents a symptom or a condition and not a disease or even an invariable syndrome itself. In order to understand the source of dementia, it becomes necessary to establish a procedure for diagnosis. Diagnosis should address a domain that starts with a specific symptom, then progresses to a symptom complex (i.e., usually identified as a syndrome) and finally culminates in a disease, which is a symptom complex due to a known cause. A symptom may be representative of either a syndrome or a disease or both, but may also stand by itself. Dementia is best conceived of as a higher-level concept encompassing a variety of prototypic sets of symptoms sufficient for diagnosis, but not restricted to a single necessary symptom complex. For example, in one case, dementia may present with deterioration of specific mental functions that are dissimilar to those shown with dementia in another case. Dementias, then, represent specific mental dysfunctions, which may vary in their symptomatic expressions.

SPECIAL CONSIDERATIONS
IN INFANTS AND CHILDREN

The identification of dementia is much more difficult with organisms not fully developed than with those that are matured. It is essential to understand normal developmental patterns prior to determining the presence of a change in these patterns as a result of disease processes. This is particularly important when evaluating the status of small infants. The development of mental functions can often be opposed by the deterioration one encounters in the dementing processes of infancy and childhood and the algebraic sum of these two opposing forces sometimes produces a confusing picture of static mental processes or even of slowly improving or developing processes Golden et al. (1983) have emphasized that injury to tertiary systems may not be expressed until 8–10 years of age. It is also important to point out that the measurement of mental functions in infants and very young children is often thought to be only partially correlated with later higher mental functions seen in older children and adults. The reasons for the low correlations are probably manyfold, but two commonly stressed problems are that higher cognitive functions are yet to develop and therefore are incapable of measurement in the very young child, and also that the intellectual changes are a result of the interaction of environment and maturation. A similar problem may also exist even in the neurological examination of infants as noted by Ellison (1983). Observation of the stage of language (babbling, using words or sentences, etc.), motor (rolling over, sitting and walking, etc.), sensory (reactions to auditory, tactile and visual stimulation) and social (smiling, reciprocal interactions, etc.) development provides an estimate of the current mental status of the infant and the young child. The extremely broad range of norms in each of these areas impedes an easy determination of the child's degree of dysfunction. Multiple and repeated assessments are necessary with a mildly dysfunctional process. Even then, as Ellison (1983) notes from the results of the National Collaborative Perinatal Project (NCPP), observed dysfunction at an early age may not be indicative of a dysfunction later. The complex variations in development tend to obfuscate subtle indicators of a disease process. As Rapin (1976, 1977) has so succinctly pointed out, one can construct a graph of the algebraic sum of the opposing processes of development and deterioration. Herskowitz and Rosman (1982) have referred to the loss of developmental milestones or a deterioration in children's intelligence as syndromes of "behaviorial regression." In certain disease processes, the deterioration may be less obvious because of the relentless progress of maturation and development. Mental functions in these situations will continue to improve and expand, but the dementing process will also continue to impede and impair. The diminution of the developmental process with time will permit the effects of deterioration to become more and more evident. In other diseases, deterioration will be so broad or rapid that this process will be overpowering and the effect will be patent.

Because of the broad range of changes in mental functions observed in normal development and the varied dysfunctions seen in diseased infants and children, less effort has been expended in establishing types of dementia for this age group than has been done for adults. Mental functions involve many neural processes, including specific as well as nonspecific subunits. The measure arbitrarily defined as *mentation* is really a global designation encompassing all sensory inputs, all associative pathways, and all motor outputs. Given this situation, assessment, whether in the pediatric neurological examination or in neuropsychological evaluation, should cover a wide range of mental functions and except for the more-severe abnormalities may need to be repeated to delineate clearly the effects of disease processes.

CORTICAL VERSUS SUBCORTICAL DEMENTIA

An obvious early misconception, that the mental functions affected in dementia were "resident" in the cerebral cortex, has been supplanted by more-recent work pointing out that progressive multiple deficits in mental function are not always associated with diseases having their maximum brunt of effect in the cerebral gray matter, but may be associated with diseases where pathology is primarily confined to more caudal areas of the central nervous system. In fact, Albert, Feldman, and Willis (1974), followed by McHugh and Folstein (1975), have differentiated in adults two major forms of dementia, one with known pathology mainly in the cerebral cortex, which they call "cortical dementia" and the other form with major pathology in subcortical regions such as the corpus striatum, thalamus, or brainstem, which is called "subcortical dementia."

Prototype adult examples of subcortical dementia are Huntington's disease, Parkinson's disease, and progressive supranuclear palsy. In these disorders, the major pathology is in the caudate nucleus, the substantia region, and the supranuclear brainstem nuclei, respectively. The prototype of cortical dementia is Alzheimer's disease. However, even this disorder may be associated with subcortical damage, as investigations have shown that the basal nucleus of Meynert may be the region of maximum damage (Whitehouse, Price, Clark, Coyle, & DeLong, 1981; Whitehouse et al., 1982), and this structure is not usually included as part of the cerebral cortex. Cummings and Benson (1984) have questioned the importance of the subcortical aspect of Alzheimer's disease as it relates to the damage found in the nucleus basalis of Meynert. Cummings and Benson (1984) still consider this disease to be a cortical dementia.

The differentiation between cortical and subcortical types of dementia is not totally accepted. There is some argument that a strict pathological differentiation is really not possible for the dementias, because all the dementias mentioned have involvement of both cortical and subcortical regions to some extent. It is further argued, by those who have a holistic view of dysmentation, that declining mental functions are due to changes encompassing the input, association, and output divisions of the central nervous system (CNS). It is considered by those who support this theory that *instrumental* functions such as perception, memory, praxias, gnosias, and phasias are represented more by the cerebral cortex, whereas the *fundamental* functions such as motivation, attention, mood, and arousal are represented more by the subcortical areas, especially those in the corpus striatum and the thalamus.

Another consideration as to the basis of mentation which must be mentioned, relates to the variety of neurotransmitter systems in the CNS. An important neurotransmitter system closely connected to an adult-onset dementia is the cholinergic system, which is believed to be deficient in Alzheimer's disease. This system is a diffuse one and basically interdigitates throughout the entire nervous system, but is especially dominant in the basal frontal nucleus of Meynert, the frontal cortex, the hippocampus, and the limbic system, where the maximum pathological effects of this particular dementia appear. In contrast, Huntington's disease appears to represent a deficiency in the gamma--aminobutyric acid neurotransmitter system, which is predominant in the striatal-neocortex and cerebellum, areas that show distinct pathological abnormalities in this disease. Possible indicators of striatal-thalamic mental dysfunction such as disturbances in mood, attention, arousal, and motivation tend to typify the clinical picture of Huntington's patients. On the other hand; the indicators of cortical dysfunction such as disturbances of memory, cognition, perception, and apraxias, aphasias, and agnosias are seen more in Alzheimer's disease. Other dementias generally found in adults also show such distinguishing features in many instances. Yet, in the childhood dementias, these features are not nearly as obvious or as easy to differentiate.

INFANTILE AND CHILDHOOD
NEURODEGENERATIVE DISEASES CLASSIFICATION

The entire topic of neurodegenerative diseases in children is an immense subject, as was pointed out by Dyken and Krawiecki (1983) in their review. Well over 750 different diseases and syndromes were identified and many, if not most, have dementia as a clinical feature. It was suggested that the infantile and juvenile neurodegenerative diseases could be conveniently classified into several diagnostic categories. The proposed categories were (1) the polioencephalopa-thies (those disorders with maximum involvement in the cerebral cortex); (2) the leukoencephalopathies (those disorders with maximum involvement of the subcortical white matter or corona radiata); (3) the corencephalopathies (those disorders with maximum involvement of the subcortical gray and white matter above the rhombencephalon, parts of the telencephalon, including the diencephalon and the mesencephalon); (4) the spinocerebellopathies (those disorders with maximum involvement of the rhombencephalon; the pons, medulla, and cerebellum; and the spinal cord); (5) the diffuse encephalopathies (those disorders where the anatomical distribution of lesions is uncertain, unconfirmed, or unknown). Those neurodegenerative disorders that have prominent dementias cluster in the polioencephalopathic subcategory, although all the categories listed have examples of disorders that have prominent dementia. It is obvious from our review that dementia in children is not merely a polioencephalonic function. Conversely, however, there is no confirmation that an easy differentiation between cortical and subcortical types of dementia as seen in adults is present in this age group.

CAUSES OF DEMENTIA

Although many of the childhood and infantile dementias are of unknown cause, a large number of the disorders appear to be related to a genetic predisposition. Almost 50% of all the neurodegenerative diseases listed by Dyken and Krawiecki (1983) are familial or otherwise definitely inherited. Such a high figure suggests that a large number of dementias are or will soon be proven to be due to genetically caused enzymatic defects. Some of the dementias, such as Tay-Sachs disease, are currently known to be produced by enzymatic defects that cause faulty cellular metabolism, death of cells, and a resultant functional deficit. The dementia of Tay-Sachs disease is caused by the absence of hexosaminidase, a ganglioside cleaving enzyme that allows an excessive accumulation of GM2-gangliosides in neurons, interfering with metabolism and causing early cellular death. These effects are seen clinically by progressive amaurosis, dementia, and progressive loss of other neurological functions. It is of historical interest and perhaps telling in regard to some of the present-day confusion about infantile dementia that Bernard Sachs, who gave the first full clinical delineation of the disease in 1881, gave the name "amaurotic familial idiocy" to the disorder. *Idiocy* suggests a static mental defect and not a progressive one. In fact, a better example of dementia in infancy would be hard to envision.

In contrast to the adult dementias, such as Huntington's disease with clear autosomal dominant inheritance, those infantile and juvenile dementias having a genetic basis are most often of an autosomal recessive type, although there are a few notable exceptions that are sex-linked. Dominant inheritance is rarer but can occur when low rates of penetrance occur or are associated with multisymptom expression, which would allow the dominant transmission of the genotype to be expressed in a phenotype not interfering with reproductive fitness, a situation that rarely occurs in dementia.

Although genetic defects are an important cause of a large number of infantile and juvenile dementias, other causes are important too. The more important are those due to persistent viral infections (i.e., "slow" viruses) and the immunopathic responses that are associated with them. It seems "slow" versus natural or wild viral infections of the CNS have a tendency to affect subcortical structures more often than the cerebral cortex, which is the focus of the usual form of encephalitis from wild viruses.

Another significant cause of infantile and juvenile dementia is ongoing exposure to toxins, whether the toxins are a drug prescribed by a physician or a chemical of exogenous origins. An example of an iatrogenic dementia of particular pertinence to the pediatric neurologist is the anticonvulsant-induced dementia related to excessive chronic use of certain anticonvulsants such as barbiturates.

An infantile or childhood dementia associated with epilepsy is believed to be particularly important in the infantile spasm syndrome and develops through a kindling process where continual electrical stimulation of a specific area, especially in the CNS, brings about permanent and progressive damage to the area stimulated.

EVALUATION OF DEMENTIA

Clinical and Neurological

The evaluation of dementia in infancy and childhood is first and foremost a clinical assessment, so that a standard medical history and physical examination are of paramount importance. Information about the psychomotor development of the patient, compilation of a social history, acquisition of details about the family history with a particular search for similar diseases in the family and collection of details about the prenatal, perinatal and postnatal periods, especially concerning immunization, nutrition, and seizures is of absolute importance to the evaluation. History about the usual childhood diseases and of medications taken in the past as well as present is important. Standard medical physical assessment is required, for all of the body's systems may contribute to the specific problem of dementia. Specific information should be obtained from multiple sources if possible, although mothers are usually the most informed of historical sources. Unfortunately, they are known to be biased somewhat, especially concerning mental processes of their offspring and not apt to observe and carefully record their child's specific behaviors. Details of the patient's intellectual status in the past and the present are required, especially in relation to that of normal controls such as normal siblings at similar ages. While such information is essential, it is important to note that it is far from reliable enough or sufficient to make precise judgements.

The neurological and mental status evaluation should be performed in detail; physical measurements taken; general physical examination performed; and intellectual status, mood, attention, speech, learning, memory, orientation, habituation, perception, cranial nerves, optic structures, equilibrium, myotatic reflexes, sensory modalities, cerebellar/coordination, and muscular tone/strenght/bulk assessed. It is important to observe for minor seizure activity. Absence continuum (or petit mal seizure status) may rarely mimic dementia.

Neuropsychological Evaluation

Standard neuropsychological assessment is important when possible. Because dementia as previously defined covers a wide spectrum of prototypic sets of multiple mental dysfunctions as well as presenting in a wide range of ages, it is obvious that assessment must be broad and yet appropriate to the developmental status of the patient. Although it is possible to select appropriate testing instruments from the wide array available, the use of two specific batteries of tests following neuropsychological principles as espoused in the quantitative approach (e.g., Reitan's batteries for children) or the qualitative approach (e.g., A. R. Luria's methods as formalized by Christensen, 1979) (see Teeter, Chapter 7, Volume 2, for a review of these tests) may be used in assessment of children. While these batteries and procedures are very useful for the assessment of the older child who is not severely impaired, they are of much less value for the infant or severely impaired older child unless special considerations are given. The use of tests designed specifically for the infant and the younger child, such as those of Cattell (1940), Brazelton (1973), and Bayley (1969) may be more appropriate in the latter case. It may also be necessary to supplement the aforementioned batteries with other psychometrically sound tests that have substantial normative data available. Reitan (1974) has emphasized that reported functional deficits may differ for differing ages, the very young with sensory-motor deficits, later perceptual deficits, and still later dysfunction manifested as language disturbance. It is easy to understand the lack of a standard battery of tests that would be appropriate for evaluating a dementing process across all conditions and ages. Swift, Dyken, and DuRant (1984) selected tests appropriate to the functional level of each patient they tested, covering the following categories of psychological and adaptive skills: gross motor skills, self-care skills, social skills, verbal intelligence and language skills, visual motor skills and nonverbal intelligence, and academic skills. These authors chose to create an index of psychological disability to permit inter- and intragroup comparisons, given the necessity of using different testing instruments. Assessment of dementia in children, and adults for that matter, presents some additional problems. Besides providing for the patient's deteriorating functions, ensuring the value of the test data requires careful consideration of the patient's stamina and frustration tolerance (Swift et al., 1984). The caretaker or parent interview is particularly valuable, and through the use of adaptive behavior instruments often provides useful data, especially for very low functioning individuals. Selection of an appropriate test of intellectual functions may be a problem when dealing with a wide range of dysfunction due to the progressive nature of dementia. Interviews and adaptive behavior scales provide information that permits the selection of instruments that are most appropriate given the particular patient's current level of functioning.

Laboratory Measures

Newer or standard electrophysiological measures may be important for the assessment of infants and children with dementia. Electroencephalography (EEG) reflects more an electrical measure of CNS status than any specific relation to dementia. Computer-assisted evoked responses to visual, aural, and somatosensory stimuli have an ever-increasing role in the evaluation of a patient with dementia. These tests reflect the ability of pathways to conduct electrical impulses and are not a direct assessment of dementia. It is important to remember that even dying pathways may still conduct electricity and it is the finer short-circuited neural pathways in association areas that may contribute more to the process of dementia than the pathways tested. Likewise, peripheral nerve conduction velocities (NCV) associated with electromyography may provide indirect evidence of the characteristics of a dementing process that may be useful in diagnosis. Some of the dementias are associated with leukodystrophies which, in turn, are associated with peripheral neuropathy, often implicated by these studies.

Cerebrospinal fluid (CSF) analyses, using both standard methods of testing (including analysis of cells [both qualitative and quantitative], protein [qualitative and quantitative], sugar, serological tests, and bacteriological tests) and special CSF determinations (such as specific enzyme analysis of special ultrastructural and histochemical studies of cells in the CSF by electron microscopy), are important in the assessment of the dementias of infancy and childhood. All of these investigations are developed to characterize the diseases or the disease category of the dementia rather than the character of the dementia itself.

One of the most important laboratory tests for the diagnosis of diseases that present as dementia is computer assisted tomography of the head (CT scan). This procedure has revolutionized the practice of neurology in the past several years, for it gives noninvasive information about the morphology of the CNS. It is important to point out, however, that dementia is a functional symptom and morphological study is supportive but only diagnostic of the diseases that cause dementia. A more recent development is the nuclear magnetic resonance (NMR) scan, which to this juncture represents only a refinement of the morphological assessment of the brain in persons who also have dementias. Newer sophisticated advancement in this technique will probably allow for functional assessment of brain activity and thus become a method of assessing dementia as well as the structural basis for it.

A development which has not as yet had an extensive usage in children is called positron emission tomography (PET scan). The PET scan utilizes radio-active-labelled metabolic substances, which are injected and then measured by tomographic techniques. One useful substance is the flurodeoxyglucose (FDG) label, which is an often-used gauge of metabolic activity. The PET-FDG scan has established in adults one of the strongest arguments for differentiating the cortical and subcortical dementias. As an example, by PET scan, Huntington's disease has been shown to be selectively metabolically inactive in the same subcortical areas as predicted by clinical and pathological study. Such is not the fact for cortical dementias like Alzheimer's disease.

The diseases of infancy and childhood presenting as dementia are many. In the previously mentioned review by Dyken and Krawiecki (1983), over 750 separate infantile and childhood neurodegenerative diseases and syndromes were listed. Fully 80% of these show evidence of dementia. The disorders are variable, and some are poorly understood. Many do not have detailed enough pathogenesis to be helpful in further analyses. In this review, the two most commonly encountered, specifically known, neurodegenerative diseases were found to be subacute sclerosing panencephalities (SSPE) and neuronal ceroid lipofuscinosis (NCL). These diseases are well enough known, the pathogenesis is well enough established, and the frequency great enough to be studiable as prototype diseases of dementia. Further details about these prototypical dementias is discussed here.

PROTOTYPICAL DISEASES

Subacute Sclerosing Panencephalitis (SSPE)

SSPE is caused by persistent infection of the brain by a measles or a measles-like virus, with the maximal damage occuring in the white matter (Dyken & DuRant, 1983; Taylor, DuRant, & Dyken, 1984). Host interactions are also important to fully explain the disease. It would appear that the virus enters the susceptible host during a particularly vulnerable period. In most children who develop SSPE, the first contact with measles occurs at less than 4 years of age. The virus or part of the virus seems to escape the natural host defense and, thereafter, harbors itself in glial cells and neurons, where the growth is slow. Spread within the nervous system appears to be by fusion rather than budding.

Faulty budding by SSPE measles virus is due to a lack of synthesis of M protein: because the virus is not able to bud and reach the extracellular space, the virus antigen is protected from the host defense reactions. Ultimately, the host cell is killed, and the virus extrudes. When this extrusion occurs in large quantities, a massive antibody response characteristic of the disease occurs. Regardless of the increased antibody, many viruses remain intracellular and protected and tend to continue to grow and to produce disease.

Clinical presentation of SSPE is fairly stereotyped (Dyken, Swift, & DuRant, 1982). Initial symptoms almost always consist of mental aberrations. These undoubtedly reflect minimal spread of the virus, particularly in the cerebral cortical gray matter, as is observed in many of the persistent viral animal models that resemble SSPE. In SSPE, a second stage develops, consisting of involuntary movements, usually myoclonic, and seizures. Later stages are characterized by continued deterioration in motor and mental abilities, and death, usually within 4 years of onset (Graves, 1984). There are few clinical variations of this course. Rare fulminating cases have been reported, with rapidly developing and progressing first-stage symptoms and signs, leading to death and similar in course to the more acute encephalitic types of animal model syndromes. Occasionally, one encounters subacute cases with a course characterized by remissions and recurrence similar to that of multiple sclerosis, but with shorter and more variable periods of remission. Also, a more-chronic course sometimes develops, with protracted, slow, but steady deterioration. In the more-extended forms, white-matter lesions predominate, whereas in the more acute varieties, a polioencephalitic picture is more likely to be encountered. Various agents or actions with either antiviral or immunopotentiating functions, or both, have been reported to have a beneficial effect on the course of the disease.

The incidence of SSPE may be decreasing in the United States, but not as rapidly as that of natural measles following the national immunization program. Currently, SSPE is not as prevalent in the United States as in some countries that have no programs of national measles immunization.

The dementia of SSPE has been extensively studied longitudinally by Swift et al. (1984) and follows a fairly predictable pattern that cuts across the lines of demarcation suggested by adult neurologists and neuropsychologists into both cortical and subcortical types. SSPE shows rather widespread effects, producing deficits in intellectual, social, motor, and adaptive abilities in all stages assessed by Swift et al. (1984). These investigators found a greater deficit in the nonverbal intellectual area than in the verbal as previously reported (Cobb & Morgan-Hughes, 1968; Donner, Waltimo, Porras, Forsius, & Soukkoven, 1972; Huttenlocher & Mattson, 1979). It is unusual for SSPE patients to be assessed very early in the progress of the disease, most of them not being diagnosed until fairly severely deteriorated.

Neuronal Ceroid Lipofuscinosis (NCL)

Zeman and Dyken (1969) coined the term NCL to refer to many of the diseases previously classified as late infantile, juvenile, and adult amaurotic familial idiocy (Zeman, Donahue, Dyken, & Green, 1970). These are relentlessly progressive disorders characterized by accumulation of lipopigments in the CNS, retina, and other tissues. Dementia, seizures, blindness, and loss of neurological function are characteristic. The cause of NCL remains unknown. Speculation on a defect in peroxidation has not been confirmed, nor is there further evidence to support a defect in polyisoprenal metabolism. The neuronal ceroid lipofuscinoses are some of the more common diseases. It has been estimated that the infantile form of the disorder is the most frequently occurring CNS degenerative disease in Finland. Skin and conjunctival biopsy in CNS usually show NCL as the most prevalent degenerative disease identified by this technique (Arsenio-Nunes, Goutieres, & Aicardi, 1981).

There are several clinical–pathological subtypes of NCL (Dyken, 1982). In all types, tissues harbor characteristic autofluorescent lipopigments that characterize ceroid and lipofuscin. These waxy pigments appear to be breakdown products generated by secondary lysosomes. This feature suggests that abnormal peroxidation of fatty acids is important in the disease and perhaps is the metabolic basis. It has been suggested that seizures may have a deleterious effect on this unstable biochemical system.

The Santavuori-Haltia (Finnish or infantile) type of NCL is characterized by early onset of a fulminating disease process with prominent mental, motor, and visual deterioration and myoclonus. The visual symptoms seem more related to the CNS than to retinal pathology. On postmortem examination, brains are severely atrophic and show autofluorescence and macrophagocytosis. Ultrastructure study shows many osmophilic granular cytoplasmic profiles, which are the probable source of the autofluorescent lipopigments. The Bielschowsky-Jansky (late infantile) form is characterized by early refractory myoclonic seizures, ataxia, and rapid deterioration of mental, motor, and visual functions. After a precipitous onset and rapid deterioration, affected infants may stabilize and linger for years in a vegetative state. Severe atrophy affects the brain. Many types of ultrastructure cytoplasmic profiles are identified within the cell body, with curvilinear types predominating. The Spielmeyer-Sjogren (juvenile) type of NCL progresses more slowly, beginning with behavioral, intellectual, or visual symptoms. Seizures are less severe. Only later in the disease process do seizures invariably worsen, proportional to, but sometimes preceding, the more rapid degeneration of all neurological functions. Examination of tissues shows numerous osmophilic cytoplasmic bodies, which are predominantly of the fingerprint type. In none of the major types of NCL are the ultrastructure cytosomal bodies specific or necessarily limited to the type of clinical presentation. Several other clinical types of NCL also have been described.

Finnish investigators have reported improvement in mental status in the Spielmeyer-Sjogren type of NCL after long-term use of an antioxidant regimen. This treatment was first suggested by Zeman (1974). The present authors' own experience with this form of treatment has been inconclusive. No effect has been observed in 2 patients with the late infantile variant, whereas 4 patients with the juvenile form may have had some slowing of the usual progressive course. Vigorous anticonvulsant treatment is indicated to counter the possible deleterious effects of uncontrolled seizures.

The dementia of NCL depends considerably on the type of NCL encountered. The different forms of NCL each have their associated symptom complexes. For example, while visual deterioration is prominent in several forms, especially the juvenile form, the adult and transitional types may have little or no visual disturbance. The several forms of NCL also differ in terms of their associated mental dysfunction. While infantile forms tend to have a rapid and steady deterioration of mental functions, the juvenile form may have an intermittent progression, with long arrests possible. The dementia encountered with the chronic juvenile form is an interesting one, which is slower than SSPE, and which is associated with more severe cognitive changes but by much fewer mood and affective changes. The adult-onset form may have prominent clinical features such as ataxia, dysarthria, and extrapyramidal motor disturbances lasting for decades, being diagnosed only at autopsy. A transitional form may have little or no obvious mental deterioration. NCL symptoms range from abnormal speech and loss of acquired knowledge to voracious eating and violent temper tantrums. Although development seems normal prior to the appearance of specific neurological symptoms, there are indications that subtle microsymptoms may precede the more classic ones. Kristensen and Lou (1983), in fact, report that the auditory memory-span of two siblings of NCL patients were observed to be impaired before the clinical symptoms became apparent. These authors suggest that mental functions may be impaired by NCL earlier than previously thought.

CONCLUSION

The infantile and childhood dementias need to be studied in the same careful manner as the adult dementias. Yet this study is much more difficult due to the fact that there are ongoing maturational changes that may obscure the deterioration produced by the disease. Instruments for psychological assessment of infants are limited in their ability to measure mental functions and not well correlated with later measurement of cognitive function. As of this time, no large-scale neuropsychological study of specific dementias associated with infancy or childhood has been completed. While several studies cited have used similar test procedures, the progressive deteriorating nature of the neurodegenerative diseases has forced the investigators even within individual studies to use different tests and then attempt to compare performance. While the method chosen by Swift et al. (1984) is a sufficient method for comparison, use of such a rating scale leads to a loss of valuable information. A close scrutiny of the actual progression of changes in mental functions that are found with these diseases will require application of a broad band of tests that have a wide range of sensitivity. Additionally, it will be important to start assessment earlier, when the disease is having its mildest effects. This will depend on early referral to the neurologist and the availability of such testing. Further research into the neuropsychological aspects of these disorders, such as the two more common neurodegenerative diseases (SSPE and NCL), seems an appropriate goal for the future.

REFERENCES

Albert, M., Feldman, R., & Willis, A. (1974). The "subcortical dementia" of progressive supranuclear palsy. *Journal of Neurology, Neurosurgery and Psychiatry, 37,* 121–130.

Arsenio-Nunes, M. L., Goutieres, F., & Aicardi, J. (1981). An ultramicroscopic study of skin dual lonjunctual biopsies in chronic neurologic disorders of childhood. *Annals of Neurology, 9,* 163–173.

Bayley, N. (1969). *Bayley Scales of Infant Development.* Cleveland, OH: Psychological Corporation.

Brazelton, T. (1973). Neonatal behavioral assessment scale. *Clinics in child development medicine* (No. 50). Philadelphia: Lippincott.

Cattell, P. (1940). *Cattell Infant Intelligence Scale.* New York: Psychological Corporation.

Christensen, A. (1979). *Luria's neuropsychological investigation: Test* (2nd ed.). Copenhagen: Munksgaard.

Cobb, W., & Morgan-Hughes, J. (1968). Non-fatal subacute sclerosing leukoencephalitis. *Journal of Neurology, Neurosurgery and Psychiatry, 31,* 115–123.

Cummings, J., & Benson, D. F. (1983). *Dementia: A clinical approach.* Boston: Butterworth.

Cummings, J., & Benson, D. F. (1984). Subcortical dementia: Review of an emerging concept. *Archives of Neurology, 41,* 874–879.

Donner, M., Waltimo, O., Porras, J., Forsius, A., & Soukkoven, A. J. (1972). Subacute sclerosing panencephalitis as a cause of chronic dementia and relapsing brain disorder. *Journal of Neurology, Neurosurgery and Psychiatry, 31,* 180–185.

Dyken, P. (1982). Neuronal ceroid lipofuscinosis. in K. Swaiman & F. Wright (Eds.), *The practice of pediatric neurology* (2nd ed., pp. 902–914). St. Louis: Mosby.

Dyken, P., & DuRant, R. (1983). The cause, pathogenesis and treatment of subacute sclerosing panencephalitis. In J. Hadden, L. Chedid, P. Dukar, F. Spreafico, & D. Willoughby (Eds.), *Advances in immunopharmacology 2* (pp. 205–210). Oxford: Pergamon.

Dyken, P., & Krawiecki, N. (1983). Neurodegenerative diseases of infancy and childhood. *Annals of Neurology, 13,* 351–364.

Dyken, P., Swift, A., & DuRant, R. (1982). Long-term follow-up of patients with subacute sclerosing panencephalitis treated with inosiplex. *Annals of Neurology, 11,* 359–364.

Ellison, P. (1983). The relationship of motor and cognitive function in infancy, pre-school and early school years. *Journal of Clinical Child Psychology, 12,* 81–90.

Golden, C., Moses, J., Jr., Coffman, J., Miller, W., Strider, F., & Graber, B. (1983). *Clinical neuropsychology: Interface with neurologic and psychiatric disorders.* New York: Grune & Stratton.

Graves, M. C. (1984). Subacute sclerosing panencephalitis. *Neurological Clinics of North America, 2,* 267–278.

Herskowitz, J., & Rosman, N. (1982). *Pediatrics, neurology and psychiatry—common ground.* New York: Macmillan.

Huttenlocher, P., & Mattson, R. (1979). Isoprinosine in subacute sclerosing panencephalitis. *Neurology, 29,* 763–771.

Kristensen, K., & Lou, H. (1983). Central nervous system dysfunction as early sign of neuronal ceroid lipofuscinosis (Batten's Disease). *Developmental Medicine & Child Neurology, 25,* 588–590.

McHugh, P., & Folstein, M. (1975). Psychiatric syndromes of Huntington's chorea: A clinical and phenomenologic study. In D. Benson & D. Blumer (Eds.), *Psychiatric aspects of neurologic disease* (pp. 267–285). New York: Grune & Stratton.

Rapin, I. (1976). Progressive genetic–metabolic diseases of the central nervous system in children. *Pediatric Annals, 5,* 313–349.

Rapin, I. (1977). Progressive genetic–metabolic diseases of the central nervous system. In A. Ruduloph (Ed.), *Pediatrics* (16th ed.), pp. 1892–1939). New York: Appleton-Century-Crofts.

Reitan, R. (1974). Cerebral lesions in young children. In R. Reitan & L. Davison (Eds.), *Clinical neuropsychology: Current status and applications* (pp. 53–89). Washington, DC: Hemisphere.

Swift, A., Dyken, P., & DuRant, R. (1984). Psychological follow-up in childhood dementia: A report of studies in subacute sclerosing panencephalitis (SSPE). *Journal of Pediatric Psychology.*

Taylor, W., DuRant, R., & Dyken, P. (1984). Treatment of subacute sclerosing panencephalitis: An overview. *Drug Intelligence and Clinical Phramacy, 18,* 375–381.

Wells, C. (1977). Dementia: Definition and description. In C. Wells (Ed.), *Dementia* (pp. 1–14). Philadelphia: Davis.

Whitehouse, P., Price, D., Clark, A., Coyle, J., & DeLong, M. (1981). Alzheimer's disease: Evidence for selective loss of cholinergic neurons in the nucleus basalis. *Annals of Neurology, 10,* 122–126.

Whitehouse, P., Price, D., Struble, R., Clark, A., Coyle, J., & DeLong, M. (1982). Alzheimer's disease and senile dementia: Loss of neurons in the basal forebrain. *Science, 215,* 1237–1239.

Zeman, W. (1974). Studies on the neuronal ceroid-lipofuscinoses [Presidential address]. *Journal of Neuropathology and Experimental Neurology, 33,* 1–12.

Zeman, W., Donahue, S., Dyken, P., & Green, J. (1970). The neuronal ceroid-lipofuscinoses (Batten–Bogt Syndrome). In P. Vinken & G. Bruyn (Eds.). *Handbook of clinical neurology* (Vol. 10, pp. 522–617). Amsterdam: North-Holland.

Zeman, W., & Dyken, P. (1969). Neuronal ceroid-lipofuscinosis. *Pediatrics, 44,* 570–583.

Chapter 10

Validity and Reliability of Noninvasive Lateralization Measures

SIDNEY J. SEGALOWITZ

Department of Psychology
Brock University
St. Catharines, Ontario,
Canada L2S 3A1

INTRODUCTION

It has become very popular in the lay public and among educational diagnosticians to account for behavioral and learning problems in terms of brain models. Thus, teachers have described children as "right-brained" types, by way of trying to understand the problem that these children show in language arts (Ley & Kaushansky, in press). Similarly, clinicians in developmental clinics, in order to check the possibility of neurological involvement, seek some measures of brain lateralization for language such as dichotic listening. In the absence of any evidence for apparent neurological disorder (such as CT scan or EEG abnormalities) and given a child with normal performance IQ on a Wechsler Intelligence Scale for Children—Revised (WISC-R) but a depressed verbal IQ and difficulty in reading, it may be reasonable to suspect a functional difficulty in terms of brain organization, rather than tissue ill-health. It is tempting to infer, from a language difficulty, some abnormality of the language hemisphere, or some abnormality in the organization of language in the brain. As Bryden and Saxby (see Chapter 4 of this volume) argue, such a position relating hemisphere specialization and developmental issues is popular although difficult to support empirically.

CHILD NEUROPSYCHOLOGY, VOL. 1

It would be ideal to determine the pattern of hemispherc specialization in a specific child by means of some test. Unfortunately, giving a dichotic listening, visual half-field, or any other test to the child may not be adequate to infer brain organization in that individual. The strength of the conclusion concerning brain lateralization depends on the validity of the measure (what the resulting score actually reflects) and its reliability. These two issues are reviewed in this chapter.

VALIDITY OF LATERALIZATION MEASURES

There is no doubt that language is asymmetrically represented in the brain and that in the vast majority of people, it is the left hemisphere that is most involved in language function (Bryden, 1982; Segalowitz, 1983). The clinical evidence that disorders of phonology, syntax, and semantics are more likely to occur with damage to the left than to the right hemisphere is overwhelming (Segalowitz, 1983; Blumstein, 1981), although there are other processes associated with communication that have a basis in right-hemisphere functioning (Foldi, Cicone, & Gardner, 1983). Given this foundation, the validity of the various measures purporting to reflect hemispheric dominance for language stems from several sources: (1) a good correlation between the measure and some definitional index of cerebral specialization, such as the incidence of aphasia after unilateral brain damage; (2) their robustness in producing left-hemisphere superiority on language tasks when appropriate (e.g., with right handers) and a less-strong effect when not expected (e.g., with left handers); and (3) agreement with other measures already accepted as reflecting language dominance. Similarly, a right-hemisphere superiority effect should be obtained when certain nonverbal processes are tested, although the strength of this effect and the prevalence even among right handers may be somewhat less (Hecaen, DeAgostini, & Monzon-Montes, 1981).

These three sources of validation for lateralization tasks are not of equal value. The best test of a measure involves the first criterion: whether or not it correlates well with a clinically validated measure of hemisphere function. In addition to the incidence of functional loss after unilateral damage, a second clinically definitive test is the Wada test of sodium amytal injection (Wada & Rasmussen, 1960). Unfortunately, very few standard laterality measures are validated against either of these. First, not many researchers have access to sodium amytal-tested patients. In these patients, it can be clearly known whether or not a patient has left-hemisphere, right-hemisphere, or bilaterally represented language. Other functions are rarely examined. Second, some measures may not be used profitably with brain-damaged patients—that is, after the function in question is lost—and testing the patient before a stroke or trauma occurs requires enormous resources. Thus, the usefulness of many lateralization measures depends on the preceding items 2 and 3, coupled with several aspects of face validity, including the nature of the stimuli, the processing required, and the known physiological requirements of the task. In contrast to these measures, although the mechanism of the dichotic-listening task is less well accepted than those of other lateralization measures, the test has been better validated against definitive clinical measures.

Dichotic Listening

The dichotic-listening test consists of having subjects listen through headphones to two different sounds simultaneously, one to each ear. The sounds should be of equal loudness, onset, and duration, as differences in these factors will affect the ear advantage shown (Berlin & Cullen, 1977; Bryden, 1982). When the stimuli are speech sounds, the right ear has an advantage among right-handers, who presumably have language represented in the left hemisphere (Rasmussen & Milner, 1977). Conversely, some nonverbal sounds have produced a left-ear advantage. The generally accepted model of dichotic listening is that when there is simultaneous input to the two ears, each ear has faster and more reliable transmission to the contralateral hemisphere, although other hypotheses have been suggested about the physiological mechanisms involved (Kinsbourne, 1972; Geffen & Quinn, 1984).

The original validation of the dichotic-listening test involved giving the test to a clinical population, whose language representation was known from sodium-amytal testing. Kimura (1961) found that on average, patients with left-hemisphere language had a right-ear advantage for reporting dichotically presented digits and those with right-hemisphere language had a left-ear advantage. The effect was independent of hand preference. Although there are many parameters in her test that have come under close scrutiny (Bryden, 1982), the basic finding has held up. More recently, for example, Geffen and Caudrey (1981) validated a dichotic-listening monitoring task against a patient group whose language laterality had been ascertained by testing after unilaterally administered electroconvulsive therapy.

Visual Half-Field

The other major lateralization testing measure is the visual half-field technique. This test involves presenting information to one visual field only. Because of the crossing of the retinal projections from each nasal visual half-field, each hemisphere receives direct information from only the opposite visual half-field, through both eyes (Bryden, 1982; Beaumont, 1982). There is some controversy as to whether or not there is a central field that is shared by both hemispheres[1]; however, such a shared field would be relatively small. The visual half-field task requires fixating on a central point, perceiving a stimulus presented for less than 150 msec, and then responding to it.

The task has been validated against split-brain patients who show an ability to read aloud words in the right visual field but not in the left visual field (Sperry, 1968). Because the left visual field projects directly to the right hemisphere, a split-brain patient who has no corpus callosum intact cannot transfer the information to the left, speaking hemisphere. Numerous studies have been done with the visual half-field technique on normal subjects, with results more or less in the expected direction. The many results not conforming to the simple expectation indicate that there are factors other than visual half-field projection that affect the results (Bryden, 1982; Beaumont, 1982).

Other Measures

Validation of the other measures used to assess hemisphere specialization rely mainly on the last 2 criteria listed at the beginning of this section. Face validity has played a large role in the development of these measures. For example, manual tasks such as the dichhaptic measure (Witelson, 1974) and dual-processing finger-tapping tasks (Kinsbourne & Cook, 1971) have not been validated against clinically verified lateralization measures, although the contralateral control of the hand not only is well-known clinically (Penfield & Rasmussen, 1968), but also has been demonstrated in split-brain patients (Sperry, 1968).

Psychophysiological measures also have a face validity of sorts, but the interpretation is often difficult, such as for asymmetric galvanic skin response (GSR) (Lacroix & Comper, 1979), event-related potentials (ERPs) (Gaillard & Ritter, 1983) and some brain blood-flow measures (Wood, 1980). One popular measure that allows the subject to be engaged in normal cognitive tasks is asymmetric EEG alpha. Such slow-wave activity is taken to reflect the level of "idling" or noncognitive involvement. Asymmetric measures indicate that one hemisphere is more cognitively engaged in the task than the other (Galin, Johnstone, & Herron, 1978). Validation of this measure can be found in a series of tests with sodium-amytal-tested and split-brain patients whose language laterality was known (Butler & Glass, 1976). During mental arithmetic, the subjects consistently showed less alpha on the side known to be dominant for language.

As with the dichotic listening and visual half-field techniques, however, it

---

[1]Anatomical studies of visual pathways of monkeys suggest at least a 1° area of overlap (Stone, Leicester, & Sherman, 1973; Bunt, Minckler, & Johanson, 1977), but behavioral studies with human split-brain patients suggest no overlap (Gazzaniga, 1970; Blakemore, 1970; Mitchell & Blakemore, 1969). Both may be correct because some connections in the visual system may be nonfunctional due to contralateral inhibition (Guillery, 1972).

seems that no two laboratories use the same testing materials and procedure. The history of the field would lead one to question the construct validity of these new measures. Often it is the case that the manipulation of some seemingly unimportant factor changes the effect radically and forces us to re-examine the theoretical bases of our notion of lateralization (Hardyck, Tzeng, & Wang, 1978). Thus, it is difficult to be confident of the validity of any particular laterality test without extensive testing of it. New variations are not guaranteed to share the validity of the old form. Partly for this reason, diagnostic use of the noninvasive laterality measures to determine hemisphere specialization has always been a chancy affair. Performance on all of the noninvasive measures are influenced by the subject's strategies, previous knowledge, and so forth, and therefore any measure of lateralization from such tasks reflects more than brain organization. This aspect of validity is discussed here at greater length later.

There is a constructive aspect to the variability of testing methods across laboratories, and that is that with the many measures available, we are in a better position to examine the complexities of hemisphere specialization for subtle aspects of cognitive information processing. When agreement is found across numerous measures, one can feel some confidence in the finding.

RELIABILITY OF LATERALIZATION MEASURES

Any psychometrically useful test must have a high demonstrated level of test–retest reliability. As clinical or diagnostic tools, the noninvasive measures of hemisphere specialization rate rather poorly. Individual measures correlate poorly with the results of other tests, and correlate only moderately with retests on the same measure. This low reliability may stem from (1) strategy or attentional shifts with practice, and (2) inconsistencies in what the tests measure.

Because there is a plethora of test materials for each lateralization technique, it is impossible to generalize with respect to a single technique. It may be that some more reliable task will be devised at any moment, or that if two tasks are similar but not exactly identical they will differ in their reliabilities. This low individual reliability does not mean that group tests are equally unreliable. On the contrary, group reliability is rather high for many of the tasks. For most research purposes, group reliability is all that is needed. For diagnostic work, individual reliability is of prime concern.

Dichotic Listening

More test–retest reliability checks have been carried out on dichotic listening tasks than on any other lateralization measure. The results range from discouraging to rather hopeful. We will examine the various dichotic listening tasks along two dimensions: stimulus choice and response procedure. The range of stimuli includes those that require perception of nonsense syllables, of digits, of a long list of words, of environmental sounds, of music, and of synthesized sounds. The response procedure may involve reporting orally or on a written form what was heard (free recall), matching the target stimuli to a set of choices (matching), reporting what appeared in one ear only on some trials and then the other ear on other trials (directed attention), reporting whether or not a particular word belongs to a preset category (semantic categorization), or indicating when a particular target or targets are heard (monitoring). It is clear that a vast array of possible dichotic-listening tasks exists, and not all have been examined with respect to reliability. When such test–retest comparisons are done, one can derive either a Pearson product–moment correlation coefficient from the results, based on some derived lateralization index, such as right ear − left ear (RE − LE) correct, or a ratio measure such as (RE − LE) / (RE + LE) or similar score (Marshall, Caplan, & Holmes, 1975; Bryden & Sprott, 1981). This reflects how well testing predicts both the direction and degree of the laterality result on the next testing. Another way of reflecting reliability is to construct a contingency table indicating how well one testing predicts the direction on the next testing—that is, how consistent subjects are across the two test sessions.

Despite the fact that at least 95% of right-handers have language represented in the left hemisphere, traditional dichotic listening tasks only produce a right-ear advantage in from 60 to 85% of the right-handed subjects. This usually produces a statistically significant right-ear advantage over the left ear. This reduction from the expected 95% may be because of a large fluctuation in individual performance on the task or because of some stable neuropsychological reason. Blumstein, Goodglass, and Tartter (1975) examined this issue of stability by testing 36 right-handed male subjects twice on 3 dichotic-listening tapes: one of consonant–vowel (CV) nonsense syllables where the consonants varied, a similar tape where the vowels varied, and a third where 2 short musical melodies were presented simultaneously and the subject had to identify them among four following melodies. The group effects were clear: The consonants tape produced a statistically very strong right-ear advantage, the vowels tape a weaker right-ear advantage, and the music tape a very strong left-ear advantage. These group results were consistent over both test sessions, which were at least 1 week apart. However, the test–retest correlations were far from useful in a predictive way: .74 for consonants, .21 for vowels, and .46 for music. In addition, in the three conditions, from 19 to 29% of the subjects changed ear advantage from the first test session to the second. This inconsistency may be due to a number of factors, discussed here later, and it should be seen in light of the 10–14% of subjects who consistently showed the "wrong" asymmetry.

Porter, Troendle, and Berlin (1976) similarly tested 8 subjects once a week for 8 weeks on a similar consonant-oriented CV tape. Six subjects showed a consistent right-ear advantage, one a consistent left-ear advantage, and one an inconsistent ear advantage. Ryan and McNeil (1974) also found the consonant-oriented CV tape to be a good group measure, while the test–retest correlation was at most 0.84.

Bakker, Van der Vlugt, and Claushuis (1978) presented children from kindergarten to grade five with four dichotic-listening tapes with digits as stimuli. One tape had 2 pairs on each trial, another 3 pairs and the others 4 pairs. Consistent ear advantages were found 75–81% of the time (depending on which tape is used), but the consistency was not due to the right-handers in the group. The right-handers, left-handers, and inconsistent-handers all were within the 75–81% consistency range. The test–retest correlations (depending on tape and age range) varied from 0.25 to 0.94, with no consistent effect due to tape or age. These results and those from other studies examining reliability of dichotic listening are given in Table 1.

A number of factors seem to be important in affecting the resulting reliability of dichotic-listening testing. One factor influencing reliability may be, not surprisingly, the amount of time between test session. For example, Schulman-Galambos (1977) found only 10% of her subjects were inconsistent, but the figure is based on a comparison of performance on the first half versus the second half of the test (in the same session). Similarly, Orsini (1984) found a correlation of 94% when the two tests were 1 hour apart, but Hines, Fennell, Bowers, and Satz (1980) found much lower reliability on the same tape when the retesting followed by 1 day or more. Wexler and Halwes (1983) also retested their subjects the day after the first testing and had a high test–retest correlation of 0.85. In contrast, Eling, Marshall, and van Galen (1981) retested their subjects at least 6 months later and the correlations were much smaller. Of course, there were also other differences between these studies that may account for the difference in reliabilities, such as age of subjects and the task requirements.

Another factor concerns the choice of stimuli. It appears that the tasks that focus on the phonetic level of the speech sounds, as opposed to word meaning or word identification, produce higher reliabilities. This may be because such stimuli allow for fewer differences in subjects' strategies, thus reducing the possibility that individual subjects change the cognitive processes they brought to perform the task. In addition, it may be that phonetic aspects of speech are more closely tied to left-hemisphere processes, whereas word processing may allow some degree of right hemisphere involvement.

This factor receives additional support from a study by Obrzut, Obrzut, and Boliek (1985). They presented children with three dichotic listening tests with varying stimuli: words, digits, and CV syllables. They presented each type in three conditions: with instructions for free recall, for directing attention to the right ear, and for directing attention to the left ear. For the words and digits tapes, the directed-attention instructions profoundly changed the ear advantage,

TABLE 1

Summary of reliability studies on dichotic listening[a]

Authors	Stimuli	Correlation	% of Ss consistent	Consistently deviant subjects
Bakker, Van der Vlugt, & Claushuis (1978)	Digits: 2 pairs	.25–.94	78.5%	
	3 pairs	.50–.86	75%	
	4 pairs (16 trials)	.50–.83	81%	
	4 pairs (32 trials)	.67–.91		
Blumstein, Goodglass, & Tartter (1975)	Consonants CV	0.74	71%	11%
	vowels CV	0.21	54%	14%
	music	0.46	81%	14%
Caroll (1978)	Words (English)	.65–.80		
	words (Spanish)	.49–.92		
Eling (1983)	Monitoring for rhyme:			
	% correct	.73	80%	
	reaction time (RT)	.70	70%	
	Semantic category:			
	%	.56	72%	
	RT	.45	60%	
Eling, Marshall, & van Galen (1981)	Monitoring for rhyme	−.02 to .53	60–80%	
	Semantic category	−.09 to .14	65–90%	
Fennel, Bowers, & Satz (1977a)	Words (left handers)	.29–.82 (within ear accuracy)[b]		
Fennel, Bowers, & Satz (1977b)	Words (right handers)	.45–.90 (within ear accuracy)[b]		
Geffen & Caudry (1981)	Monitoring for /dog/	—	81% (accuracy) 73% (RT)	
Hines, Fennel, Bowers, & Satz (1980)	Words	.35–.77 (left-handers) .62–.82 (right-handers)		
Hines & Satz (1974)	Digits	.86 (split-half)		
Koomar & Cermak (1981)	Consonant CV	—	93%	
	Digits	—	80%	
	Consistency across both tasks		53%	
Orsini (1984)	Words (same as Hines, Fennell, Bowers, & Satz, 1980)	.94	97%	

TABLE 1 (*Continued*)

Authors	Stimuli	Correlation	% of Ss consistent	Consistently deviant subjects
Pizzamiglio, Pascalio, & Vignati (1974)	Digits	—	30%	
Porter, Troendle, & Berlin (1976)	Consonant CV	—	87.5%	12.5%
Ryan & McNeil (1974)	Consonant CV	0.80		
Schulman-Galambos (1977)	Words	—	90%	—
Shankweiler & Studdert-Kennedy (1975)	Consonant CV	.70		
Teng (1981)	Word	−.60		
	Syllable	.60		
	Digits (free recall)	.36		
	Digits (directed attn)	−.11		
Wexler & Halwes (1983)	Fused rhymed words	.85		
Wexler, Halwes, & Heninger (1981)	Consonant VCV	.91		
Zurif & Bryden (1969)	Digits	.49 (between free recall and directed attention conditions)		

[a] When a range of values is given for correlation entries, the study involved a number of subject groups, e.g., at different ages.

[b] Correlations on degree of ear advantage given in Hines, Fennell, Bowers, & Satz (1980).

as one would expect. In the CV condition, however, directed attention hardly changed the responding score at all, with the right-ear advantage remaining throughout.

How Shall an Individual Subject be Judged?

Consistency of ear advantage can be adjudged in a number of ways, the most common one being a reflection of which ear had an absolute advantage. As indicated earlier, this does not produce good consistency on retest. Other criteria exist, though, for deciding whether or not a subject has a left-ear advantage or a right-ear advantage: one could either use a dividing point different from zero asymmetry or allow for an undecided group when the ear difference does not reach a specified size. For example, Wexler and Halwes (1983) reported that 49% of their right-handed subjects had an ear difference on their fused-rhymed-words tasks great enough to be significant at the $p < .10$ level on a chi-square test. Of these, 98% had a right-ear advantage. Loosening up the criteria to a $p < .30$ confidence level allows 62% of the subjects to be classified, of whom 97% have right-ear advantages. With classification of all subjects, 85% had the expected right-ear advantage. By making the contingency for an acceptably large right-ear advantage more exacting, one can be more sure of decisions on individual subjects. Wexler and Halwes (1983) suggested a criterion of $p < .10$ as appropriate for producing a distribution of left-ear advantages and right-ear advantages that is in agreement with the neurological literature for speech dominance. The disadvantage of this increased certainty is that a large percentage of subjects are not classified at all, which may obviate the usefulness of the technique in clinical settings.

Visual Half-Field

The visual half-field technique is probably as popular a technique for measuring lateralization among university students as dichotic listening, but the equipment required for it makes it less useful in other settings (e.g., schools, hospitals). The variety of stimulus configurations possible is at least as great as for the dichotic listening paradigm, but fewer test–retest reliability studies have been done, and those produce reliability levels quite a bit below those for dichotic listening.

Hines and Satz (1974) report a split-half correlation of .46 for visual half-field asymmetries for digits, while Hines et al. (1980) reported test–retest correlations ranging from 0.35 to 0.82. In general, the more time between test sessions, the lower the correlation. See Table 2 for a summary of these results.

Other Measures

The test–retest reliability of various other measures has been reported. Hiscock and Kinsbourne (1980) followed up a set of children a year after the original testing. They looked for the asymmetrical effect of a verbal interference task on left- versus right-hand finger-tapping. Although the number of children showing the predicted effect was consistent over age groups (3 to 11 years) and test session, the correlations between the lateralization effects shown in the two sessions was only 0.06 to 0.10. Green (1985), however, found considerably higher correlations in a similar paradigm with adult subjects who received the test and retest in the same session ($r = 0.77$ and 0.47 on two verbal tasks).

Bakan and Strayer (1973) reported $r = 0.78$ for conjugate lateral eye move-

TABLE 2

Summary of reliability studies on visual half-field (VHF) tasks[a]

Authors	Stimuli/task	Correlation
Chiarello, Dronkers, & Hardyck (1984)	Lexical decision	.69–.81 (depending on metric used)
Fennel, Bowers, & Satz (1977a)	Letters (left-handers) (Correlations on degree of VHF asymmetry given in Hines, Fennel, Bowers & Satz, 1980)	.16–.91 within VHFs.
Fennel, Bowers, & Satz (1977b)	Letters (right-handers) (Correlations on degree of VHF asymmetry given in Hines, Fennel, Bowers & Satz, 1980)	0.0–.86 within VHFs.
Hines, Fennel, Bowers, & Satz (1980)	Letters	.62–.82 (right-handers) .35–.77 (left-handers)
Hines & Satz (1974)	Digits	.46 (split-half)
Segalowitz & Orr (unpublished data)	CVC nonsense syllables	
	Right-handers	.32–.67
	Left-handers	.41–.77
	Clock faces:	
	Right-handers	.19–.64
	Left-handers	−.35 to .19
Zurif & Bryden (1969)	Letters	.51 (between free report and ordered report conditions)

[a] When a range of values is given for correlation entries, the study involved a number of subject groups or conditions.

ments (CLEMs) when subjects explained the meanings of proverbs. Unfortunately, because no comparable right hemisphere task was given, there is no way of knowing whether or not the CLEM score may be reflecting general movement patterns of the individual subjects rather than a metric of cerebral specialization.

The experimental literature on the averaged ERPs taken from EEG provides an enormous number of stimulus–task paradigms, with recording site also varying as a key parameter. Although some clinically standard techniques do provide highly reliable ERPs across subjects (Callaway, Tueting, & Koslow, 1978), reports of test–retest reliability of hemisphere asymmetry-related ERPs are rare (Low, Rogers, Purves, & Dunn, 1979). This is probably partly due to the difficulty of obtaining such neuroelectric asymmetries in the first place and the small degree of asymmetry compared to the size of the entire signal.

EEG alpha band (8–12 hz) amplitude differences have been examined for reliability. Ehrlichman and Wiener (1979) tested 11 right-handed subjects on two occasions each, 1 week apart on four tasks judged to require left-hemisphere processing and on four for the right hemisphere processing. The differences in the left–right ratios were compared across test sessions, producing an $r = 0.88$. Similarly, Amochaev and Salamy (1979) tested 6 subjects on 3 occasions each on 7 tasks. Although these authors did not report the test–retest correlations, the left–right asymmetry alpha values were provided. Writing, block design, maze, and arithmetic tasks had correlations over the first and second test sessions of 0.50, 0.61, 0.89, and 0.91, respectively.

Cross-Task Correlations

If one expects the dichotic listening and visual half-field tasks to reflect hemisphere specialization, then confidence would be bolstered if these tasks produced similar results. Such cross-modal lateralization testing has been examined a number of times with poor results (see Table 3). Generally speaking, the percentage of people showing the same lateral advantage on both tasks is far from 100%, and in fact approaches 50–60%. This lack of agreement may be due to several factors. First of all, each test often has a low reliability, as shown in the previous section. Second, the tasks may tap neurolinguistic processes that are lateralized somewhat differently. Reading and listening, for example, may each require

TABLE 3

Summary of reliability studies correlating dichotic listening results with VHF results[a]

	Stimuli			
Authors	Dichotic listening	VHF	Correlation	% Consistency
Bryden (1965)	Digits	Letters	.19	54%
Bryden (1973)	Digits	Letters		42%
Fennel, Bowers, & Satz (1977a)	Words	Letters		50–70%
Fennel, Bowers, & Satz (1977b)	Words	Letters		25–81%
Hines, Fennel, Bowers, & Satz (1980)	Words	Letters	.39	
Hines & Satz (1974)	Digits	Digits	(right-handers)	63%
			(left-handers)	63%
Zurif & Bryden (1969)	Digits	Letters	.01–.18	

[a] When a range of values is given for correlation entries, the study involves a number of subject groups.

accessing the language system, but the specific language-related decoding processes may vary across people in how much they rely on the processes of each hemisphere. Third, the nonlanguage requirements of the tasks differ considerably: dichotic listening involves difficulties in output and memory besides the decoding difficulty; visual half-field tasks strain the system more on input and on interpreting a degraded stimulus (because they are presented to the periphery for an unusually short period of time) than on memory (Bryden, 1982). One should not be surprised, then, that the results of dichotic listening and visual half-field testing are often divergent. The reliability for each is relatively low, and their validity (what each measures) differs.

PROBLEMS WITH NONINVASIVE LATERALIZATION MEASURES AS DIAGNOSTIC TOOLS

As mentioned, there is a considerable discrepancy between the distribution of hemispheric specialization for language in the population as measured by the noninvasive lateralization tasks discussed and by the figures from the clinic. Moreover, the patient data do not seem to support the existence of a large group of bilaterally represented people, who might correspond to the subjects who are inconsistent upon retest with dichotic listening or some visual half-field task. There is no reason to think that the reliability of the clinical data is anything less than 100%, although obviously it is impossible to test whether or not specific brain damage produces a consistent effect in an individual. The conclusion, then, must be one of the following: (1) there is a high error of measurement in most lateralization tasks; (2) the tests measure aspects of brain organization that reflect processes beyond those of the hemispheric specialization one is interested in; or (3) the pattern of hemispheric specialization for the cognitive requirements of the task changes within individuals over the hours or days between testings. There is no known physiological basis or evidence for the third possibility, except in developmental studies involving much greater periods of time (Goldman, 1974).

Both of the first two are probably at play. In fact, it may be difficult to distinguish them empirically because some uncontrolled aspect of performance in a dichotic listening test, for instance, may add to the experimental error term, although in principle the aspect may be controlled. For example, it may be that some subjects approach the retest situation differently from others. Unless their attentional strategy is controlled (as in directed-attention instructions; see Bryden, Munhall, & Allard, 1983), some may purposefully change attentional direction just to try to improve their performance, or to make it more interesting. Others may not change strategy at all. Such changes would, of course, lower test–retest reliability, yet this test–retest variation in asymmetry does not reflect anything about brain organization.

There is good evidence that attentional asymmetries exist that are not related to hemispheric specialization of function. Levine, Banich, and Koch-Weser (1984) found that subjects have a generalized visual half-field asymmetry that contributes to the asymmetry shown in a visual half-field task. Similarly, Bryden (1978) discusses how, in a dichotic-listening task, left- and right-handers tend to report more from the ear on the same side as their preferred hand independent of the hemisphere that actually is language dominant. If such trait characteristics influence the ear or visual half-field advantage on lateralization tests, one should expect that the number of people showing left-hemisphere language on noninvasive lateralization measures should differ from the clinical results.

All measures are susceptible to such individual differences (Segalowitz & Bryden, 1983; Segalowitz, 1985). Even psychophysical measures, such as EEG, are influenced by lateral attentional processes (Watson, Andriola, & Heilman, 1977). Any attempt, then, to make a clinical judgment for an individual on the basis of a single lateralization score presumes that these sources of variation may be ignored. Single-case analysis of lateralization is a difficult task because (1) the asymmetry must be shown to be stable, and (2) the asymmetry must be shown to reflect hemisphere specialization for the function under investigation and not some artifact of strategy. The first factor may be accounted for by multiple testing, such as giving a dichotic listening task six times on different days. The second factor requires the use of a relative measure—that is, a score that reflects the performance of each hemisphere for the cognitive function in question without the strategy artifacts usually included along with it.

Thus, for example, if it is speech lateralization that concerns us, one should include a similar task with nonverbal stimuli. Any difference in asymmetry between these two tasks must be due to speech processing and not some artifacts that influence attentional bias. Statistical methods can then be applied to these results (see Dywan & Segalowitz, in press, for a fuller discussion of these issues). If, however, the reliability for one of the tasks is low compared to the other, the difference score is going to show low stability as well. Any attempt to interpret lateralization scores for an individual requires attention to these issues.

SUMMARY

The most popular lateralization measures have shown considerable stability as group measures and, for the most part, have been shown to reflect validly cerebral specialization. The stability, and therefore usefulness, of the measures as indications of the pattern of hemisphere specialization in individuals is considerably poorer on the whole, although there is no reason to conclude that in principle a psychometrically useful measure of brain lateralization is unattainable. Until that time, however, indices using noninvasive lateralization methods should be treated statistically only, although this can be done in the context of a clinical case study.

REFERENCES

Amochaev, A., & Salamy, A. (1979). Stability of EEG laterality effects. *Psychophysiology, 16,* 242–246.
Bakan, P., & Strayer, F. F. (1973). On reliability of conjugate lateral eye movements. *Perceptual and Motor Skills, 367,* 429–430.
Bakker, D. J., Van der Vlugt, H., & Claushuis, M. (1978). The reliability of dichotic ear asymmetry in normal children. *Neuropsychologia, 16,* 753–757.
Beaumont, J. G. (Ed.). (1982). *Divided visual field studies of cerebral organization.* London: Academic Press.
Berlin, C. I., & Cullen, J. K. (1977). Acoustic problems in dichotic listening tasks. In S. J. Segalowitz & F. A. Gruber (Eds.), *Language development and neurological theory.* New York: Academic Press.
Blakemore, C. (1970). Binocular depth perception and the optic chiasm. *Vision Research, 10,* 43–47.
Blumstein, S. E. (1981). Neurolinguistic disorders: Language–brain relationships. In S. B. Filskov & T. J. Boll (Eds.), *Handbook of clinical neuropsychology.* New York: Wiley.
Blumstein, S., Goodglass, H., & Tartter, V. (1975). The reliability of ear advantage in dichotic listening. *Brain and Language, 2,* 226–236.
Bryden, M. P. (1965). Tachistoscopic recognition, handedness and cerebral dominance. *Neuropsychologia, 3,* 1–8.
Bryden, M. P. (1973). Perceptual asymmetry in vision: Relation to handedness, and speech lateralization. *Cortex, 9,* 418–432.
Bryden, M. P. (1978). Strategy effects in the assessment of hemispheric asymmetry. In G. Underwood (Ed.), *Strategies of information processing.* London: Academic Press.
Bryden, M. P. (1982). *Laterality: Functional asymmetry in the intact brain.* New York: Academic Press.
Bryden, M. P., Munhall, K., & Allard, F. (1983). Attentional biases and the right-ear effect in dichotic listening. *Brain and Language, 18,* 236–248.
Bryden, M. P., & Sprott, D. A. (1981). Statistical determination of degree of laterality. *Neuropsychologia, 19,* 571–582.
Bunt, A., Minckler, D., & Johanson, G. (1977). Demonstration of bilateral projection of the central retina of the monkey with horseradish peroxidase neuronography. *Journal of Comparative Neurology, 171,* 619–630.
Butler, S. R., & Glass, A. (1976). EEG correlates of cerebral dominance. *Advances in Psychobiology, 3,* 219–272.
Callaway, E., Tueting, P., & Koslow, S. H. (1978). *Event-related brain potentials in man.* New York: Academic Press.
Caroll, F. (1978). *Cerebral lateralization and adult second language learning.* Unpublished doctoral dissertation, University of New Mexico, Albuquerque.
Chiarello, C., Dronkers, N. F., & Hardyck, N. F. (1984). Choosing sides: On the variability of language lateralization in normal subjects. *Neuropsychologia, 22,* 367–373.
Dywan, J., & Segalowitz, S. J. (in press). The role of the case study in neuropsychological research. In J. Valsiner (Ed.), *The role of the individual subject in scientific psychology.* New York: Plenum.

Ehrlichman, H., & Wiener, M. S. (1979). Consistency of task-related EEG asymmetries. *Psychophysiology, 16,* 247–252.

Eling, P. (1983). Consistency of ear advantage: An improvement due to increase in presentation rate. *Neuropsychologia, 21,* 419–423.

Eling, P., Marshall, J., & van Galen, G. (1981). The development of language lateralization as measured by dichotic listening. *Neuropsychologia, 19,* 767–773.

Fennell, E. B., Bowers, D., & Satz, P. (1977a). Within-modal and cross-modal reliabilities of two laterality tests among left handers. *Perceptual and Motor Skills, 45,* 451–456.

Fennell, E., Bowers, D., & Satz, P. (1977b). Within-modal and cross-modal reliabilities of two laterality tests. *Brain and Language, 4,* 63–69.

Foldi, N. S., Cicone, M., & Gardner, H. (1983). Pragmatic aspects of communication in brain damaged patients. In S. J. Segalowitz (Ed.), *Language functions and brain organization.* New York: Academic Press.

Gaillaird, A. W. K., & Ritter, W. (Eds.). (1983). *Tutorials in event-related potential research: Endogenous components.* Amsterdam: North-Holland.

Galin, D., Johnstone, J., & Herron, J. (1978). Effects of task difficulty on EEG measures of cerebral engagement. *Neuropsychologia, 16,* 461–472.

Gazzaniga, M. S. (1970). *The bisected brain.* New York: Appleton-Century-Crofts.

Geffen, G., & Caudrey, D. (1981). Reliability and validity of the dichotic monitoring test for language laterality. *Neuropsychologia, 19,* 413–423.

Geffen, G., & Quinn, K. (1984). Hemispheric specialization and ear advantages in processing speech. *Psychological Bulletin, 96,* 273–291.

Goldman, P. S. (1974). Functional development of the prefrontal cortex in early life and the problem of neuronal plasticity. *Experimental Neurology, 32,* 366–387.

Green, A. (1985). *Lateralization in monolingual and bilateral males at different levels of Spanish as a second language: Use of the concurrent activities paradigm.* Unpublished doctoral dissertation, Kent State University, Columbus, OH.

Guillery, R. W. (1972). Binocular competition in the control of geniculate cell growth. *Journal of Comparative Neurology, 144,* 177–180.

Hardyck, C., Tzeng, O. J. L., & Wang, W. S. Y. (1978). Cerebral lateralization of function and bilingual decision processes: Is thinking lateralized? *Brain and Language, 5,* 56–71.

Hecaen, H., DeAgostini, M., & Monzon-Montes, A. (1981). Cerebral organization in left-handers. *Brain and Language, 12,* 261–284.

Hines, D., Fennell, E., Bowers, D., & Satz, F. (1980). Left-handers show greater test–retest variability in auditory and visual asymmetry. *Brain and Language, 10,* 208–211.

Hines, D., & Satz, P. (1974). Cross-modal asymmetries in perception related to asymmetry in cerebral function. *Neuropsychologia, 12,* 239–247.

Hiscock, M., & Kinsbourne, M. (1980). Asymmetry of verbal–manual time sharing in children: A follow-up study. *Neuropsychologia, 18,* 151–162.

Kimura, D. (1961). Cerebral dominance and the perception of verbal stimuli. *Canadian Journal of Psychology, 15,* 166–175.

Kinsbourne, M. (1972). Eye and head turning indicates cerebral lateralization. *Science, 176,* 539–541.

Kinsbourne, M., & Cook, J. (1971). Generalized and lateralized effects of concurrent verbalization on a unimanual skill. *Quarterly Journal of Experimental Psychology, 23,* 341–345.

Koomar, J. A., & Cermak, S. A. (1981). Reliability of dichotic listening using two stimulus formats with normal and learning-disabled children. *American Journal of Occupational Therapy, 35,* 456–463.

Lacroix, J. M., & Comper, P. (1979). Lateralization in the electrodermal system as a function of cognitive/hemispheric manipulations. *Psychophysiology, 16,* 116–129.

Levine, S. C., Banich, M. T., & Koch-Weser, M. (1984). Variations in patterns of lateral asymmetry among dextrals. *Brain and Cognition, 3,* 317–334.

Ley, R. G., & Kaushansky, M. (in press). The 4Rs: Readin', 'riting, 'rithmetic and the right hemisphere: A review of the application of the brain laterality model to education. In A. A. Sheikh (Ed.). *Imagery and the education process.* Farmingdale, NY: Baywood.

Low, M. D., Rogers, S. J., Purves, S. J., & Dunn, H. G. (1979). Spontaneous and evoked cerebral electrical activity and localization of language function in children with minimal cerebral dysfunction. In D. Lehmann & E. Callaway (Eds.). *Human evoked poientials.* New York: Plenum.

Marshall, J. C., Caplan, D., & Holmes, J. M. (1975). The measure of laterality. *Neuropsychologia, 13,* 315–321.

Mitchell, D., & Blakemore, C. (1969). Binocular depth perception and the corpus callosum. *Vision Research, 10,* 49–54.

Obrzut, J. E., Obrzut, A., & Boliek, C. A. (1985). *The effect of stimulus type and directed attention on dichotic listening with children.* Paper presented at the 13th annual International Neuropsychological Society Meeting, San Diego.

Orsini, D. L. (1984). *Early brain injury and lateral development.* Unpublished doctoral dissertation, State University of New York, Stony Brook.

Penfield, W., & Rasmussen, T. (1960). *The cerebral cortex of man.* New York: Hafner.

Pizzamiglio, L., Pascalio, C., & Vignati, A. (1974). Stability of dichotic listening test. *Cortex, 10,* 203–205.

Porter, R. J., Troendle, R., & Berlin, C. I. (1976). Effects of practice on the perception of dichotically presented stop-consonant–vowel syllables. *Journal of the Acoustical Society of America, 59,* 679–682.

Rasmussen, T., & Milner, B. (1977). The role of early left-brain injury in determining lateralization of cerebral speech functions. *Annals of the New York Academy of Sciences, 299,* 355–369.

Ryan, W. J., & McNeil, M. (1974). Listener reliability for a dichotic task. *Journal of the Acoustical Society of America, 56,* 1922–1923.

Schulman-Galambos, C. (1977). Dichotic listening performance in elementary and college students. *Neuropsychologia, 15,* 577–584.

Segalowitz, S. J. (Ed.). (1983). *Language functions and brain organization.* New York: Academic Press.

Segalowitz, S. J. (1985). *A paradigm for measuring individual differences in brain lateralization.* Mimeo, Brock University, St. Catharines, Ontario.

Segalowitz, S. J., & Bryden, M. P. (1983). Individual differences in hemispheric representation of language. In S. J. Segalowitz (Ed.), *Language functions and brain organization.* New York: Academic Press.

Shankweiler, D., & Studdert-Kennedy. M. (1975). A continuum of lateralization for speech perception? *Brain and Language, 2,* 212–225.

Sperry, R. W. (1968). Hemisphere deconnection and unity in conscious awareness. *American Psychologist, 23,* 723–733.

Stone, J., Leicester, J., & Sherman, M. (1973). The naso-temporal division of the monkey's retina. *Journal of Comparative Neurology, 150,* 33–348.

Teng, T. (1981). Dichotic ear difference is a poor index for the functional asymmetry between the cerebral hemispheres. *Neuropsychologia, 19,* 235–240.

Wada, J., & Rasmussen, T. (1960). Intracarotid injection of sodium amytal for the lateralization of cerebral speech dominance: Experimental and clinical observations. *Journal of Neurosurgery, 17,* 266–282.

Watson, R. T., Andriola, M., & Heilman, K. M. (1977). The EEG in neglect. *Journal of Neurological Science, 34,* 343–348.

Wexler, B. E., & Halwes, T. (1983). Increasing the power of dichotic methods: The fused rhymed words test. *Neuropsychologia, 21,* 59–66.

Wexler, B. E., Halwes, T., & Heninger, G. R. (1981). Use of a statistical significance criterion in drawing inferences about hemispheric dominance for language function from dichotic listening data. *Brain and Language, 13,* 13–18.

Witelson, S. F. (1974). Hemispheric specialization for linguistic and nonlinguistic tactual perception using a dichotomous stimulation technique. *Cortex, 10,* 3–17.

Wood, F. (Ed.). (1980). Noninvasive blood flow studies. *Brain and Language, 9*(1).

Zurif, E. B., & Bryden, M. P. (1969). Familial handedness and left–right differences in auditory and visual perception. *Neuropsychologia, 7,* 179–187.

Chapter 11

Integrating Neuropsychological and Cognitive Research: A Perspective for Bridging Brain–Behavior Relationships

MARLIN LANGUIS

Department of Educational Theory and Practice
College of Education
Ohio State University
Columbus, Ohio 43210
and Brain Behavior Laboratory
Columbus, Ohio 43210

MERLIN C. WITTROCK

Department of Educational Psychology
College of Education
University of California at Los Angeles
Los Angeles, California 90024

INTRODUCTION

In the final analysis, the integration of brain processes with learning behavior requires effective approaches in three areas: precise neurocognitive assessment, a diagnostic capability to discriminate among learners and to classify subgroups,

CHILD NEUROPSYCHOLOGY, VOL. 1

and intervention, directly related to assessment and diagnosis, that emphasizes metacognitive approaches and puts learning under the control of the learner. The chapter is organized, generally, to consider each of the three areas. However, a neurocognitive point of view is defined first.

At its essence, a neurocognitive perspective builds on cognitive psychology and the constructivist view of learning that was defined by Wittrock (1974) in his generative model of learning and subsequently explicated in a series of publications (Wittrock, 1978, 1980, 1981, 1985a, 1985b). A neurocognitive perspective attempts to integrate brain mechanisms, basic cognitive processes, and learning strategies.

The notion that the brain is directly responsible for thinking and learning is well accepted today. Until recently, however, covert mental processes were inferred indirectly from the learner's task performance. The mystery of neurocognitive processes has, at last, begun to yield to research in cognitive neuroscience. The exponential development of computer technology now enables the researcher to investigate the mind in action. The development of topographic brain mapping technology permits direct study of covert learning processes. For example, brain imaging systems such as the brain electrical activity mapping (BEAM) system developed by Duffy, Burchfiel, and Lombroso (1979), the Brain Atlas system, and similar systems provide topographic mapping of brain electrical activity as the learner performs cognitive tasks. The momentum of brain research continues to increase.

The fact that thinking is brain-specific suggests two reasons for optimism. The late Norman Geschwind (1983) commented lucidly, "Knowing that one's brain is organized and processes differently from another's gives us the freedom to accept ourselves and our uniqueness and to make the first necessary step to doing something positive about it." The mind enlightened about its own processes may be free at last to explore its full potential. The second reason for optimism is related to the first. Promising results associated with the applications of classical biofeedback techniques for a period of more than 5 years with a number of learning-disabled and hyperactive learners has been reported by Lubar (1985). Working from a broad cognitive model, Languis, Letteri, Pennell, and McQueen (1984) proposed that a learner can, by using information about his or her brain and applying systematic metacognitive strategies, change brain functioning and improve learning efficiency and independence. It just may turn out that the brain is our most plastic and malleable organ. And it may respond to our "self-control" not only during childhood, but also throughout the lifespan. Perhaps old dogs can learn new tricks after all.

On the other hand, the application of cognitive neuroscience to education is at a very early stage. Brain research has been focused predominantly on (1) understanding neurophysiological substrates of cognitive processes and (2) diagnosing medical problems in the brain. Neither of these foci lead directly to elucidating psychological dimensions of learning, much less educational applications. As a result, many important questions remain to be answered. A beginning has been made, but bridging the gap between basic cognitive neuroscience and educational practice will require substantial time and effort. Languis and Kraft (1985) suggested a set of guidelines for asking relevant questions for addressing the problem. Hynd and Obrzut (1981) defined a program for the preparation of the school psychologist who could provide leadership in neuropsychological and neuroeducational applications.

Nevertheless, psychologists, educators, and others in the helping professions stand to profit greatly from emerging insights about how humans learn, think, and imagine. Brain research provides a hard-science basis for explaining the cognitive and learning processes of students (Languis, Naour, Martin & Buffer, in press). It is in harmony with the constructivist view that learning is an active process with defined components. Learning may be systematically and deliberately orchestrated by the individual through the use of effective learning strategies. Put simply, learning to learn can be learned. In a very real sense, brain research is helping to make learning transparent. It is, perhaps, the optimal tool for metacognition. Brain research, combined with effective pedagogy, provides a powerful system for teaching learning, which is the ultimate curriculum of the school.

Research in cognitive psychology is currently focused on cognitive and learning processes and strategies underlying thinking and learning across the curriculum. Minstrell (1984) and Osbourne and Wittrock (1983) found that students possess naive conceptions and misconceptions about science phenomena that are highly resistant to change. However, dealing with the misconceptions metacognitively has shown promise in increasing science-concept mastery. Differences have been found in basic cognitive processes between more- and less-competent learners on IQ tests (Glazer, 1981) and in complex reading tasks (Brown, Bransford, Ferrarra, & Compione, 1983). Competent learners retrieve and organize information faster and from a larger relevant memory store than do less-competent learners. In addition, they possess a larger repertoire of strategies, and they effectively choose the appropriate strategy for the task at hand. They plan and metacognitively monitor their approaches and progress toward goals. Letteri (1980) has demonstrated that generalizable cognitive strategies may be systematically taught, and executive metacognitive skills may be developed to produce cognitive efficiency and transfer across curriculum domains.

METHODS OF NEUROCOGNITIVE ASSESSMENT

To measure the human EEG, sensors are attached to the scalp over 20 or more locations that are of greatest interest. Very small electrical voltages, detected by these sensors, are amplified by a polygraph and filtered before being printed on strip chart paper. The written record is visually inspected and interpreted by a trained neurologist. The neurologist is confronted with a heroic task in accurately interpreting the volume and complexity of EEG information. Brain electrical activity, generated by aggregates of neurons, is displayed as brainwave patterns. During medical assessment, brainwaves typically are collected while the individual is passively relaxing.

On the other hand, during neurocognitive assessment, the individual is asked to perform cognitive tasks. Accurate interpretation of brain electrical activity patterns is difficult for medical purposes. For neurocognitive assessment, accurate visual interpretation of the printed paper record of the EEG is impossible. A crucial concern in all neurophysiological measurement of brain electrical activity is the control and elimination of artifact (electrical signals that originate from sources other than the brain) (Torello & McCarley, 1986). Therefore, the brainwaves are subjected to a variety of computer-mediated signal analysis techniques, including the evaluation of data for artifact.

Three basic methods of neurocognitive measurement and analysis of the human EEG have been used: (1) brainwave frequency method, (2) event-related potential (ERP) method, and (3) probe-ERP method. Each method is discussed in the pages that follow. Next, a method for displaying, analyzing, and interpreting any of the three methods of neurocognitive assessment is reported. That method is topographic brain mapping, a technique by which brain electrical activity is displayed as multicolored pictures (maps) of the brain many times a second.

EEG Brainwave Frequency Method

The first method is an analysis of the prevalence of brainwave frequency patterns in the ongoing EEG. Fast Fourier transform (FFT) power spectral analysis is applied to brain electrical activity collected while the learner performs a cognitive task such as reading text for comprehension, performing a mental-rotations spatial task, responding to a Piagetian conservation task, or responding to an item from a cognitive-style instrument. The resulting data is the percentage of delta, theta, alpha, or beta EEG frequency bands found in selected time epochs during the task performance. The EEG frequency-band analysis may be evaluated over each scalp location of interest.

The measurement of brainwave frequency patterns has been used extensively in neurocognitive research. The EEG can be recorded while people are actually engaged in a variety of complex cognitive tasks such as reading, writing, or calculating in a fairly naturalistic setting. On the other hand, many artifacts are present in the ongoing EEG and are hard to remove using this method of brain activity measurement. Next, it is a very general and gross measure of brain activity. Within the EEG lie many subtle and complex patterns which the delta, theta, alpha, and beta frequency patterns are not sufficiently precise to tease out. Finally, it is not at all clear that basic cognitive processes can be associated with patterns in the EEG frequency domains. Therefore, the application of brainwave frequency analysis should be used in neurocognitive applications as a general tool, perhaps as a first-level assessment technique. However, it may be used effectively in combination with the ERP and the probe-ERP method (discussed here later) and especially in association with topographic brain mapping. In fact, most neurocognitive brain-imaging systems provide both brain frequency and ERP options.

Neurocognitive Applications of EEG Brainwave Frequency Method

Selected examples of brain frequency pattern measurements follow to illustrate the range of neurocognitive applications of this method.

Dunn (1985a, 1985b) has used EEG measurements to explicate his bimodal theory. According to bimodal theory, the human brain has at least two qualitatively different modes of thought: the *analytic mode,* which is a logical, linear, and sequential processing system, and the *holistic mode,* which is a simultaneous, parallel, or gestalt processing system. These modes are not a function of a simple left- versus right-hemisphere dependency.

Analytics learn and recall word lists and expository text in a more highly logical manner and produce less alpha than holistics during an eyes-open baseline and during learning and recall tasks, especially when they are asked to learn in an alert state. In contrast to analytics, holistics always produce more alpha during the baseline and learning tasks (especially during the encoding of material which they later recall), and they appear to use a more paralogical learning strategy (Dunn, Gould, & Singer, 1981). Analytics consistently generate less alpha than holistics from both cerebral hemispheres during these tasks. Also, both groups tended to produce more alpha from their left hemisphere during the reading of expository text, compared with baseline brain activity, suggesting that the right hemisphere may have been more activated than the left for both groups. This finding is similar to that obtained by Kraft, Mitchell, Languis, and Wheatley (1980), who measured alpha–beta brainwave ratio patterns of 6- to 8-year-old students asked to read silently, answer comprehension questions, and perform Piagetian conservation tasks.

The difference between analytics and holistics, however, does not appear to be caused by analytics having greater reading ability. Reddix and Dunn (1984), using abstract, high imagery poetry, found that male holistics were able to grasp the underlying meaning of the poem, whereas, male analytics were not. The opposite pattern tended to occur for females, although that pattern was less clear. Languis and Naour (1985) suggested a vector model of sex differences that may underlie the rather confusing literature on gender differences. The vector model of gender differences proposes that sex differences result from both neu-rodevelopmental and experiential factors that give direction and magnitude to femininization and masculinization vectors in individuals, especially at develop-mentally sensitive periods. Further, the model explicates the role of levels of sex hormones, especially testosterone, in the eventual expression of cognitive and learning patterns (style) observed in males and females. Thus, differential brain organization may lead to qualitative differences in cognitive style. If so, a uni-versal instructional approach applied to all students may not be appropriate.

Naour, Languis, and Martin (in press) investigated brain electrical activity patterns in the ongoing EEG during the performance of six cognitive tasks. Groups ($N = 6$) of third- and sixth-grade normal and learning-disabled right-handed boys were assessed. Brain activity was measured from Wernicke's area over the left hemisphere and the homologous area over the right hemisphere. Analysis of the delta, theta, alpha, and beta brainwave activity patterns in the group did not reveal hemispheric aysmmetries. However, across tasks, greater theta activity was observed in the learning-disabled students, compared with normals, especially after the first 10 seconds of task performance. In addition, the overall pattern of brain activity in sixth-grade learning-disabled students resembled that of third-grade normals, suggesting a developmental component in the learning-disability students studied.

Lyons (in press) evaluated a model relating brain functioning patterns, cog-nitive-style variables, and personality variables. Further, she examined patterns in learning and teaching behaviors in 16 female preservice elementary teachers. Brain activity patterns over Wernicke's area and the right hemisphere homologue were assessed during five cognitive tasks and were analyzed using FFT. The Rod and Frame and the Group Embedded Figures test of field dependence–indepen-dence were used, and the sensing–intuition component of the Myers Briggs Type Indicator (MBTI) was used to assess the personality variable.

Overall, the variables correlated positively. High left-hemisphere beta activity correlated with field independence and intuition; right-hemisphere beta corre-lated with field dependence and sensing. Moreover, characteristic learning and teaching behaviors were found to closely parallel the cognitive profile of indi-viduals in the study.

Event-Related Potential (ERP)

The ERP method employs a signal-averaging paradigm. A large number of short epochs of EEG (approximately 1 second long), precisely time-locked to the presentation of a target stimulus, are collected and computer averaged. Target stimuli may be visual, auditory, or tactile. Embedded within the EEG is a waveform, smaller in voltage than delta, theta, alpha, and beta waves. It is called the *event-related potential* (ERP). The ERP, though small, may be measured by the technique of signal averaging. Because the brain waves in the ongoing EEG occur randomly and are not time-locked to the presentation of the target stimulus, they average out to a straight line for the same reason that waves caused by two pebbles dropped into water cancel out one another. What remains is the enhanced ERP waveform.

What is the significance of the ERP for cognitive researchers and educators? The ERP includes a cluster of components that have been associated with basic cognitive processes. John (1963) classified ERPs into two types: exogenous and endogenous. Both types have been associated with cognition. However, the group of ERP waveforms that may be detected within approximately the first 40 milliseconds (msec) following the onset of sensory stimuli are basically associated with the integrity of the sensory processing system. For the most part, exogenous ERPs are generated at synapses in lower brain centers, are stable, and do not require the subject's cognitive participation. For example, ERPs from auditory clicks may be reliably measured whether the individual is awake and alert, drowsy, or even sleeping. On the other hand, endogenous ERP components occur from about 100 to 500 msec following the stimulus. These later ERPs are associated with cognitive processing of the stimulus event. Endogenous ERP components are influenced by the cognitive demands of the task and by the psychological state of the learner (e.g., the degree of focused attention). Because the endogenous ERP waveform components are sensitive to the learner's cognitive characteristics, they are of substantive interest to cognitive researchers. Much remains to be learned about the precise meaning of ERP waveforms. However, increasing evidence suggests that ERPs may serve as reliable markers of internal cognitive processes. As this pattern becomes clearer, ERPs may play a significant role in research as indices of higher cognitive processes.

Each endogenous waveform component is labeled by its characteristic latency in msec following the onset of the target stimulus and by its positive or negative electrical property (e.g., N100, N200, P300, N400). It is somewhat unfortunate that endogenous waveform components bear a specific latency label because the latency of a given waveform component does vary somewhat across subjects with different cognitive characteristics and within a subject under varying physiological or psychological states. Nevertheless, latency labels for endogenous ERP components serve to identify waveform components.

The N100 Component of the ERP

The N100 is a negative-going waveform that peaks most robustly about 100 milliseconds after an auditory stimulus. It has been associated with processes of selective attention (Hillyard, Hink, Schwenk, & Picton, 1973; Picton & Hillyard, 1974). The amplitude of the N100 is greater when auditory or visual stimuli are attended than when the stimuli are ignored by the subject. The N100 is clearly observed in the probe-ERP method discussed later in this chapter.

However, the N100 is not the only ERP component associated with attention. The N100 may be related to early rather than late stages of selective attention processing. The early phase may be a process of filtering relevant from irrelevant stimuli, whereas the late phase may be a more detailed stimulus evaluation process. As a potential neurocognitive marker for selective attention, the N100 may be an extremely useful tool for cognitive assessment.

The P300 Component of the ERP

The P300 ERP is the waveform that has been studied most extensively. First reported and named in 1965, by Sutton and associates (Sutton, Braren, Zubin, & John, 1967), it can at times be so robust that it may be detected in the ongoing EEG. Under those somewhat rare circumstances, the use of signal-averaging techniques may be unnecessary to observe the P300. It is of greatest amplitude at the midline over the central-parietal regions of the scalp. The P300 is strongest when an individual is required to attend to an event that occurs only now and then. For example, frequently occurring stimuli (tones of 1000 hz) are presented with infrequently occurring stimuli (tones of 3000 hz), which the subject must count. This so-called "oddball" paradigm is very effective in eliciting the P300 waveform.

The cognitive meaning of the P300 is best described as a marker of the individual's evaluation of a stimulus event. As ERP P300 evidence accumulates, it is becoming clear that the P300 involves the updating of memory and may be generated in the hippocampus and associated brain structures. In a general sense, the P300 indexes a decision-making process within the brain. Both the amplitude and latency of the P300 are influenced by task and subject characteristics.

P300 Amplitude. The amplitude of the P300 waveform is related to the unpredictability of the stimuli presented. The amplitude of the P300 ERP increases as the probability and predictability of a target stimulus event decreases. However, stimuli must also have relevance for the subject (i.e., the subject must attend to and count the oddball stimuli) to elicit a P300 (Duncan-Johnson & Donchin, 1982). Consequently, it appears that there is an attentional cognitive resource to which the P300 is sensitive. In addition, Squires, Squires, and Hillyard (1975) have shown that if an individual is confident of his or her decision in discriminating a stimulus, and if the probability of that stimulus is low, the P300 will have the greatest amplitude. Because less expected or surprising outcomes result in robust P300 waveforms, the amplitude may be related "to the amount of prior uncertainty resolved by a stimulus" (Ruchkin & Sutton, 1973).

P300 Latency. The issue of P300 latency and how it relates to performance is considerably more complex than is amplitude. More-difficult discrimination tasks result in greater latencies for both P300 and reaction time (Ritter, Simpson, & Vaughan 1972). Conversely, easier discriminations resulted in both decreased

P300 latency and reaction time. Furthermore, Duncan-Johnson and Donchin (1982) demonstrated that P300 and reaction time covaried with the probability of the target. The expectancy of a stimulus may affect both stimulus evaluation and response time. Ford, Roth, Mohs, Hopkins, and Kopell (1979) showed that in elderly people, P300 latency was equivalent to younger persons in a Sternberg task. However, reaction-time latencies were longer for the elderly. It appears that decreases in Sternberg task performance seen in the elderly were not the result of decrements in information processing in the brain, but were associated with delays in motor output systems.

It should also be noted that the P300 may be part of a complex waveform with components that include the N200. However, there are differences between these two components. The N200 appears to be considerably more modality-specific than the P300. Ritter and colleagues (1972) noted that with increased task demands, both the P300 and N200 latencies were increased (longer evaluation time) along with the reaction-time latency, and that the N200 latency had a higher correlation to reaction time than did the P300 latency. It may be that the N200 is the first stage in the memory updating or stimulus-evaluation process and that the P300 indicates the completion of that process. Studies also indicate that there may be subcomponents within the P300, which may be variously labeled as P300a, P300b, and so forth. Overall, the P300 waveform is of great interest in neurocognitive research and appears to have substantive promise in the study of brain–behavior relationships (Donchin, 1984).

N400 Component of the ERP

A specific ERP component (N400) has been identified that is associated with semantically incongruous words appearing at the end of otherwise meaningful sentences (Kutas & Hillyard, 1980). According to Kutas and Hillyard, the N400 may be a psychophysiological marker of the re-evaluation of semantic information in what was once a predictable sentence (e.g., "Mary had a little lamb; its fleece was white as *telephones*."). In this study, semantically appropriate sentence endings did not invoke the N400 but instead resulted in a triphasic positive waveform. The relationship of the N400 ERP to other aspects of language processing is not entirely clear. However, these preliminary results are supportive of the effective use of ERP techniques to study higher cortical functions like semantic processing.

Applications of the ERP Method

In ERP studies completed at the Brain Behavior Laboratory, the ERP method has been used to evaluate differences in groups of individuals with defined cognitive characteristics.

Torello (1984) developed, validated, and utilized a two-channel microcomputer-based system to measure and analyze the exogenous, cognitive components of the ERP waveform. Twelve normal adult males (CA 18–42) and six adult (CA 16–42) brain-injured (moderate–severe head trauma) patients 6 to 12 months post-injury were assessed. Electrodes were placed at Pz, according to the 10/20 international system and referenced to a left earlobe electrode. Eye blink and movement artifact was evaluated from measurements taken from paired electrodes placed over the supra-orbital ridge of the left eye and lateral to the orbit of the same eye. The Stroop task was used as the experimental protocol.

The average amplitude of the P300 waveform was significantly reduced ($p < .05$), and the average latency of the P300 was increased ($p < .05$) for the brain-injured population compared with normals. The average response latency (reaction time) was significantly longer ($p < .05$) for the brain-injured population compared with normals. Trial-by-trial analysis of target stimuli revealed inconsistency in processing the task in the brain-injured subjects, especially toward the end of the testing period, suggesting difficulty for these individuals in maintaining focused attention on the task and difficulty in marshalling the attentional resources to perform the task efficiently.

Duffy, Denkla, Bartels, and Sandini (1980) and Duffy, Denkla, Bartels, Sandini, and Kiessling (1980) have shown a significant difference in the left temporal P300 waveform in an homogeneous dyslexic group of subjects compared with age-matched controls. A number of tasks (listening to music and speech, remembering abstract figures, paired-associate learning, reading, and relaxing with the eye open or closed) were administered to these subjects, and EEG was collected simultaneously. Striking differences were seen in patterns of EEG activity between the two groups. Several discrete brain areas were identified in the dyslexics that were significantly different from the norm. These areas included the media frontal lobe on both sides of the brain, the left lateral frontal lobe, the left midtemporal lobe, the left posterior quadrant (including Wernicke's area), and the right posterior quadrant. These brain regions correspond to areas classically associated with speech and reading in normals. Thus, though the brain dysfunction that occurs in pure dyslexia is not localized, a single area appears to involve cortical systems involved in speech and reading.

Simmons, Languis, and Drake (1985) sought to identify P300 ERP differences between a heterogeneous dyslexic population compared with controls, and using a variety of cognitive tasks. Nineteen dyslexic individuals were compared with 16 control subjects. Four odd-ball paradigm tasks requiring color, sound, letter, and word recognition were used. Brain electrical activity was recorded from Fz, Pz, the left temporoparietal (Wernicke) area and the right-hemisphere homologue. Eye and muscle artifact was excluded, and P300 response latencies and amplitudes were measured and compared between dyslexic and normal controls.

The dyslexic group showed significant amplitude reductions in the P300 over the left temporoparietal region on all tasks. Other electrodes showed no consistent differences between dyslexics and controls.

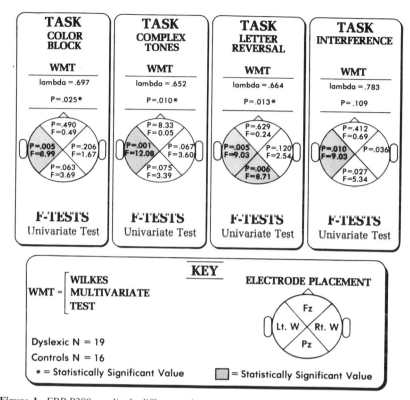

Figure 1. ERP P300 amplitude differences between college-age dyslexic and control students.

Color, sound, and letter discrimination tasks produced an overall dyslexic-group reduction in P300 waveform amplitude compared to the normal subjects. The letter-stimulus task elicited the greatest deviation at individual-electrode sites. The data suggest that observed changes in the P300-wave in dyslexics is consistently found in the left temporoparietal lobe and that global differences vary with the eliciting task.

Differences in the left temporoparietal (Wernicke's) area were found in both the Duffy, Denckla, Bartels, and Sandini (1980) and the Simmons et al. (1985) ERP studies. Postmortem autopsy studies of four dyslexics, by Galaburda, Sherman, Rosen, Aboitiz, and Geschwind (1985) revealed numerous neuronal ectopias in layer I of the cortex in the temporoparietal region of the dominant hemisphere. Hynd an Cohen (1983) reviewed additional studies indicating neurodevelopmental and hemispheric aysmmetry differences between dyslexics and normals. The evidence from these studies is consistent and confirmatory. It appears that neurocognitive differences may be found between learning-disabled students when compared to controls using ERP-assessment techniques.

These differences may provide greater insight into the brain areas that are involved in learning disabilities. Furthermore, the use of brain-activity measures, like P300, may detect changes in brain function that may not be noticeable behaviorally at an early age. Aberrant brain activity could alert an educator to a child at risk for dyslexia before such a disability manifests itself in poor school performance and the associated psychological problems become firmly entrenched. The development of appropriate strategies and approaches could be initiated early, possibly in relation with programs such as reading recovery at age 6 years (Clay, 1979a, 1979b), in order to prevent or reduce the severity of the predicted learning disability. Lyons, Languis, and Rogers (1985) found, in a group of 115 adult dyslexics surveyed, that serious learning difficulties were initially experienced by these individuals in the first and second grade of school.

Shockley (1984) assessed ERP cognitive patterns in autistic learners and age-matched controls. ERP waveforms (N100, N200 and P300) were measured in nine autistic males (CA 12 year 11 months to 22 years) and nine age-matched controls. Autistic subjects were identified by DSM-III and a comprehensive psychological assessment. Scalp electrodes were placed at Pz, referenced to linked mastoids with grounding at central forehead. Eye artifact was removed via trial-by-trial editing of target events. Three cognitive ERP tasks were assessed: tone omission, visual color blocks, and high–low tones. Each subject was assessed twice on separate days, with the order of tasks counterbalanced.

No differences were observed between the first and second assessment on any of three cognitive ERP-protocol tasks. The amplitude of the P300 waveform was significantly attenuated in the autistic population compared with controls in the auditory (high–low tones) task but not in the visual (color blocks) or the tone-omission tasks. The amplitude of the waveform at 200 msec was greater than the P300 waveform in autistic subjects. However, the amplitude of both the N100 and N200 waveform was reduced in the autistic population compared to normal controls. No differences in waveform latencies or in performance latency (button press to target stimuli) were observed between the two groups.

Shibley and Shockley (1984) used a multifactored assessment protocol to develop a comprehensive performance profile for the same nine autistic males used in the Shockley (1984) study. Factors in the assessment protocol were neurocognitive ERP brain activity patterns in visual and auditory tasks, the Block Design and Digit Symbol subscales of the Wechsler Adult Intelligence Scale—Revised (WAIS-R), the Crawford Small Parts Dexterity Test, and performance in assembling and soldering an electronics circuit board.

The following results were found: high performers on one factor were generally high performers on other factors in the assessment protocol. Low performers were likewise consistent across assessment factors. The highest correlation was observed between the ERP and the WAIS-R subscales, and the greatest variability was observed in the Crawford Small Parts Dexterity Test. Finally, the on-the-job performance of the autistic subjects in the assembly and soldering of an electronics circuitboard was higher than would be predicted from the subjects' standardized test performance. Shibley and Shockley interpreted the results by noting that when the autistic subjects' attention was focused on any task, their performance was relatively high and consistent.

ERP assessment of the influence of a megavitamin intervention regime for autistic individuals was conducted by Languis and Shockley (1984). Late waveform components were measured from seven autistic males (CA 15–23) during the performance of a visual (color block) and auditory (high–low tone) task. Complete data were collected from six of the subjects. All measurements were taken in the Ohio State University (OSU) Cognitive Neuroscience Brain Behavior Laboratory. Brain electrical activity was collected at four scalp locations (Fz and Cz central sites and Wernicke's area over the left hemisphere and the right-hemisphere homologue with the ground electrode placed on the forehead). The active brain sites were referenced to linked mastoids. Impedance was measured at all scalp locations immediately preceding and following each assessment session. All impedance values were below 5 Kohm. Electrodes were placed over the supra-orbital ridge over the left eye and at the corner of the right eye to monitor and control for eye-blink and eye-movement artifact.

Each subject was assessed at 1-month intervals in a double-blind study in which the experimental intervention conditions (placebo, multivitamin, B6, and B6 and multivitamin) were assigned randomly to each subject each month.

The results were evaluated for evidence of change in the P300 waveform (normalization) toward that of age-matched controls in Shockley's (1984) study of the same autistic population. The results indicate considerable variation among subjects so that generalizations across the subject population are not warranted. Individual subject patterns suggested a general normalization of the amplitude of the P300 waveform for only two subjects. For those individuals, the vitamin intervention showing the most influence on P300 amplitude was B6, followed by placebo, multivitamin maintenance, and finally by B6 and multivitamin combined. The evidence of a vitamin regime on ERP brain processing patterns in autistic learners remains unclear.

Languis and Simmons (1984) evaluated the consistency of the P300 waveform in a group of five normal young adults (two males and three females) by measuring the ERP to the same cognitive tasks (color blocks and high–low tones) for 4 consecutive days. The subjects were asked to maintain consistent patterns of sleep, nutrition, life stress, et cetera. The intra-individual variation of the amplitude of the P300 waveform for the two tasks did not vary more than $\pm$ 5% between consecutive trials for these individuals. When the individual's psychological and physiological factors are held as constant as is possible, it appears that the P300 elicited in neurocognitive tasks is quite consistent under test–retest conditions.

Applications of P300 measurement have also been investigated with man–machine systems (Donchin, 1984). The paradigm required a subject to classify a series of items into one of two categories. Most of the presented stimuli were not relevant to the task. The remaining, randomly presented stimuli were classified into two groups by pressing a button with either the left hand or the right hand. Most errors in classification occurred when P300 latency was longer than reaction time latencies—that is, when the subject acted before thinking. Whenever P300 latency preceded reaction-time latencies, the subject was most likely accurate in his or her response. When errors were detected using this technique and when proper feedback was given to the operator, misclassification could be avoided. If the learner is aware of his or her evaluation process, it would be possible to reduce response errors. Through detailed analyses of P300 measures, it may be possible to supplement overt behavioral response data and improve man–machine interactions.

The P300 measure can also be used to determine how demanding a task is to a subject in the cognitive domain (Wickens, Kramer, Vanesse, & Donchin, 1983). In order to determine the information-processing capacity for a given subject, two tasks are simultaneously presented in this paradigm. The secondary task is the counting of infrequently occurring, high-frequency tones presented in a sequence of a high- and low-pitched auditory stimuli. As we stated previously, the P300 amplitude for this kind of task is inversely related to the probability of the high-frequency tone. However, when this simple discrimination is performed concurrently with a primary task, such as a perceptual–motor tracking task using a computer monitor and joystick controls, the P300 amplitude to the secondary task decreases with increasing demands of the primary task. Selective attention to the secondary task decreases when the cognitive load for the primary task increases. Thus, the availability of resources to accommodate both tasks is reduced as one task increases in difficulty. One may be able to construct a system of instruction where P300 and performance criteria are used to determine the processing demands of a particular task. Through the use of P300 measures, decisions concerning the learner's readiness to accept increasing task demand could be made with increased precision. Perhaps, more efficient and accurate design in curriculum and instruction variables may be possible. These variables include complexity of task demands, rate of presentation, and sensory modality for task presentation (Andreassi, 1980).

Torello (1984) proposed a set of potentially useful ways to apply the ERP and probe-ERP methods to educationally relevant concerns. Torello suggested that by evaluating the robustness or attenuation of the P300 concurrently with the level of the learner's task performance, effective judgments may be made concerning task difficulty for the learner, learner motivation, and learner confidence. By combining evidence of covert neurocognitive processes with observable task performance, greater depth of diagnosis and accuracy may be achieved.

Moreover, by monitoring change in the P300 and task performance as level of task complexity or the length of the work session varies, one could establish the limits of individual cognitive capacities.

The Probe-ERP Method

As discussed earlier, the spontaneous EEG and ERP methods have certain advantages. The EEG can be recorded while people are actually engaged in a variety of complex tasks in a naturalistic setting. On the other hand ERPs require repetitive, transient stimuli, precisely timed, which limits the activities that can be studied with this method. The EEG is often contaminated with artifacts that are largely eliminated by the averaging technique of the ERP. In addition, an extensive body of literature demonstrates that at least some measurable ERP components both reflect different levels of stimulus and task processing (i.e., sensory, attentive, and cognitive) and are generated from specific cortical and subcortical loci. Is it possible to devise a method to combine the advantages of the ongoing EEG and the ERP methods?

Galin and Ellis (1975) and Johnstone, Galin, Fein, Yingling, Herron, & Marcus (1984) developed the probe-ERP paradigm, combining the major advantages of the EEG and ERP. While an individual performs any of a variety of real-world cognitive tasks, task-irrelevant probe stimuli such as tone pips or light flashes are presented. The learner is instructed to attend to the primary cognitive task. The ERPs are collected and averaged from the probe stimuli. There is general agreement that the probe-ERP waveform changes as a function of task (Shucard, Shucard, and Thomas, 1977; Shucard, Cummings, Thomas, & Shucard, 1981). The conclusions of all probe-ERP studies rely on the assumption that a brain region is less responsive to the probe stimulus when that region is engaged in the primary concurrent task. The amplitude of the ERP from the probe stimuli is influenced by the amount of the brain's attentional resources devoted to processing the assigned cognitive task. The N100 waveform component of the ERP appears to be substantially influenced in the probe-ERP technique. There is a finite limit to how much information the brain can process at one time. As noted earlier, Wickens et al. (1983) found that when subjects were asked to perform two tasks concurrently, but attend differentially between one task (the primary task) and a second task (the secondary task—reduced amplitude of the ERP was associated with the secondary task). Cognitive processing of the probe stimuli is least over brain areas where the processing of the cognitive task is greatest.

On the other hand, the probe-ERP method is not without its difficulties. One serious problem is habituation to the task-irrelevant probe stimuli. Work is underway to find the most effective means to deal with the problems inherent in the probe-ERP method.

Topographic Mapping of Brain Electrical Activity

New computer methodology can condense, summarize, and display spectral, spatial, and temporal information of brain activity from 20 different scalp locations. Statistical comparisons with either a control group or data from the same subject can be made at different times, with the earlier measurements forming the baseline. The product of this automated data handling is a topographic map of electrical activity across the entire cerebral cortex. It is called the Brain Electrical Activity Map (BEAM) (Duffy et al., 1979).

Topographic mapping of brain electrical activity is analogous to the construction of a meteorological isotherm map, which provides temperature readings at any given point in the country. The same is true of the topographic map created by the Brain Atlas technique. Brain activity from 20 sensors provides enough data to interpolate the activity at any given point on the scalp, generating a sort of iso-EEG map of brain activity.

Brain mapping has been used to demonstrate that dyslexia is a neurophysiological problem with topographically specific brain areas of dysfunction. Duffy and colleagues (Duffy, Denckla, Bartels, & Sandini, 1980; Duffy, Denckla, Bartels, Sandini, & Kiessling, 1980) studied a group of dyslexia-pure subjects and their age-matched controls. The specific feature of brain activity that was always associated with the dyslexic subjects was greater alpha activity in these regions. According to many studies, increases in alpha represent related cortical inactivity (Gevins et al., 1979). Conversely, decreases in alpha have been shown to correspond to cortical activation (Davidson & Schwartz, 1977). The greater amount of alpha activity is evident in dyslexic subjects even when linguistic tasks are not being performed and thus may represent a fundamental trait difference of lowered electrical activity in specific areas of dyslexic brains.

The diagnostic utility of the brain mapping technique is evident. When numerical measures of brain electrical activity are used to develop diagnostic rules, they are shown to be 80–90% successful in classifying subjects as dyslexic or normal (Duffy, 1982; Torello & Duffy, 1985). In addition, the same neurocognitive brain-mapping information may be used in a controlled and directed program of teaching students to become competent in using generalizable cognitive strategies across the curriculum. It is important to note that brain-imaging systems have sufficient computing speed to display a brain map periodically as the task is being performed. Thus the brain-activity pattern may be displayed as the pattern emerges. Within a few seconds after the task is completed, the collected maps of brain activity during the cognitive task may be displayed in very small (millisecond) time slices. Thus, the investigator–interventionist and the learner have almost immediate access to a very detailed account of the mental events that just preceded. In our limited experience to the present, brain maps have proved to be very useful in stimulating self-reflection, and self-revelation by the learner.

A RESEARCH AND DEVELOPMENT MODEL: INTEGRATING NEUROCOGNITIVE ASSESSMENT, DIAGNOSIS, AND METACOGNITIVE INTERVENTION

In the multidisciplinary Brain Behavior Laboratory at OSU, we have informally investigated the capacity of individuals to vary the ERP waveform patterns by deliberately employing different cognitive strategies during task performance. These efforts appear to substantially influence brain-processing patterns especially when measured with the sensitivity of the Brain Atlas topographic mapping system. It is reasonable to assume that individuals can and do employ a variety of strategies under any experimental conditions. As a result, even though instructions and task training are employed in our laboratory to ensure that subjects are cooperative and consistent in task performance, a standard procedure in the Brain Behavior Laboratory is to interview each subject after electrophysiological assessment to determine what cognitive strategies may have been employed as tasks were performed. This information is considered in interpreting the assessment data. This approach argues for a comprehensive view of the individual's role in complex cognitive task performance. At the same time, it suggests that the individual has the potential capacity to exercise considerable control over brain-processing patterns. This view is both optimistic and encouraging. It suggests that metacognitive intervention might profit by taking advantage of the individual's potential capacity to influence cognitive processes in order to improve learning and to achieve greater control over it.

Exploratory experience using the Brain Atlas with the probe-ERP method (Andrews, 1985) has resulted in individual examples of identifiable differences in brain maps associated with apparently subtle notions such as the type of learning strategy an individual is using, the presence or absence of learning motivation, and difficulty in the performing of a task versus the mastery of a task. When an individual imagines learning effectively in a classroom, the brain map is different from when the individual imagines learning poorly. These differences appear to correspond with actual performance in instruction.

Andrews (1985) has proposed that important applications of this methodology could be made in many areas of learning. It is clear from his preliminary uses of this methodology that individuals who are learning conceptually different types of material are doing so in rather different ways. While this is not a new assertion, this methodology will permit direct monitoring of the brain activity during learning of a particular subject matter and the differences in an individual's methods of learning. This information may be useful to assist in the design and evaluation of the student's educational program.

The model proposed offers potential for understanding and adaptation of individual differences in learning effectiveness and style. Direct assessment may be possible in a variety of somewhat subjective areas: an individual's attentional engagement in tasks, ability to voluntarily modify processing patterns, ability to utilize various representational and processing methods (linguistic, spatial, etc.), and responsiveness to important learning variables (e.g., response to novelty, speed of automatization of skills, organizational methods). Individual students can be evaluated for a propensity and ability to use any particular learning strategy. This information will have special use in identifying the likelihood of the individual to respond effectively to any particular instructional method (e.g., phonics to an individual with poor ability to do auditory coding may not be the best approach). In addition, such information can be used to assist the individual in developing those areas of weakness through the use of those strategies that have the greatest strength. Probe-ERP monitoring of brain activity goes beyond performance tests in providing a direct assessment of brain activity (the same performance can result from differing strategies, processes, and strengths), and it could be used in assisting the individual in gaining greater self-understanding and personal control over learning effectiveness.

A within-subject research design may be an appropriate approach to investigating the effectiveness of an intervention. A learner might perform a task a number of times. Then a statistical average map of his or her brain activity could be calculated. A comparison map might be made when his or her learning is effective and when learning is less effective. Individual trials could ensue, followed by presentation of a statistical deviation map that shows differences from the best learning pattern. The learner could reflect on the things that were done on that trial, plan an approach to the next trial, perform, produce a statistical map, re-evaluate, et cetera. In this way, the individual could use the variability in her or his own performance as a vehicle to gain both greater understanding of her or his own learning and greater control over it. This, supplemented with instruction in alternative strategies and approaches, may enable the learner to adjust the variety, flexibility, performance, and ability to control his or her learning.

INTEGRATING NEUROCOGNITIVE ASSESSMENT AND DIAGNOSIS WITH METACOGNITIVE INTERVENTION

As discussed earlier, bridging brain–behavior relationships requires that neurocognitive assessment and diagnosis be integrated with an intervention program that directly utilizes neurocognitive information in a comprehensive cognitive profile of the learner. The concluding section of the chapter reports preliminary evidence related to the potential utility of the research and development model just proposed. The final part of the section provides an illustration of a metacognitive intervention program designed to develop competence in generalizable cognitive controls.

Preliminary Evidence

Is it possible that the effects of a program in directing and controlling learning strategies may be measurable both at neurophysiological and task-performance levels? Results from an exploratory study with learning-disability students by Languis et al. (1984) revealed a pattern of pre- to posttest gains in task performance and in ERP P300 waveforms following a cognitive-intervention program. The purpose of the study was to investigate relationships between cognitive augmentation experiences and the following areas: (1) changes in student performance on cognitive-control measures and (2) changes in ERP brain activity patterns during cognitive tasks.

Six right-handed learning-disabled (LD) students and two LD controls (7 males, 1 female) were the subjects. The subjects ranged from 12 to 29 years of age. Learning disability was defined as having no history of neurological insult, intelligence in the normal or above-normal range, and overall school performance 2 or more years below grade level. All subjects were pre- and posttested on the following two cognitive control measures in Letteri's (1985a) Cognitive Control Profile: (1) The Group Embedded Figures Test (GEFT) was employed to assess the analytic–global dimension, and (2) the Circles Test was used to measure the focusing–scanning dimension. Subjects were also given pre- and postassessment of ERP waveform patterns (P-300 amplitude) on four cognitive tasks: complex tones, color blocks, letter reversal, and Stroop.

ERP brain electrical activity was collected from four scalp locations (Pz, Fz, left Wernicke's area, and the right-hemisphere homologue), all referenced to linked mastoids. Electrical potentials generated by eye-blink or ocular movement were collected by a pair of electrodes placed between the lateral angle of the orbicularis oculi over the left eye and the supra-orbital margin of the right eye. All epochs in which eye artifact exceeded a prescribed value were deleted from the data. The ERP waveform was calculated by averaging artifact-free epochs following the presentation of infrequent target stimuli (20% of the time), occurring randomly among nontarget stimuli (the odd-ball paradigm).

Between pre- and postassessments (2 weeks apart), experimental subjects were given up to 2 hours daily of individual cognitive intervention experiences in analytic and focusing learning strategies by experienced interventionists. Intervention experiences placed a heavy emphasis on the use of metacognitive strategies by the students. Additionally, the students reviewed their pretest P300 ERP patterns and regularly discussed the possible relationship of brain processing patterns to their intervention experiences and their work on cognitive control strategies. Control subjects had regular contact with the laboratory setting and the interventionists for the same period of time but were given no cognitive augmentation experiences.

Each of the experimental subjects showed pre–posttest gains in scores on the cognitive control tests: the analytical–global test and the focusing–scanning test. By contrast, control subjects showed no gains or small decreases (see Table 1). These data indicate that a systematic program of augmentation in cognitive controls may influence higher performance on these measures. Such a pattern was not entirely unexpected because the intervention was, in effect, direct teaching for improvement in the areas of the tests.

However, pre–posttest gains were also found in the ERP patterns for all six experimental subjects but not in the control subjects.

These data are of considerable interest because it indicates that changes in neurocognitive functioning may occur in students who participate in a program designed to build competence in cognitive processes and learning strategies. Across all tasks, the average increase in P300 amplitude for experimental subjects was 2.77 microvolts (μv) but only .08 μv for control subjects (see Figure 2). Across all scalp locations, the increase for experimental subjects was 2.69 μv but only .12 μv for controls. The greatest ERP P300 amplitude increase was observed over Wernicke's area, followed closely by the amount of amplitude increase in the frontal lobe (Fz). The general pattern of increase in P300 amplitude for the experimental subjects in this study exceeded the expected test–retest, intra-individual variation of ERP waveforms on cognitive tasks (Languis & Simmons, 1984). By contrast, average change within the control group was well within test–retest range of intra-individual variability.

The general pattern of these ERP data suggests that systematic experiences in learning strategies may, in fact, be measureable as changes in the consistency and robustness of cognitive information-processing patterns revealed in the ERP. While it is premature to warrant such a conclusion, the pattern is clearly encouraging and deserves further investigation.

The next question addressed is whether providing the individual with information about his or her brain electrical activity, and how it changes as cognitive controls and learning strategies are mastered, can be useful in facilitating the

TABLE I

Cognitive intervention and change in performance scores on measures of cognitive control between learning disabled and normal students

Subjects	Analytical/global			Focusing/scanning		
	Pre	Post	Change	Pre	Post	Change
Experimental	$\bar{X} = 14.5$	$\bar{X} = 17.2$	$\bar{X} = +2.7$	$\bar{X} = 26.7$	$\bar{X} = 39.2$	$\bar{X} = +12.15$
$N = 6$	$SD = 4.07$	$SD = 3.01$		$SD = 8.3$	$SD = 16.67$	
Control	$\bar{X} = 13$	$\bar{X} = 13$	$\bar{X} = 0$	$\bar{X} = 59$	$\bar{X} = 53.5$	$\bar{X} = -5.5$
$N = 2$	$SD = 0$	$SD = 0$		$SD = 5.9$	$SD = 1.7$	

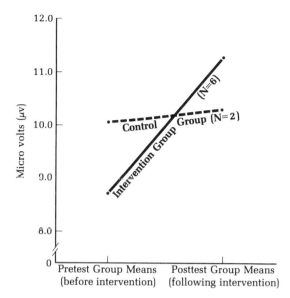

Figure 2. Academic intervention program and P300 amplitude changes in learning-disabled students.

learning-to-learn process. The research and development model proposed may be useful in addressing the question. Topographic mapping of brain electrical activity may be used as a direct part of intervention with individuals to enhance their learning. It has been amply demonstrated that expert individuals differ from novices in the selection and application of appropriate learning strategies. An individual could be shown a map that indicates the differences between his and a skilled individual's brain-activity pattern. The learner may use the information in working toward improvement of learning efficiency. The brain-map feedback information may be used by the learner to set next-level goals (a metacognitive process). With practice in mastering and applying appropriate strategies, the individual could periodically monitor changes in brain-activity pattern and use that information to influence subsequent efforts. Changes in performance and brain activity may be evaluated with self-monitoring to assist the individual in gaining metacognitive knowledge of his or her abilities and the strategies to effectively control them.

Using the Brain Atlas system in the Brain Behavior Laboratory, we have demonstrated the utility of combining brain mapping with an intervention in learning strategies. We assessed individual differences in college-age normal and learning-disabled students each doing the same cognitive task under identical conditions. The task (called high–low tones) involved listening to low tones (500 Hz) and high tones (1000 Hz) presented in a random order. High tones occurred less frequently than low tones (ratio 4 : 1). The students were instructed to press a counter button as quickly as possible each time a high tone occurred (the target event) but to ignore the low tones. The Brain Atlas collected and averaged brain activity time locked to each presentation of thirty high tones in one file and to each presentation of approximately 120 low tones in another file. Brain maps were then viewed by the experimenter and student to evaluate temporal and spatial dimensions of the student's brain processing patterns. As discussed earlier in this chapter, the high–low tones task is known to elicit a P300 waveform for the high tones only in persons processing information normally.

The two brain maps displayed at the top of the color plate show the brain processing pattern for a typical normal male college student (chronological age—26) for the "target" high tones (left map) and for the low tones (right map). In the middle of the color plate are the brain maps for a learning disabled male college student (chronological age—23) doing the same task.

It is apparent that the maps are different in four salient respects: (1) The focus of brain activity is symmetrical in the normal student but is asymmetrical in the learning disabled student; (2) The peak amplitude of the P300 waveform in the normal student is much greater than that in the learning disabled student; (3) The shape and distribution of the waveform for four scalp sites is displayed to the left of each map. The waveforms are much more coherent and are generally smoother in the normal than in the learning-disabled learner; (4) The students were instructed to ignore the low tones so the P300 waveform should not be present if attentional focus is maintained on the high tones only. The brain map for the low tones does not show a P300 waveform in the normal student but the P300 waveform is inappropriately present in the brain map for the learning-disabled student.

The two brain maps at the bottom of the color plate are of the same learning-disabled male college student after approximately 3 months intervention experiences involving a college course on metacognition and training in a set of learning strategies. The brain maps indicate a change in brain processing to a more normalized pattern in three areas: (1) greater symmetry, (2) more coherent waveform distribution across scalp sites, and (3) greater attentional focus as indicated by a more normalized pattern of processing of the low tones. The peak amplitude of the P300 waveform remained much the same as in the previous assessment. The student also displayed improved academic, cognitive, and affective performance in association with the intervention and brain mapping experiences.

The brain maps shown on the color plate are presented as examples to illustrate the utility of brain mapping assessment and monitoring change associated with a learning strategies intervention. Much additional research will be required to establish the precise nature and extent of differences in brain processing patterns between individuals or groups. Change in brain processing within or between

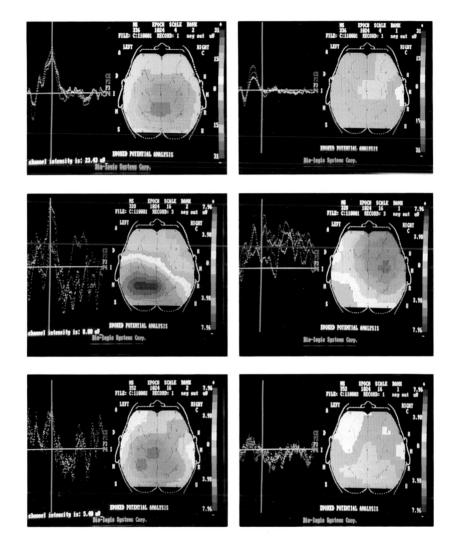

Color Plate. Brain mapping assessment of auditory ERP P300 waveform differences in a normal and learning-disabled college student.

individuals associated with cognitive interventions is a virtually uncharted area. Nevertheless, brain mapping appears to hold substantive promise for persons interested in neurocognitive research and practice in the future.

METACOGNITIVE AND COGNITIVE-CONTROL INTERVENTION

Studies of teaching learning strategies have defined the nature of those strategies with reasonable clarity (Weinstein and Mayer, in press; Kirby, 1984). The evidence is encouraging that students can be taught to improve their competence in learning strategies. However, the long-term effects of teaching these strategies to learners is not entirely clear (Kirby, 1984; Holley & Dansereau, 1984). Two major concerns appear regularly in programs applying cognitive skills and learning strategies. The first is that some learners become discouraged with the effort required to continue to use new strategies in their educational experiences, and sometimes they revert to old, inefficient learning habits. It appears that a certain level of confidence, competence, and comfort with the new strategies is required for learners to keep using them independently. The second is the familiar problem of achieving transfer of the strategy to novel situations. What follows is a brief description of a program that addresses both problems.

Letteri (1980) has developed an assessment battery (cognitive control profile) that reliably and validly describes and predicts level of achievement for children in middle elementary grades to high school. Seven cognitive controls were chosen on the basis of high validity, reliability, and correlation with mathematics and reading areas achievement. The seven controls are

Field Dependence–Independence (Witkin, Dyke, Paterson, Goodenough, & Karp, 1962)
Focusing–Scanning (Gardner & Long, 1962)
Breadth of Categorization (Bruner, 1961)
Cognitive Complexity vs. Simplicity (Kelly, 1955)
Reflectiveness vs. Impulsivity (Kagan, 1965)
Leveling vs. Sharpening (Gardner, Holzman, Klein, Linton, & Spence, 1959)
Tolerance vs. Intolerance (Klein, Gardner, & Schlesinger, 1962)

The controls operate in concert at every stage of the information processing. In fact, they are the prime operators that not only control the flow of the new information through the system but also determine the accuracy with which information is retrieved from the system and therefore the accuracy of the performance based on this information.

When an individual is tested for cognitive controls, the result of each test is compared to a norm table for that individual's age or grade level. Students are then classified as Type I, Type II, or Type III. The profile predicts achievement levels in standardized and teacher-made tests with a 95–99% accuracy for all grade and age levels and also accounts for as high as 87% of the achievement scores. This means that among other factors considered (age, sex, place in family, etc.), the cognitive profile is the most important contributing factor to the achievement.

In Type II and Type III individuals, the cognitive controls are modifiable through a program called cognitive augmentation. Letteri (1979, 1980, 1985a, 1985b) has documented the influence on school achievement of a program of cognitive intervention in learning strategies. Students in the Letteri program have increased an average of 3.65 grade levels in standardized-achievement tests and have gained an average of two letter-grades on teacher-made tests. Usually substantive results occur after approximately 3 months of the intervention program with 2 hours of individual instruction per week.

Materials and strategies for teaching each of the cognitive controls have been developed. Group studies in schools, as well as clinical studies of students, indicate that any of the controls can be changed. Once the individual has developed the skill to an appropriate level, transfer is made to academic tasks. This is done gradually, integrating the academic content into the control training, but it is done as early as possible during the intervention program so the individual does not perceive the control as an isolated skill or strategy. Moreover, the student is involved in a partnership with the interventionist at every point. A metacognitive approach is used throughout in which setting goals, metacognitive knowledge, self-awareness, reflection, monitoring, and maintaining executive control are consistently emphasized.

The following section provides an overview of two cognitive-control strategies and the materials employed in intervention extracted from two selected seventh-grade case studies: Student A & B (Letteri, 1985a).

Analytic–Global (Field Dependence–Independence):

The first step in analysis augmentation is to segment geometric figures into parts in many different ways. The individual must describe the parts in many different ways. The individual must describe the parts verbally, where they are located in the main figure, and then reproduce these parts in the drawing. For young children, this can be accomplished using manipulative materials.

Student B's response indicated a global response. The student saw the picture as a whole, and while the four parts were there, the proportions and perspective were not correct. This is the result of a disorganized search and scan process.

A series of exercises were completed with the student, with instructions necessary to help the student develop better control of his analysis of presented information. The student was, for example, encouraged to segment the circle in different ways. Guidelines such as: "Is there another way you could look at the parts of the circle"? "Could you start at the top and move to the bottom"? "Do you see the different segments if you look at the circle diagonally"?

Transfer of Analysis

Transfer of analysis is made to the individual's academic tasks. For example, mathematics word problems or map study in social studies are used for this transfer. Doing the map study requires the student to find specific information from a concentrated and complex source. To do this effectively and efficiently, the student must find some way of segmenting the map so the parts of it can be searched for the desired information.

This task requires a highly ordered and controlled searching process. With reminders about how the geometric shapes were segmented (during the augmentation session), students use the same procedures in segmenting the map into sections and scanning those sections for the desired information and continuing through the entire map in this organized and controlled fashion until all tasks are completed. The map can be segmented from the top to the bottom (or reverse); from the left to the right (or reverse); or split into smaller sections and each section searched. All of these operations require a plan, and the plan must be executed accurately and consistently. These operations and plans are the skills that are taught during the augmentation program and that are transferred to the academic tasks of the student. Segmenting a geometric form is not the skill taught. The operations, plans, and controls required for segmenting are the skills taught in analysis augmentation, and these can be transferred to a wide variety of tasks and problems.

Focusing

Once the student has learned to segment information, finding the relevant data on which to focus and disregarding irrelevant data is needed. Activities for developing this focusing skill include work on a variety of stimuli. The student is asked to focus on specific components, beginning with very simple figures (triangle, square, circle) and to select these from the maze of data on the cards. Then the more complex instructions are given, which combine several characteristics (red triangle, large; blue circle, small). Students are encouraged to think aloud as they do the tasks. The skill of both combining several components and searching rapidly and accurately through a maze of irrelevant data to select the relevant data is emphasized in this strategy.

Transfer Focusing

Mathematics word problems are an obvious area to transfer the focusing cognitive control. Students seem to have difficulty in segmenting mathematics word problems and in focusing on the relevant data for successful completion of the problem. For example, Student B read a math word problem from his text-book requiring calculation of the percentage of successful shots in the basket compared to those attempted. He was asked, "Well, what have you found?" The student responded, "I would not have him on my team." "Why not?" asked the interventionist. Student B replied, "Because he takes too many shots. He is a ball hog!" With continued guidance and experience, the student applied the control learned in the initial focusing exercise to the task problem by picking out the data needed to solve the problem while ignoring the irrelevant data. Discussions between the student and interventionist are consistently used to assist the student in reflecting on, monitoring, and gaining control of the learning process.

CONCLUSION

Integrating neuropsychological and cognitive research poses a major challenge to cognitive researchers and practitioners in the helping professions. The range of approaches and current evidence in using electrophysiological approaches in neurocognitive research and application has been reviewed and critiqued. A research and development model for assisting individuals in achieving excellence in learning has been suggested. The model provides an approach to integrating neurocognitive assessment, diagnosis, and intervention. The model is presented in a framework that emphasizes a constructivist view of learning (Wittrock, 1974, 1978) and the development of competence in cognitive strategies by the learner (Wittrock, 1980, 1981, 1985a, 1985b).

For some professional colleagues, the model proposed may appear to represent a drastically divergent perspective. In reality, the model for assisting individuals in achieving excellence in learning is incompatable with only one learning theory: strict behaviorism.

On the other hand, it is congruent with major contemporary conceptions of the fundamental nature of cognitive and learning processes: First, it agrees with the fundamental construct in cognitive neuropsychology that embedded within the human information-processing system and common to all learners are a fundamental set of basic cognitive processes. Second, it draws from psychophysiology notions relating basic cognitive processes to measurements of brain electrical activity during the performance of cognitive tasks; Third, it is consistent with the notion, fundamental to cognitive psychology, that learning is a constructive process in which the learner is actively involved at every point and that there exist substantive and qualitative differences in the learning strategies and style that individuals employ. Finally, it is congruent with the idea fundamental to the metacognitive movement in education and psychology that it is possible for an individual to become aware of and to exercise control over her or his basic cognitive and learning processes.

The uniqueness of the model, at one level, lies in its proposed integration of neurocognitive measurement of brain electrical activity (in the form of topographic brain maps) in the metacognitive intervention program for individual learners. Much work needs to be done to define the appropriate use of brain-imaging techniques in neurocognitive applications before such practices become routine. Topographic mapping of brain electrical activity in applied psychological or educational settings may seem esoteric. But it really is not that unusual. The technology exists, and the cost and complexity of use is rapidly decreasing in line with the exponential rise of computer technology. A larger problem in implementation is the appropriate education of the user.

At a more general level, the unique contribution of the model may lie in the integration of several related, but heretofore typically separate, learning conceptions. The model surely illustrates the need for multidisciplinary collaboration among researchers and practitioners in education, psychology, medicine, computer science, engineering, et cetera (Buffer, 1985). An advantage of the model, as proposed, is that it is amenable to empirical test and evaluation. Perhaps, in some meaningful and useful way, the model may foreshadow promising directions for the years ahead. Applying the model to mainstream practice lies many years ahead. Hynd and Obrzut (1981) have cogently explicated the issues and implications of incorporating neuropsychological assessment in the American educational system. Lyons and Languis (1985) identified similar issues and needs in teacher education. The problems are great. But the opportunities and challenges are greater.

REFERENCES

Andreassi, J. L. (1980). *Psychophysiology: Human behavior and physiological response*. New York: Oxford University Press.

Andrews, D. B. (1985, June). Contemporary approaches to the study of learning. Paper presented at the Center for the Study of Learning Conference. Columbus, OH.

Brown, A. L., Bransford, J. D., Ferrarra, R. A., & Compione, J. S. (1983). Learning, remembering, and understanding. In J. Flavell & E. Markman (Eds.), *Carmichael's manual of child psychology*. New York: Wiley.

Bruner, J. S. (1961). Cognitive risk and environmental change. *Journal of Abnormal Psychology*, 62, 231–241

Buffer, J. J. Jr. (1985). A multidisciplinary approach to human development and learning. In M. L. Languis (Ed.), *Learning and the brain: Theory into practice*. Vol. 24, No. 2, pp. 145–148. Columbus: Ohio State University.

Clay, M. M. (1979a). *Reading: The patterning of complex behavior*. Auckland, New Zealand: Heinmann.

Clay, M. M. (1979b). *The early detection of reading difficulties*. Auckland, New Zealand: Heinmann.

Davidson, R. J., & Schwartz, G. E. (1977). The influence of musical training on patterns of EEG asymmetry during musical and non-musical self-generation tasks. *Psychophysiology, 16*, 58–63.

Donchin, E. (1984). *Cognitive psychophysiology*. Hillsdale, NJ.: Lawrence Erlbaum Associates.

Duffy, F. H. (1982). Topographic display of evoked potentials: Clinical applications of brain electrical activity mapping (BEAM). *Annals of the New York Academy of Sciences, 398*, 183–196.

Duffy, F. H., Burchfiel, J. L., & Lombroso, C. T. (1979). Brain electrical activity mapping (BEAM): A method for extending the clinical utility of EEG and evoked potential data. *Annals of Neurology, 5*, 309–321.

Duffy, F. H., Denckla, M. B., Bartels, P. H., & Sandini, G. (1980). Dyslexia: Regional differences in brain electrical activity by topographic mapping. *Annals of Neurology, 7*, 412–420.

Duffy, F. H., Denckla, M. B., Bartels, P. H., Sandini, G., & Kiessling, L. S. (1980). Dyslexia: Automated diagnosis by computerized classification of brain electrical activity. *Annals of Neurology, 7*, 421–428.

Duncan-Johnson, C. C., & Donchin, E. (1982). The P300 component of the event related potential as an index of information processing. *Biological Psychology, 14*, 1–52.

Dunn, B. R. (1985a). Bimodal processing and memory from text. In V. M. Rentel, S. Corson, & B. R. Dunn (Eds.), *Psychophysiological aspects of reading and learning*. New York: Gordon & Breach.

Dunn, B. R. (1985b, April). *Brain organization and cognitive style: Facts, fancies, and possibilities*. Invited paper presented at the 11th Western Symposium in Learning, Western Washington University, Bellingham.

Dunn, B. R., Gould, J. E., & Singer, M. (1981). *Cognitive style differences in expository prose recall* (Tech. Rep. No. 2101). Urbana: University of Illinois, Center for the Study of Reading.

Ford, J. M., Roth, W. T., Mohs, R. C., Hopkins, W. F., III, & Kopell, B. S. (1979). Event related potentials recorded from young and old adults during a memory retrieval task. *Electroencephalography and Clinical Neuropsychology, 47*, 450–459.

Galaburda, A. M., Sherman, G. F., Rosen, G. D., Aboitiz, F., & Geschwind, N. (1985). Developmental dyslexia: Four consecutive patients with cortical anomalies. *Annals of Neurology, 18*, 222–233.

Galin, P., & Ellis, R. (1975). Asymmetry in evoked potentials as an index of lateralized cognitive processes: Relation to EEG alpha asymmetry. *Neuropsychologia, 13*, 45–50.

Gardner, R. W., & Long, R. I. (1962). Control defense and centration effect. *British Journal of Psychology, 53*, 129–140.

Gardner, R. W., Holzman, P. S., Klein, G. S., Linton, H. B, & Spence, D. P., (1959). Cognitive control: a study of individual consistencies in cognitive behavior. *Psychological Issues 1* (4), 1–185.

Geschwind, N. (1983). *Biological foundations of cerebral dominance conference*. Boston: Harvard School of Medicine.

Gevins, A. S., Zeitlin, G. M., Doyle, J. C., Yingling, C. D., Schaeffer, R. E., Callaway, E., & Yeager, C. L. (1979). Electroencephalogram correlates of higher cortical functions. *Science, 203*, 665–668.

Glazer, N. (1981). Ethnicity and education: Some hard questions. *Phi Delta Kappan, 62*, 386–389.

Hillyard, S. A., Hink, R. F., Schwenk, V. I., & Picton, T. W. (1973). Electrical signs of selective attention in the human brain. *Science, 182*, 177–180.

Holley, C. D., & Dansereau, D. S. (Eds.) (1984). *Spacial learning strategies.* New York: Academic Press.

Hymes, D., Dunn, B. R., Gould, J. E., & Harris, W. (1977, May). *Effects of mode of conscious processing on recall and clustering.* Paper presented at the meeting of the Southeastern Psychological Association, Hollywood, FL.

Hynd, G. W., & Cohen, M. (1983). *Dyslexia: Neuropsychological research theory and clinical differentiation.* New York: Grune & Stratton.

Hynd, G. W., & Obrzut, J. E. (Eds.). (1981). *Neuropsychological assessment and the school-age child.* New York: Grune & Stratton.

John, E. R. (1963). Neural mechanisms of decision making. In W. S. Fields & W. Abbott (Eds.), *Information storage and neural control* Springfield, IL: Charles C. Thomas.

Johnstone, J., Galin, D., Fein, G., Yingling, C. Herron, J., & Marcus, M. (1984). Regional brain activity in dyslexic and control children during reading tasks: visual probe event-related potentials. *Brain and Language, 21*, 233–245.

Kagan, J. (1965). Impulsive and reflective children: Significance in conceptual tempo. In J. D. Krumboltz (Ed.), *Learning and the educational process* (pp. 609–628). Chicago: Rand McNally.

Kelly, G. A. (1955). *The psychology of personal constructs* (Vol. 1). New York: Norton.

Kirby, J. (1984). *Cognitive strategies and educational performance.* New York: Academic Press.

Klein, G. S., Gardner, R. W., & Schlesinger, N. J. (1962). Tolerance for unrealistic experience: A study of the generality of a cognitive control. *British Journal of Psychology, 53*, 41–55.

Kraft, R. H., Mitchell, R. O., Languis, M. L., & Wheatly, G. H. (1980). Hemispheric asymmetries during six- to eight-year-olds performance of Piagetian conservation and reading tasks. *Neuropsychologia, 18*, 637–643.

Kutas, M., & Hillyard, S. A. (1980). Reading senseless sentences: Brain potentials reflect semantic incongruity. *Science, 207*, 203–205.

Languis, M. L., & Kraft, R. H. (1985). The neuroscience and educational practice: Asking better questions. In V. Rentel, S. Corson, & B. R. Dunn (Eds.), *Psychophysiological aspects of reading and learning processes.* New York: Gordon & Breach.

Languis, M. L., Letteri, C., Pennell, L., & McQueen, P. (1984). *Cognitive augmentation and information processing patterns in learning disabled students.* Unpublished manuscript, Ohio State University, Columbus.

Languis, M. L., & Naour, P. J. (1985). Sex differences neuropsychological function: A vector model. In C. Telzrow & L. Hartlage (Eds.), *The neuropsychology of individual differences: A developmental perspective.* New York: Plenum.

Languis, M. L., Naour, P. J., Martin, D. J., & Buffer, J. J. (Eds.). (in press). *Cognitive science: Contributions to educational practice.* Columbus, OH: ERIC Clearinghouse for Science, Mathematics, and Environmental Education.

Languis, M. L., & Shockley, K. C. (1984, April). *Megavitamin intervention and event related potentials in autistic learners.* Paper presented at the Nutrition and Behavior Conference, Ohio State University, Columbus.

Languis, M. L., & Simmons, J. (1984). *Intra-individual test–retest consistency in the P300 event related potential.* Unpublished manuscript, Ohio State University, Columbus.

Letteri, C. A. (1979). The relationship between cognitive profiles, levels of academic achievement and behavior problems. In R. Rutherford & A. Prieto (Eds.), *Monograph in behavior disorders: Severe behavior disorders of children and youth* (pp. 74–85). Reston, VA: Council for Children with Behavior Disorders.

Letteri, C. A. (1980). Cognitive profile: Basic determinant of academic achievement. *Journal of Education Research, 73*, 195–199.

Letteri, C. A. (1985a). Teaching students how to learn: Cognitive profile analysis, augmentation, transfer. In M. L. Languis (Ed.) Learning and the Brain *Theory into Practice, 24,* 112–122.

Letteri, C. A. (1985b). In M. L. Languis, P. J. Naour, D. J. Martin, & J. J. Buffer (Eds.), *Cognitive science: Contributions to educational practice.* Columbus, OH: ERIC Clearinghouse for Science, Mathematics and Environmental Education.

Lubar, J. (1985). Biofeedback and learning disabilities. In M. L. Languis (Ed.), *Learning and the brain: Theory into practice* Columbus: Ohio State University College of Education.

Lyons, C. (in press). Brain functioning, cognitive style, and personality variables in learning and teaching behaviors of preservice teachers. In M. L. Languis, P. J. Naour, D. J. Martin, & J. J. Buffer (Eds.), *Cognitive science: Contributions to educational practice.* Columbus, OH: ERIC Clearninghouse for Science, Mathematics, and Environmental Education.

Lyons, C. A., & Languis, M. L. (1985). Cognitive science and teacher education. In M. L. Languis (Ed.), *Learning and the brain: Theory into practice* (Vol. 24, pp. 127–131). Columbus: Ohio State University.

Lyons, C. A., Languis, M. L., & Rogers, J. (1985 August). *Indepth study of the developmental and environmental context of dyslexics and their families.* Paper presented at the American Psychological Association Conference, Los Angeles.

Minstrell, J. (1984). Teaching for the development of understanding of ideas: Forces on moving objects. *AETS Yearbook.*

Naour, P. J., Languis, M. L., & Martin, D. J. (in press). Developmental component in brain electrical activity of normal and disabled boys. In M. L. Languis, P. J. Naour, D. J. Martin, & J. J. Buffer (Eds.), *Cognitive science: Contributions to educational practice.* Columbus, OH: ERIC Clearinghouse for Science Mathematics, and Environmental Education.

Osborne, R. J., & Wittrock, M. C. (1983). Learning science: A generative approach. *Science Education, 67,* 489–509.

Picton, T. W., & Hillyard, S. A. (1974). Human auditory evoked potentials II. Effects of attention. *Electroencephalography and Clinical Neurophysiology, 36,* 191–200.

Reddix, M. D., & Dunn, B. R. (1984). *EEG alpha production correlates of cognitive style differences and recall of metaphor from poetry* (Referred Tech. Rep.). Urbana: University of Illinois, Center for the Study of Reading.

Ritter, W., Simpson, R., & Vaughan, H. G., Jr. (1972). Association cortex potentials and reaction time in auditory discriminations. *Electroencephalography and Clinical Neurophysiology, 33,* 547–555.

Ruchkin, D. S., & Sutton, S. (1973). Visual evoked and emitted potentials and stimulus significance. *Bulletin of the Psychonomic Society, 2,* 114–146.

Shibley, R. E., & Shockley, K. C. (1984, March). *Electrophysiological event-related potential indices of cognitive processing in autistic learners.* Paper presented at the American Educational Research Association Conference, New Orleans.

Shockley, K. C. (1984). *Differences in P300 event related potentials in autistic and normal youth.* Unpublished master's thesis, Ohio State University, Columbus.

Shucard, D. W., Cummings, K. R., Thomas, D. G., & Shucard, J. L. (1981). Evoked potentials to auditory probes as indices of cerebral specialization of function—Replication and extension. *Electroencephalography and Clinical Neurophysiology, 52,* 389–393.

Shucard, D. W., Shucard, J. L., & Thomas, D. G. (1977). Auditory evoked potentials as probes of hemispheric differences in cognitive processing. *Science, 197,* 1295–1298.

Simmons, J., Languis, M. L., & Drake, M. (1985, August). *Neurocognitive event-related potential assessment of dyslexic and normal college students.* Paper presented at the American Psychological Association Conference, Los Angeles.

Squires, K. C., Squires, N. K., & Hillyard, S. A. (1975). Decision-related cortical potentials during an auditory signal detection task with cued observation intervals. *Journal of Experimental Psychology: Human Perception and Performance, 104,* 268–279.

Sutton, S., Braren, M., Zubin, J., & John, E. R. (1967). Evoked potential correlates of stimulus uncertainty. *Science, 150,* 1187–1188.

Torello, M. W. (1984). *The development and implementation of a two channel system to measure event related potentials in normal and brain injured adults.* Unpublished doctoral dissertation, Ohio State University, Columbus.

Torello, M., & Duffy, F. (1985). Using brain electrical activity mapping to diagnose learning disabilities. In M. L. Languis (Ed.), *Learning and the brain: Theory into practice* (Vol. 24, pp. 95–100). Columbus: Ohio State University.

Torello, M. W., & McCarley, R. W. (in press). The use of topographic mapping techniques in clinical studies in psychiatry. In F. H. Duffy (Ed.), *Topographic mapping of brain electrical potentials.* Boston: Butterworth.

Weinstein, C. E., & Mayer, R. E. (in press) The teaching of learning strategies. In M. C. Wittrock (Ed.), *Handbook of research and teaching,* 3rd ed. New York: Macmillan.

Wickens, C., Kramer, A., Vanesse, L., & Donchin, E. (1983) Performance of concurrent tasks: A psychological analysis of the reciprocity of information-processing resources. *Science, 221,* 1080–1082.

Witkin, H. A., Dyk, R. B., Paterson, H. F., Goodenough, D. R., & Karp, S. A. (1962). *Psychological differentiations.* New York: Wiley.

Wittrock, M. C. (1974). Learning as a generative process. *Educational Psychologist, 11,* 87–95.

Wittrock, M. C. (1978). The cognitive movement in instruction. *Educational Psychologist, 13,* 15–29.

Wittrock, M. C. (1980). Learning and the brain. In M. C. Wittrock (Ed.), The Brain and Psychology, pp. 371–403. New York: Academic Press.

Wittrock, M. C. (1981). Reading comprehension. In F. J. Pirozzolo & M. C. Wittrock (Eds.), Neuropsychological and cognitive processes in reading, pp. 229–259. New York: Academic Press.

Wittrock, M. C. (Ed.). (1985a). *Handbook of research on teaching and learning.* Washington, DC: American Educational Research Association.

Wittrock, M. C. (1985b). Teaching learners generative strategies for enhancing reading comprehension. In M. L. Languis (Ed.), *Learning and the brain: Theory into practice* (Vol. 24, pp. 123–127). Columbus: Ohio State University.

Index

A

Alzheimer's disease, 178, *see also* Dementia
Antilocalizationists, 119
Aphasia, 84–86
  childhood, 84–86
  plasticity, 84–85
Auditory brainstem response (ABR), 45
Auditory evoked potentials' (AEP), 66
Auditory evoked response (AER), 95, 108–109
  components, 110
  lateralization of function, 108–109
  multivariate analysis, 95
  predicting language development, 109–111
Autism, 220–221
Autoimmune disease, 165–166, *see also* Developmental dyslexia
Autonomic responses, 46–47

B

Brain Atlas, 224–225, 229–230, Color Plate (Chapter 11)
Brain behavior relationships, 118–121
  Luria's conceptualization, 120–121, *see also* Luria's theory
Brain damage, 66–69, 114, 218, *see also* Brain injury
  causes in children, 157
  early versus late, 68–69, *see also* Kennard Principle
  patterns, 67
Brain Injury, 7, *see also* Brain damage
  effects in children, 7–8
  epidemiology, 8
  language disturbance, 67

Brain organization, 74
  aphasia, 74
Brain vesicles, 18–28
  diencephalon, 23–24
    epithalamus, 23–24
    hypothalamus, 23–24
    thalamus, 23–24
  mesencephalon, 23
  metencephalon, 21–23
    pons and cerebellum, 22–23
  myelencephalon, 18–21
  subdivisions of, 18
  telencephalon, 24–28
    corpus striatum, 24–25
    neopallium, 25–28
    paleopallium and archipallium, 25
Brain weight, 28–29, *see also* Myelination
  development of, 28–29
  rate of growth, 28

C

Central processing unit, 126–128
  two components, 126
Central nervous system, 141–150
  plasticity, 141–150
  recovery of function, 141–150
Cerebral asymmetry, 57–58
Cerebral hemispheres, 159–160
  rate of development, 159
Cerebral lateralization, 73–90, *see also* Lateralization measures
  concerns about, 73
  future research efforts, 89–90
  stuttering, 89
Child neuropsychology, 2–10
  clinical child neuropsychology, 2

Child Neuropsychology (*cont.*)
  definition of, 3–4
  developmental factors, 5
    critical periods, 5
    plasticity, 5
  research, 1
  research procedures, 4–7
  theory, 1
Cognitive development, 56, *see also* Informa-
    tion-Integrative model
  piagetian stages, 56
Cognitive neuroscience, 210–211
  application in education, 210
Cognitive Processes, 95–112, 117, 121, *see
    also* Information-Integration model
  developmental changes, 117
Cognitive research, 209–235
Commissurotomy, 145
Cortex, 143–149
  development of, 143
Cortical layers, 60–63
  density, 61
  patterns, 61–62
Cortical maturation, 55–69
  Developmental neurolinguistic model, 69
Cranial nerves, 20–21, 24, 46
  nuclei, 20–21

D

Delirium, 176
Dementia, 9, 175–188, *see also* Neu-
    rodegenerative diseases in children
  causes of, 180–181
  cortical, 178–179
    Alzheimer's, 178
  cortical versus subcortical, 178–179
    differentiation, 179
  definition of, 175–176
  delirium, 176
  developmental considerations, 177–178
  evaluation of, 181–184
    electrophysiological, 183–184
    laboratory measures, 183–184
    neuropsychological, 182–183
  infants and children, 177–178
  neuronal ceroid lipofuscinosis (NCL), 186–
    187
    clinical presentation, 188
  primary degenerative, 176

subacute sclerosing panencephalitis (SSPE),
    184–185
  clinical presentation, 185
subcortical, 178
  Huntington's, 178–179
  Parkinson's, 178
  progressive supranuclear palsy, 178
Developmental aphasia, 144, *see also* Aphasia
Developmental dyslexia, 144, 155–170, 218–
    220, *see also* Learning disabilities; Read-
    ing disabilities
  allergies, 165–166
  animal model, 155, 166–170
    testosterone, 166
  autoimmune disease, 165–166
  autopsy studies, 219
  cases (autopsies), 160–163
  gender effects, 168–169
  neuronal ectopia and dysplasia, 163–164
  neuropathology, 160–165
    etiology, 164–165
    hemispheric effects, 164–165
Developmental milestones, 177
  behavioral regression, 177
Developmental neurolinguistics, 55–69
  anatomical change and asymmetry, 57–58
  discipline of, 57
  myelination, 59–60
  neurodensity and layer width, 60–62
  research, 63–64
Developmental neuropsychology, 10, *see also*
    Cerebral lateralization
Dichotic listening, 65, 66, 79–81, 87, 146,
    199–202
  ear advantage, 199–200
  lateralization index, 196
  reliability factors, 197–198
  test–retest reliability, 195–196
Dyslexia, *see* Developmental dyslexia

E

Electroencephalography (EEG), 66, 183, 211–
    214, 218
  10/20 international system, 218
Equipotentiality, 57, 64, 66, 119, 157, 158
Event related potential (ERP), 214–223, 226
  applications of, 217–222
  components of, 215–217
  probe, ERP method, 222–226

Evoked potentials (EP's), 146–147
Evoked response, 42, 44

F

Factor analysis, 128–129
Fibers, 25
  commissural, 25
  types, 25
Field dependence–independence, 232–233
Fissures, 26–27, 143
  longitudinal fissure, 26
  parietooccipital sulcus, 26
  Sylvian (lateral) fissure, 26
Footedness, 77
Frontal Lobe, 62
Functional Asymmetries, 27–28, see also Cerebral lateralization

H

Handedness, 75–79, 85, 165–166
  aphasia in children, 85–86
  development of, 75–79
  difficulties with definition, 75
  in infancy, 75–76
  in preschoolers, 77
  methods of measurement, 75
  relation to eye dominance, 77–78
  relation to reading and language, 78
Hand preference, 73, see also Handedness
Hemidecordectomies, 68
Hemispherectomy, 144, 146, 158
Hemispheric specialization, 64–69, see also
  Cerebral lateralization
  brain-damaged populations, 66–69
  normal population, 64–66
  speech perception, 64–65
High amplitude sucking (HAS), 42, 65, 96,
  see also Laterlization measures
Huntington's Disease, 178, 179, 180, see also
  Dementia

I

Infants, 95, 100, 109, 158–159
  anatomical asymmetries, 158–159
  brain, 158

Information-Integration model, 121–137, see
  also Cognitive processes
  application of, 130–137
  components, 126–130
  cognitive processes, 135–137
    memory span, 135–136
  control of behavior, 123–124
  cross-cultural studies, 130–131
  empirical evidence, 128–130
  information processing—two forms, 124–
    125
  language and reading skills, 133–135
    reading disability, 133–135
  Luria's functional units, 122–123
  mentally retarded, 136
  relationship to Piagetian theory, 131–132
  research methods, 128
Information processing, 117, 123, 124–125,
  see also Cognitive processes
  simultaneous and successive, 124–125
Intervention, metacognitive, 226–234

K

Kennard principle, 142, see also Brain
  Damage

L

Language Acquisition, 56, see also Aphasia
  models of, 56
  stages of, 56
Language, 156–160
  adult, 156
  anatomical asymmetries, 156–157
    planum Temporale, 156
    volume, 156–157
  children, 157–160
    bilateral representation, 158
    equipotentiality theory, 157
    lateralization at birth, 157–158
    functional asymmetries, 156
Language development, 55–57
  hemispheric equipotentiality, 55
  lateralization, 55–56
  tenets, 55–56
Lateralization in mice, 169
Lateralization measures, 191–205, see also
  Cerebral lateralization; Perceptual
  asymmetries

Lateralization measures (*cont.*)
  problems in clinical diagnosis, 203–204
  reliability, 195–203
    conjugate lateral eye movements
      (CLEMS), 200–201
    cross-task correlations, 202–203
    dichotic listening, Laterlization Index,
      195–200
    electroencephalographic measures, 201–
      202
    finger tapping, 200
    visual half-field techniques, 200
  Validity of, 192–195
    dichotic listening, 193
    event-related potentials (ERP's), 194
    finger-tapping tasks, 194
    sources of, 192–193
    visual half-field studies, 193–194
Learning disabilities, 160–170, 210, 220, 227,
    see also Developmental dyslexia
  animal model, 166–168
  in mice, 169
Linguistic development, 9, *see also* Language
    acquisition
Lobes, 26–27, *see also* Brain vesicles
Longitudinal study, 109
Luria's model, 119, 125
Luria's theory, 29–32
  arousal unit, 29–30
  organizational and planning unit, 31–32
  sensory-input unit, 30–31
    primary fields, 30
    secondary fields, 30–31
    tertiary fields, 31

M

Motor functions, 32–38, *see also* Reflexes
  automatic reflexes, 37–38
  development of, 32–38
  fetal and neonatal reflexes, 33–34
  misconceptions, 32
  primitive reflexes, 34–37
Multiple sclerosis, 185, *see also* Dementia
Myelination, 29, 58–59, 60, *see also* Brain
    weight
  process of, 59–60

N

Neurocognitive assessment, 211–224, *see also*
    Lateralization measures
  methods, 211–224
  electroencephalographic (EEG), 212–214
    learning disabilities, 214
    modes of thought, 213–214
  event related potential (ERP), 214–223
    autism, 220, 221
    components of, 215–217
    developmental dyslexia, 218–220
    learning disabilities, 220
    probel-ERP method, 223
    topographic brain mapping, 224
    Brain Atlas, 224
Neurocognitive research, 210–211
  defined, 210
Neurodegenerative diseases in children, 179–
    187, *see also* Dementia
  classification of, 179–180
Neurolinguistics, 55–69, *see also* Develop-
    mental neurolinguistics
Neuropsychological development, 9, 13–48,
    see also Luria's theory
  theoretical framework, 14
Neuropsychological research, 6
  obstacles, 6
Neurulation, 14–18
  closing of neural tube, 18
  flexures, 17
  formation of neural tube, 15–16
  motor and sensory precursors, 17–18
  neural crest, 16–17
  sequential stages of, 15–16

P

Parkinson's disease, 178, *see also* Dementia
Perceptual asymmetries, 79–84, *see also* Lat-
    erlization measures
  dichotic listening, 79–81
    developmental aspects, 80–81
    effects of gender, 81
  other asymmetries, 84
  tactile asymmetries, 81–82
    dichhaptic stimulation
  visual asymmetries, 82–84
    tachistoscopic method, 82–83

Phrenology, 118
Place of articulation, 105–108
  back and front consonants, 104
  infants, 105–108
Plasticity, 9, 56, 57, 141–150, *see also* Recovery of function
  definition of, 142
Preterm infants, 43–45
Progressive supranuclear palsy (PSP), 178, *see also* Dementia
Psychophysiological indices, 95–112
Public law, 94–142
  The Education for All Handicapped Children's Act, 1

R

Reading disability, 133–134, 137, *see also* Developmental dyslexia
Reading and laterality, 86–89, *see also* Developmental dyslexia
  developmental lag hypothesis, 87
  genetics, 86
  subtypes, 88
Recovery of function, 141–150, *see also* Plasticity
  definition of, 142–143
  dependent on, 150
  fine-motor function, 149–150
  limbic structures, 150
  nonlinguistic, 149–150
Reflexes, 34, 36, 37–38, *see also* Motor functions
  asymmetrical tonic neck reflex (ATNR), 36
  Babkin reflex, 34
  body righting reaction, 37
  equilibrium reaction, 38
  Galant Reflex, 35
  Grasp reflex, 34
  labyrinthine righting reaction, 37
  Landau reflex, 36
  optical righting reaction, 37
  positive supporting reflex, 34–35
  protective extensor thrust (Parachute) reaction, 38
  righting reactions, 37
  rooting reflex, 34
  sucking reflex, 33

  swallow, 33
  withdrawal and extension reflexes, 34–35
Regional cerebral blood flow, 146–149
  ^{133}Xenon inhalation technique, 148
Reorganization, 149, *see also* Plasticity; Recovery of function
Reye's syndrome, 8

S

School psychologist, 211
Sensory function, 38–46
  development of, 38–46
    postnatal sensory function, 42–46
      sensory processing in infants, 43–45
      postterm sensory processing, 45–46
    prenatal sensory function, 39–42
      audition, 41–42
      cutaneous receptors, 39–40
      labyrinthine receptors, 40
      olfaction, 41
      proprioceptive receptors, 40
      taste, 40–41
      vision, 42
Special education programs, 1
Subacute sclerosing panencephalitis (SSPE), 184–185, *see also* Dementia
Syntactic ability, 66

T

Tachistoscopic research, 65, 66, *see also* Lateralization measures
Tay-Sachs disease, 180
Testosterone, 214, *see also* Developmental dyslexia
Tone onset time (TOT), 100–101
Topographic brain mapping, 210, 229
Tourette's syndrome, 8

V

Voicing contrasts, 96–104
  electrophysiological techniques, 97–104
  evoked potentials, 97–98
  tone onset time (TOT), 100–101
  voice onset time (VOT), 96–97

Voice onset time (VOT), 96–104
   definition of, 96
   developmental pattern, 100
   waveform components, 101–104

W

Wada test, 65